IMAGES
of America

Stoughton in the 20th Century

On the Cover: A parade takes place in Stoughton Square in the 1940s. This parade followed Route 138 (Washington Street), past the businesses in the Stoughton Building and the State Theatre. (Courtesy of the Stoughton Historical Society.)

IMAGES
of America

STOUGHTON IN THE 20TH CENTURY

David Allen Lambert and
Brenda Lea Lambert

ARCADIA
PUBLISHING

ISBN 978-1-4671-2312-9

Published by Arcadia Publishing
Charleston, South Carolina

Printed in the United States of America

Library of Congress Control Number: 2014949819

For all general information, please contact Arcadia Publishing:
Telephone 843-853-2070
Fax 843-853-0044
E-mail sales@arcadiapublishing.com
For customer service and orders:
Toll-Free 1-888-313-2665

Visit us on the Internet at www.arcadiapublishing.com

This book is dedicated to the veterans of Stoughton past and present.

Contents

Acknowledgments

I have lived in Stoughton my entire life, and I am incredibly proud to call this wonderful place my home. My love of history began when my second-grade teacher, Mrs. Davis, pushed me to pursue my interest in the subject. At that point, I also turned to my dad, a Stoughton historian, about the history of Stoughton. It was around that same time that I became involved with the Stoughton Historical Society and discovered many fascinating stories about the place I call home. I would like to thank, first, my father, David Allen Lambert, who taught me, and still continues to teach me to learn from history. Also, I would like to thank my mother, Anne-Marie, my sister Hannah, and my aunt Carol. Most of all, I thank every teacher I have had in the Stoughton Public Schools. You all pushed me to study hard, work hard, and never stop learning. To any kid with an interest in history, by all means pursue it. Go out and discover your local history. Find the stories and chase after the missing pages.

—Brenda Lea Lambert

Like my daughter, I have lived in Stoughton my entire life. At the age of 11, I met the late Edward "Ye Olde Ed" Meserve, the president of the Stoughton Historical Society. He introduced me to local historians Howard Hansen and John C. Stiles, whose photographs are found throughout this book. I volunteered evenings and after school at the society, learning about the rich history of Stoughton. At this young age, I was embraced and nurtured in the field of local history by these gentlemen. I would like to acknowledge the influence of these and countless other members of the Stoughton Historical Society, living and deceased. We would like to thank the society, whose rich collection of photographs has once again made another volume in this series possible. Unless otherwise noted, photographs appear courtesy of the Stoughton Historical Society. The photography of George Adolph Gerard, John C. Stiles, Chet Cohenno, Frank Maioli, Carol-Ann Lea, and others make this a time capsule of 20th-century Stoughton. I would like to acknowledge the amazing assistance and inspiration of my daughter and coauthor, Brenda Lea Lambert. I acknowledge my family for their help—specifically my wife, Anne-Marie, for assistance in getting photographs of current views of Stoughton. I would also like to acknowledge the assistance of Patricia Basler, director of the Stoughton Public Library, and Dwight MacKerron, Brian Daley, and Richard Fitzpatrick of the Stoughton Historical Society. And a special thank-you goes to Caitrin Cunningham, our acquisitions editor at Arcadia Publishing, for assistance.

—David Allen Lambert

INTRODUCTION

Stoughton was nearly 200 years old at the dawn of the 20th century. The boundaries had changed in the 18th century with the creation of the towns of Sharon (formerly Stoughtonham) and Canton. Transformation occurred again in 1888, when the section known as East Stoughton was incorporated into the town of Avon, Massachusetts. Stoughton, which started the 19th century as an agricultural community, had transformed itself into a booming factory town. Stoughton created shoes, boots, garments, rubber-fabricated goods, shoe lasts, and other items that were sent on the rail lines to Boston and beyond. Fortunes of old farming families were transformed, and the flow of immigrant labor to help make the shops and factories in Stoughton successful continued well into the 20th century. The trolley lines and busy storefronts in Stoughton Square are different now than a century ago. Trolleys have been replaced with the traffic of automobiles and buses. Stoughton commuters still take the trains daily into Boston under the shadow of the granite clock tower at a train station hand-constructed a century before.

Sermons of one church in the beginning of the 19th century were transformed to that of many faiths and languages, creating a diversified Stoughton in the 20th century. From the sound of a marching band, to the introduction of silent movies at a Stoughton theater, to renting movies on DVD from a local video store, entertainment came to Stoughton residents over the years. A home-cooked meal was often supplemented with takeout food from Stoughton Town Spa and other establishments by mid-century. The buzz of an airplane overhead would make one stop and look, and a camera over the plane's wing would catch a glimpse of an expanding Stoughton. The town knew what personal loss meant when the *Titanic* sank in 1912, taking the life of local businessman George Quincy Clifford. One of the community's residents, Nicola Sacco, would be forever remembered throughout the world for his involvement in one of the most controversial trials and executions in America. This community heard the news of war and answered the call. Many young men and woman of Stoughton were mustered to arms in two world wars, as well as to the battlefields of Korea, Vietnam, and other places. Throughout the 20th century and into the 21st, Stoughton has remained a close and united community. The history of Stoughton in the 20th century could be written in hundreds upon hundreds of pages. The names and faces of this community each tell a remarkable story of personal history, and these in turn become the overall history of Stoughton.

My first Stoughton history book, *Beyond the Blew-Hills*, was written by the late Stoughton historian John E. Flynn. In the chapter "The Years Beyond," my late friend Ed Meserve relates the following, which I think is a fitting way to close this introduction:

> History does not end with the closing of a book, for as long as the sun rises the world will continue to change and history will be made. Sometimes we do not see history when it occurs but merely as events of passing interest. But news today whether it be of local or world interest becomes history tomorrow.

Your own chapter of Stoughton history is that which historians of the future will seek to explain in the 21st century. We live in an age of e-mails, text messages, and cell phones. With these same phones, we snap photographs and post them to social media, or take hundreds of photographs with digital cameras. Have you stopped to think how many important e-mails you have printed out? Or how many digital photographs you have actually printed? What time capsule are we leaving historians and genealogists of the 22nd century?

I encourage the reader to collect his or her own Stoughton photographs and stories and share them with family. Remember to donate copies or originals to the Stoughton Historical Society, to help it preserve the worthwhile past for future generations.

One

Stoughton Buildings

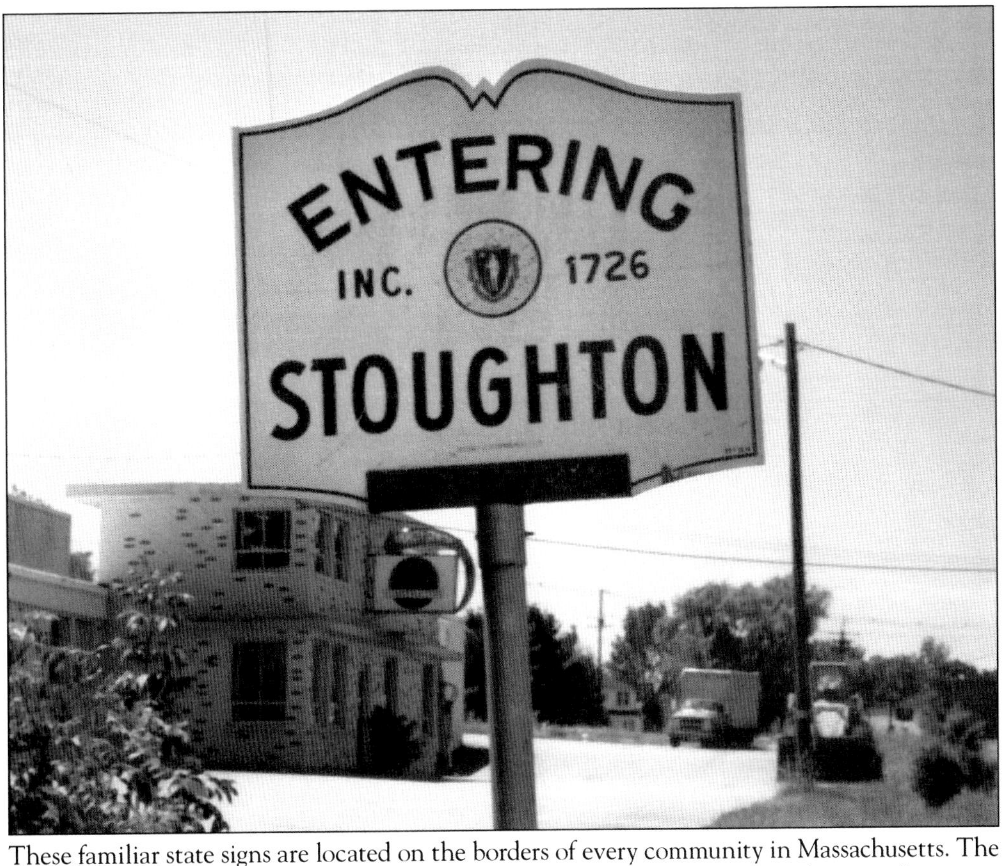

These familiar state signs are located on the borders of every community in Massachusetts. The town of Stoughton, incorporated in 1726, was once larger in size. Stoughton became the parent of the towns of Sharon (formerly Stoughtonham), Canton, and Avon.

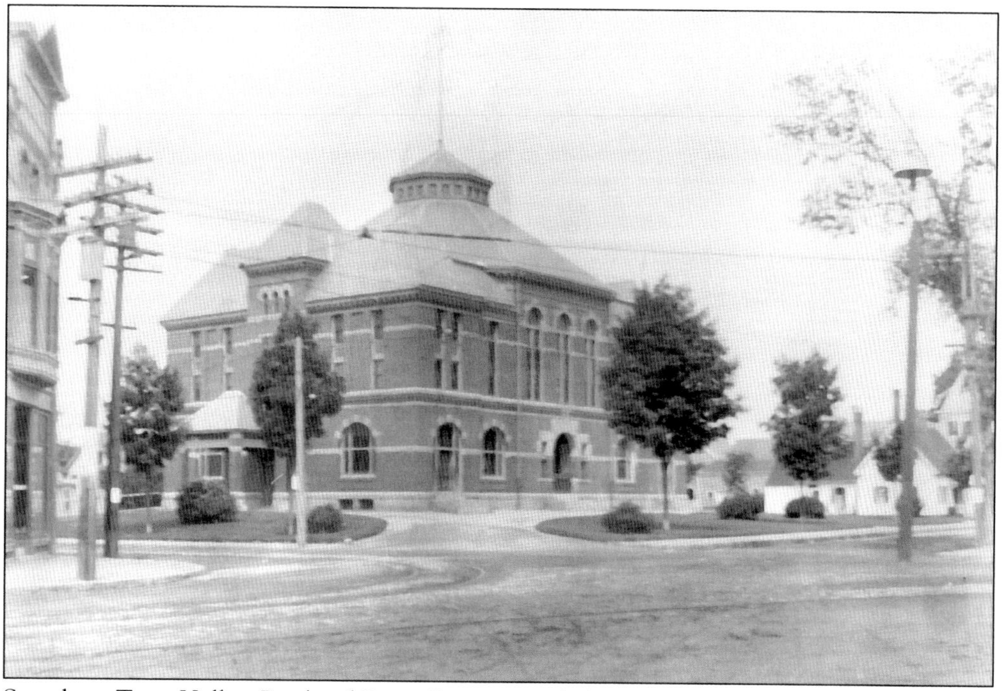

Stoughton Town Hall, at Pearl and Porter Streets, was dedicated on November 22, 1881. Over 130 years later, this structure is still utilized as a town hall. It was designed by architectural firm Joseph W. Coburn & Co. of Boston. Besides housing town offices, it was the home of the Stoughton Public Library until 1904, the Stoughton Fire Department until 1927, and the Stoughton Police Department until 1959. Construction began on the town hall on April 29, 1880, at the site of Robert Porter's home, which was razed to make way for the new building.

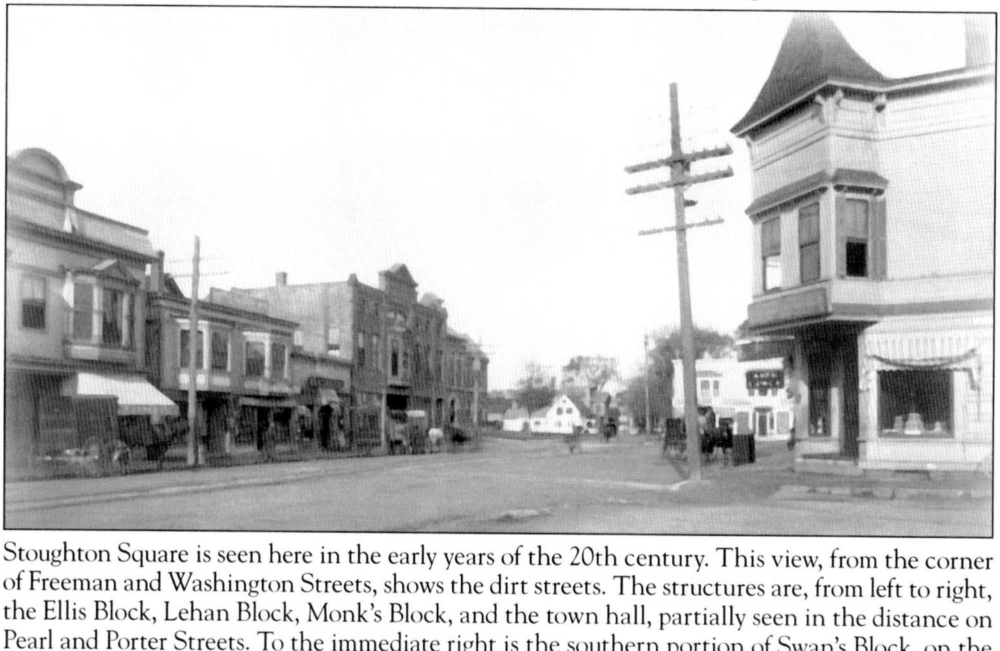

Stoughton Square is seen here in the early years of the 20th century. This view, from the corner of Freeman and Washington Streets, shows the dirt streets. The structures are, from left to right, the Ellis Block, Lehan Block, Monk's Block, and the town hall, partially seen in the distance on Pearl and Porter Streets. To the immediate right is the southern portion of Swan's Block, on the corner of Freeman Street.

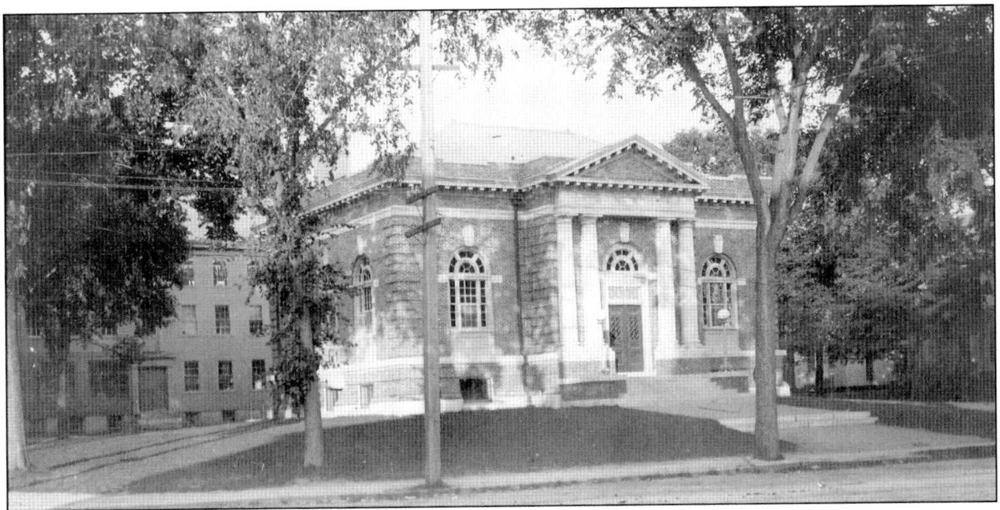

The Lucius Clapp Memorial Building at 6 Park Street was designed by architect Walter Atherton and dedicated on June 17, 1904. It stands on the site of a 1768 schoolhouse and Abraham Capen's Tavern, built in 1799. This structure served as the home of the Stoughton Public library from 1904 to 1969, and it was briefly the home of the Stoughton Youth Commission. Within the walls of this structure are now maintained the historical and genealogical archives of the community. The Stoughton Historical Society, founded in 1895, now shares this historic site with the office and archives of the Old Stoughton Musical Society. In this photograph, the former Atherton Boot Factory (left) can be seen on Pleasant Street, where Randolph Savings Bank is now located.

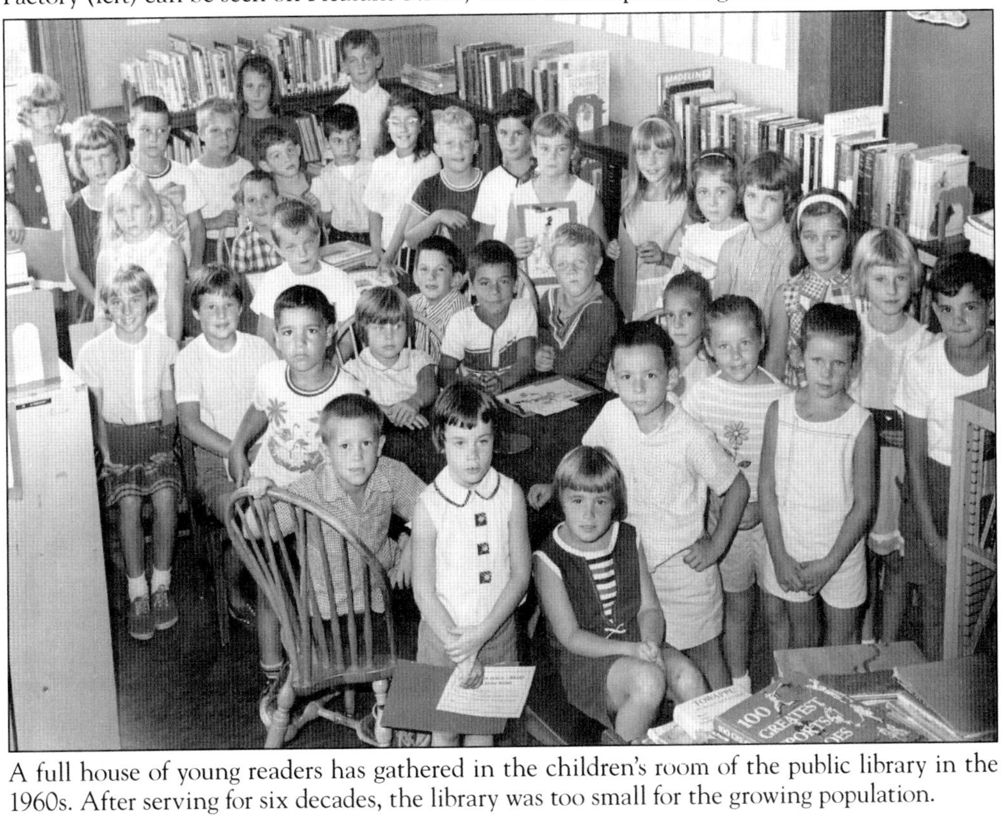

A full house of young readers has gathered in the children's room of the public library in the 1960s. After serving for six decades, the library was too small for the growing population.

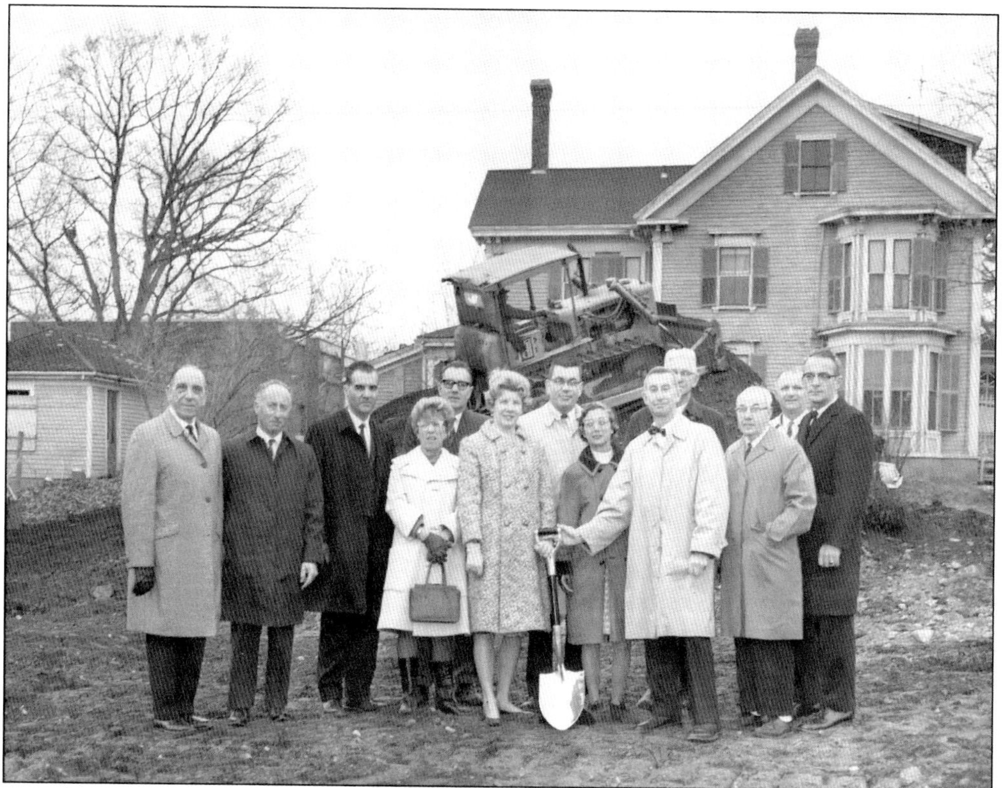

Stoughton officials and library trustees attend ground-breaking ceremonies at the corner of Walnut and Park Streets for the current Stoughton Public Library in 1969. In 1967, the town of Stoughton received the second-highest federal grant for a public library under the Library Services and Construction Act. Shown in the first row are, from left to right, two unidentified persons, Charles Yaitanes, Valerie Crockett, Anne Peterson, Dorothy Woodward, Francis M. Daly, and Orrin Hansen.

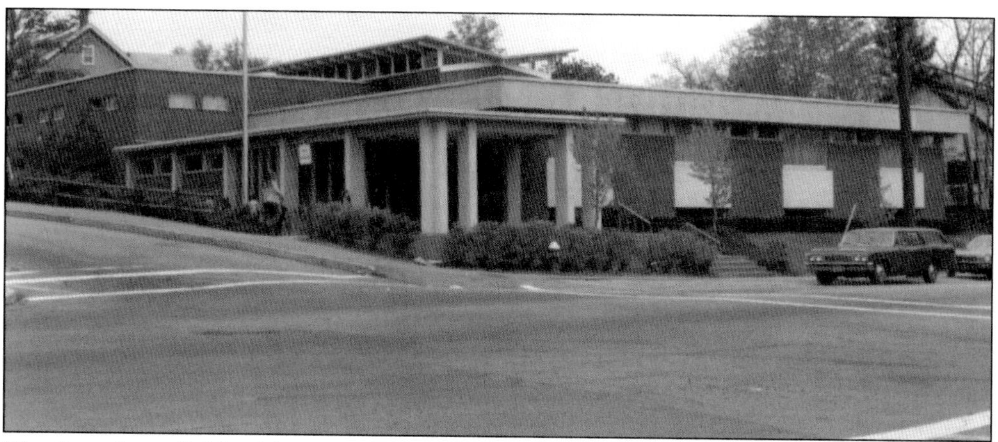

The Stoughton Public Library at 84 Park Street was designed by Richmond and Goldberg Architects. It opened on May 18, 1969. The library has served the community at this location, beginning with printed books through to the age of the Internet. Many programs here enrich the community, from children's story hour by Margaret "Peggy" Sewyck, to English-language tutoring for new immigrants settling in Stoughton.

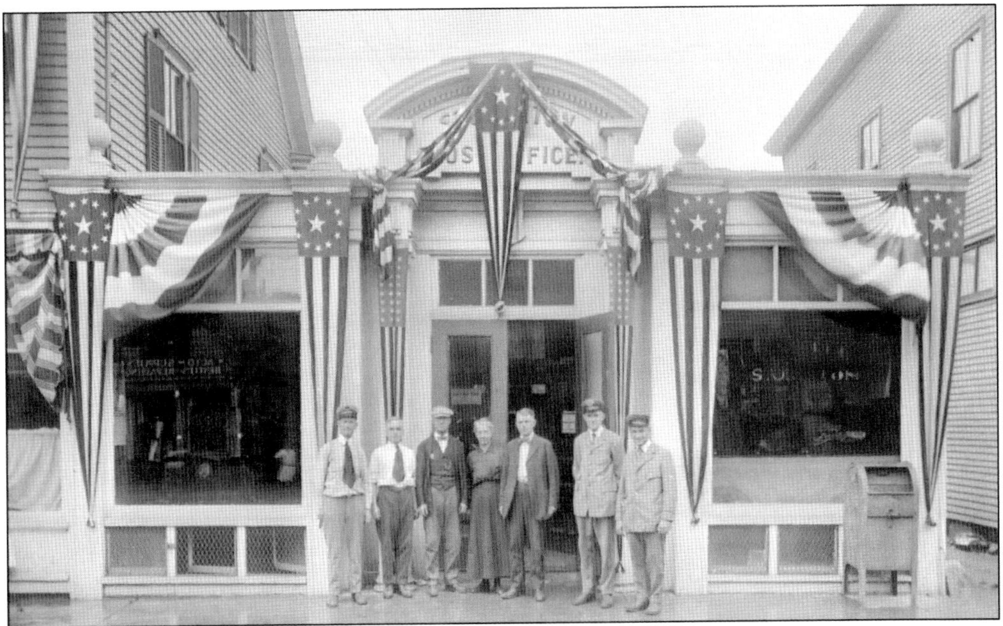

In 1919, the Stoughton Post Office was located on Wyman Street. This home of the post office opened in 1911 and it remained the location until 1939. Shown here are, from left to right, William Dwyer, George Ring, William Southworth, Minnie Hussey (assistant postmaster), Christopher Farrell (postmaster), Walter Curry, and Frank O'Neil. This building and the one to the left of it were lost to fire in 1960.

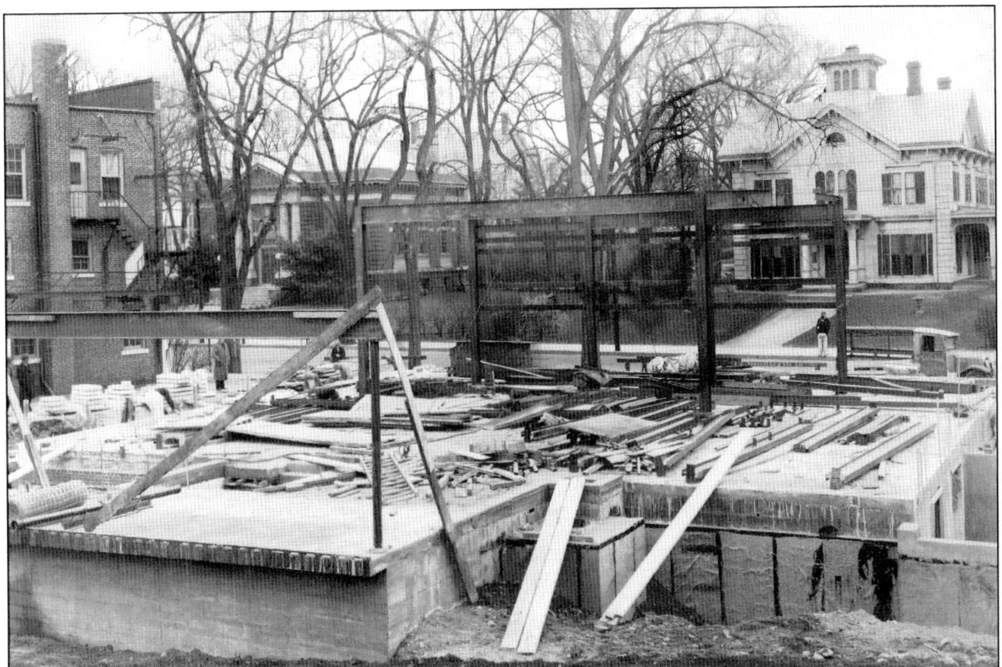

Construction during the WPA era produced the next post office, at 19 Park Street. From left to right in the background are the Stoughton Trust Company, the Stoughton Public Library, and the Chicatabut Club. The new post office would be dedicated on February 4, 1939.

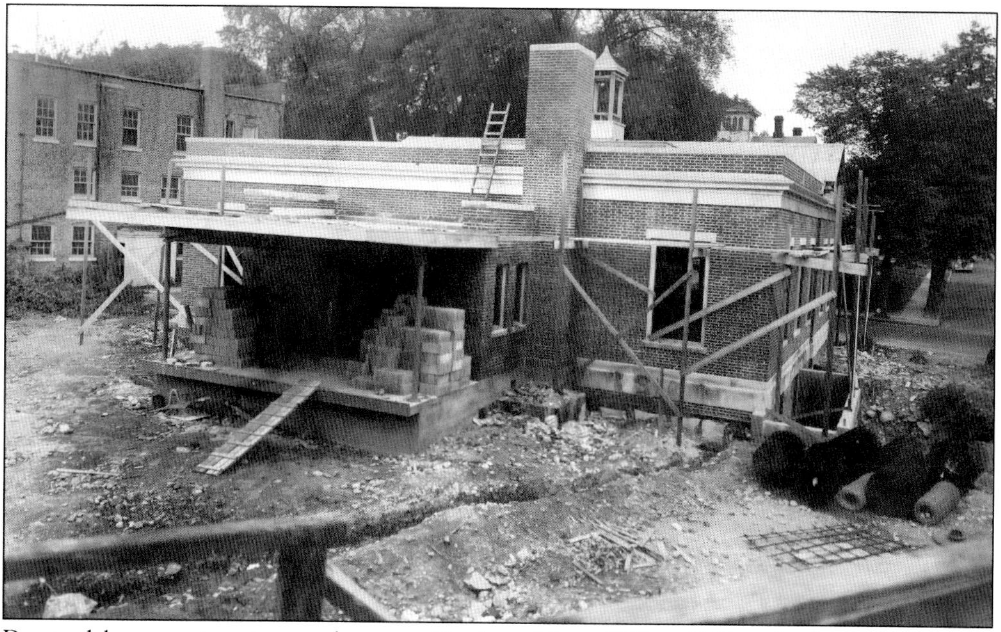

Due to delays, construction on the post office lasted from 1937 to 1939 at this location. On this site once stood the majestic columned home of Stoughton town clerk and businessman Martin Wales. The 19th-century house graced Stoughton Square at Washington and Park Streets, until the Stoughton Trust Company was built on its front lawn in 1916. This building was razed to make way for the post office.

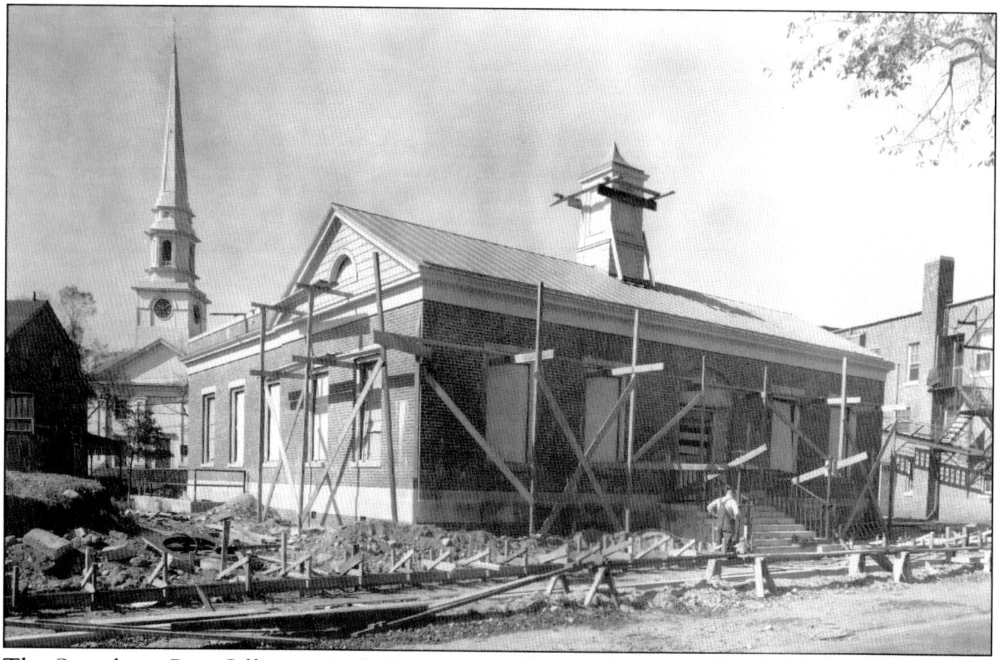

The Stoughton Post Office on Park Street is nearly completed. This building would serve the community from World War II and through the Korean War and Vietnam War years. The post office was at this location until 1976. In recent years, this building has been an antiques store, a karate studio, and a dentist's office.

The current Stoughton Post Office, located at 31 Porter Street, opened in 1976. This site was once the home of James Lehan's Ford dealership. The business was purchased by James Kourafas from the Lehan family and moved to larger accommodations at 1776 Washington Street. The company was renamed Dentch Ford. (Authors' collection.)

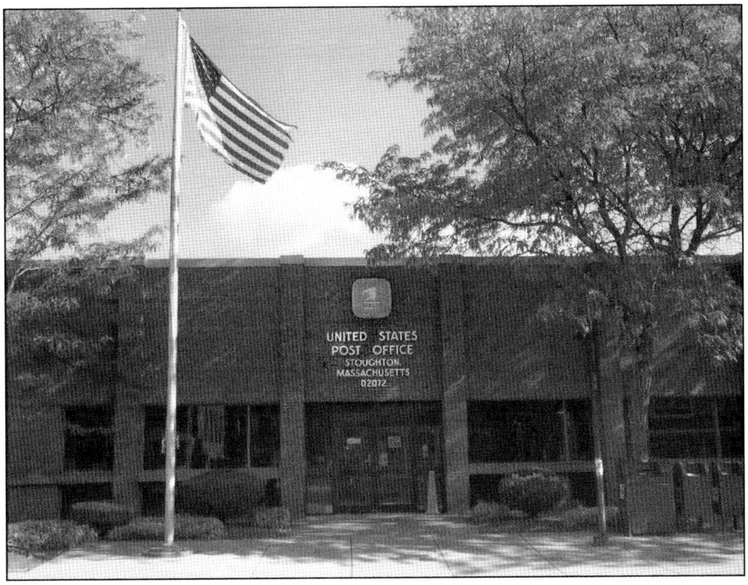

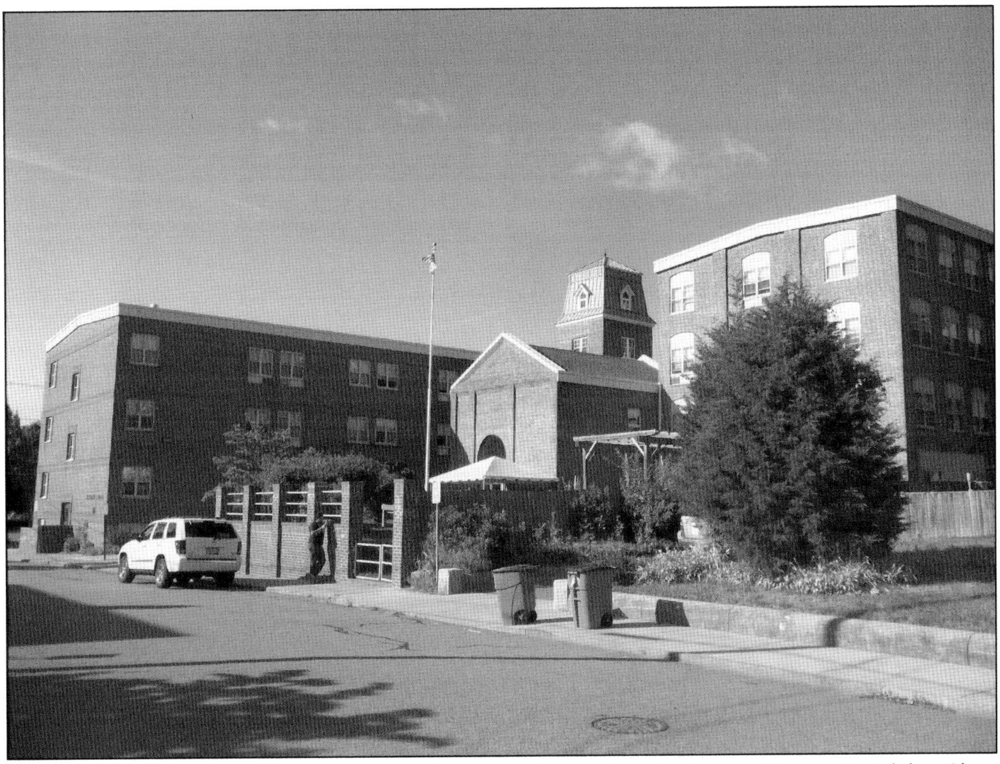

The offices of the Stoughton Housing Authority are located in the former George E. Belcher Shoe Last Factory at the corner of Pleasant and Capen Streets. The once bustling floors of this factory have been home to many Stoughton residents since being converted to housing in the 1970s. On April 15, 2012, a bronze plaque was dedicated by town historian (and coauthor of this book) David Allen Lambert and others at 4 Capen Street, on the side of the structure. The funds for the plaque were raised on Facebook to honor the memory of George Quincy Clifford, who, while president of the Belcher Last Factory, perished aboard the RMS *Titanic*. (Authors' collection.)

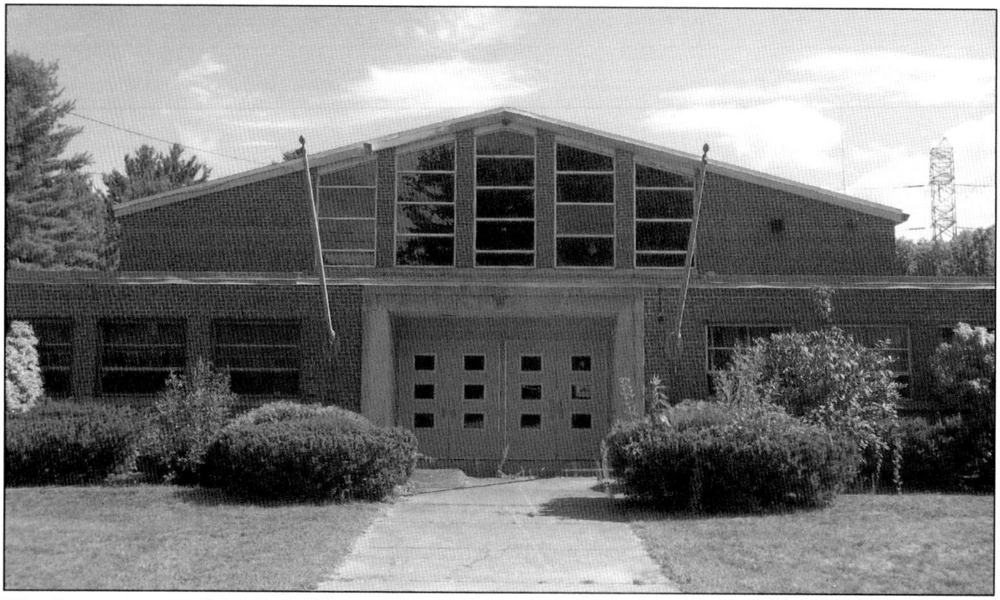

The former home of the Stoughton National Guard Armory was located near the intersection of Pleasant and Turnpike Streets. This structure was a training center for the National Guard when it opened on January 1, 1960, and it continued in this capacity for several decades, until around 2009. The state was going to auction this building off, but local state legislators and Stoughton selectmen fought to keep the structure. The Town of Stoughton purchased it for $1. In recent years, it has housed equipment owned by the town. (Authors' collection.)

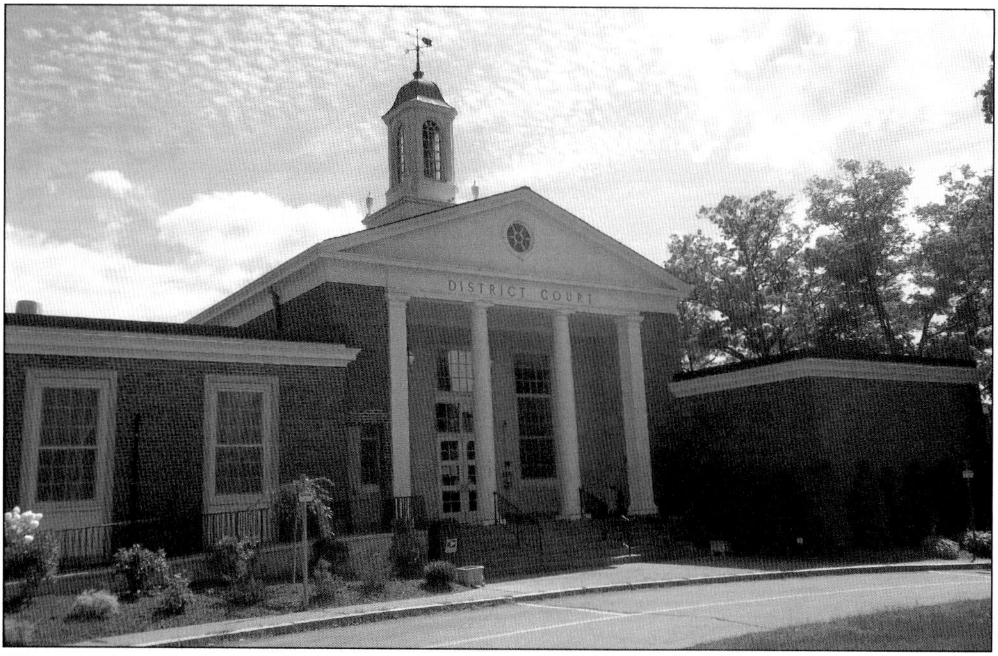

The Stoughton District Court structure opened in 1962 at 1288 Central Street. The courthouse for Norfolk County had formerly been in the second floor of the Swan's Building until relocating to this location. Here, the gavel has fallen under the hands of various judges, including former town manager and judge Francis T. Crimmins Jr. (Authors' collection.)

Two

Places of Worship and Schools in Stoughton

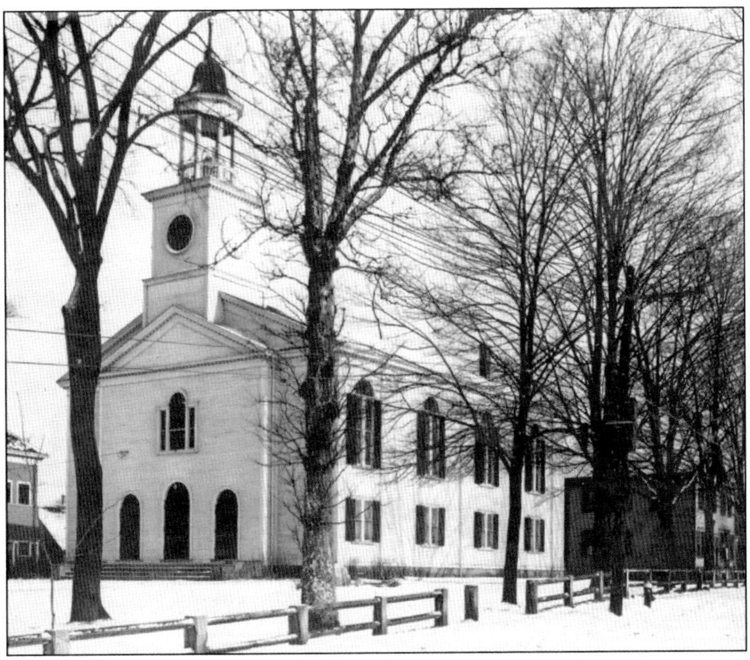

The former First Parish Universalist Church stood at the corner of Pleasant and Washington Streets. Building began on this structure in July 1806, and it was dedicated on June 2, 1808. Within the walls of the Church of Christ occurred the split that created the Universalists and Congregationalists on July 10, 1822. The building was altered and remodeled in 1848 and enlarged in 1870.

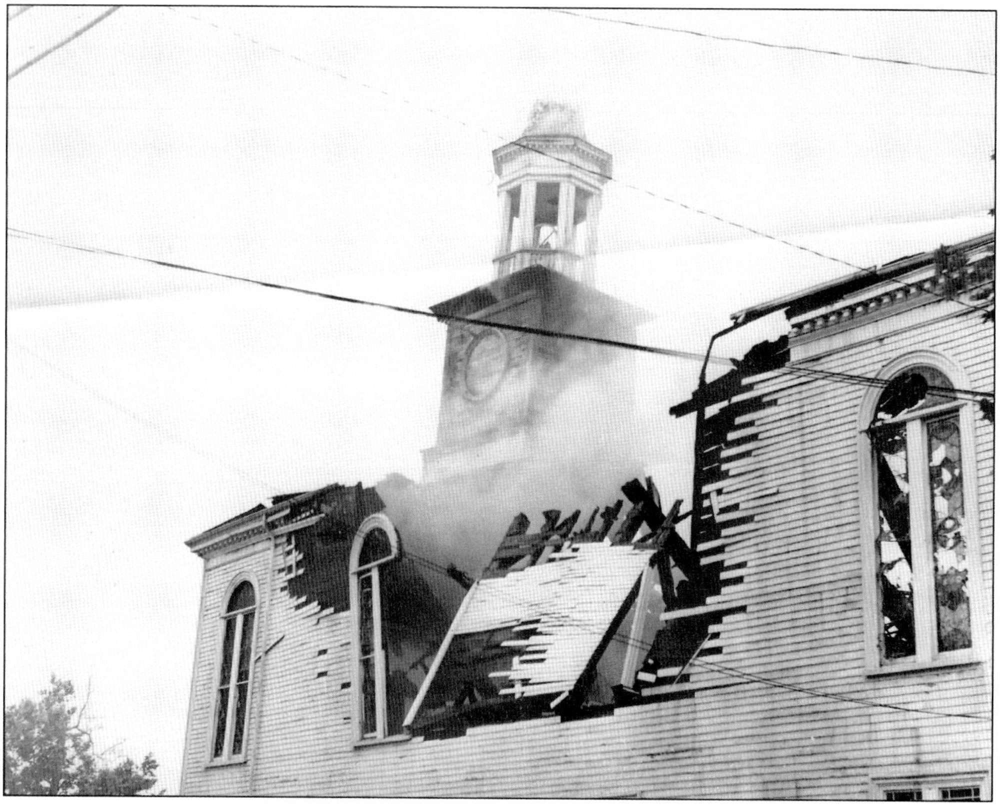

The destruction of the Universalist church at 790 Washington Street came at the hands of a fire on June 29, 1966.

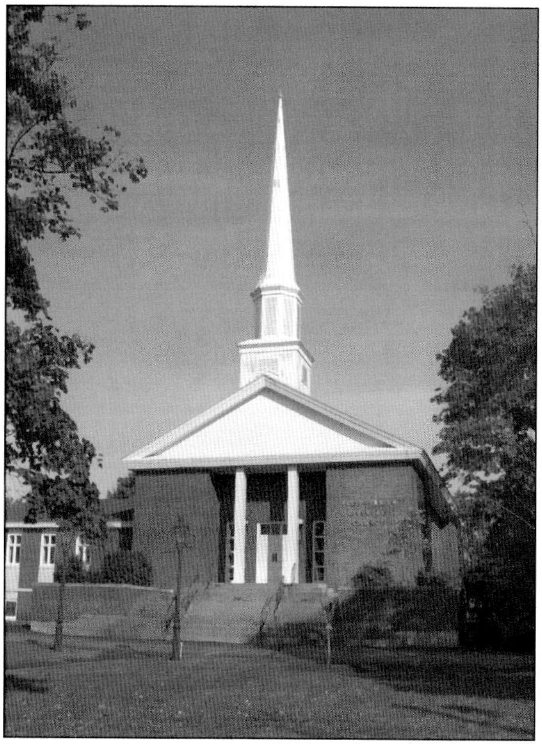

The current building for the First Parish Universalist Church was dedicated in April 1970. Portions of the original granite posts that surround the church green still remain. The church green, formerly where soldiers mustered, is now where town residents gather for Saturday farmers' markets. (Authors' collection.)

This was the second home of the First Congregational Church, dedicated on January 28, 1852, at 819 Washington Street. This structure was destroyed by fire on March 9, 1942. The site has for many decades been occupied by a gas station. The old parsonage of Rev. Albert Perry still stands next to the former church location. This photograph was taken by the well-known Stoughton photographer George A. Gerard. (Authors' collection.)

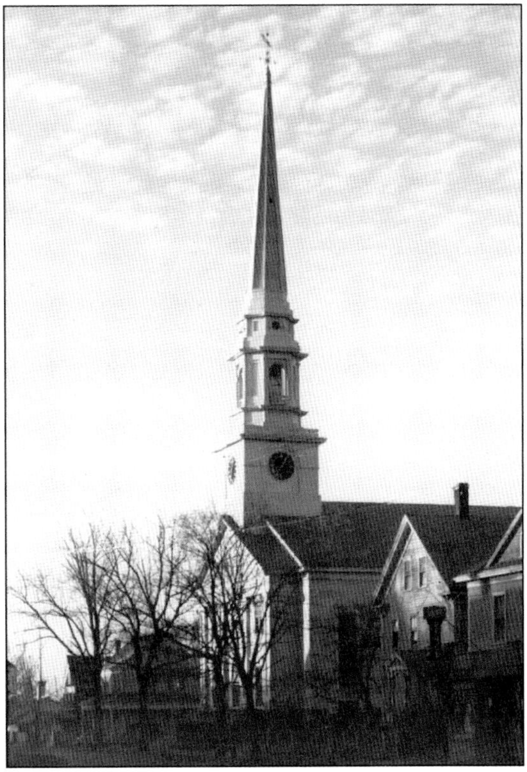

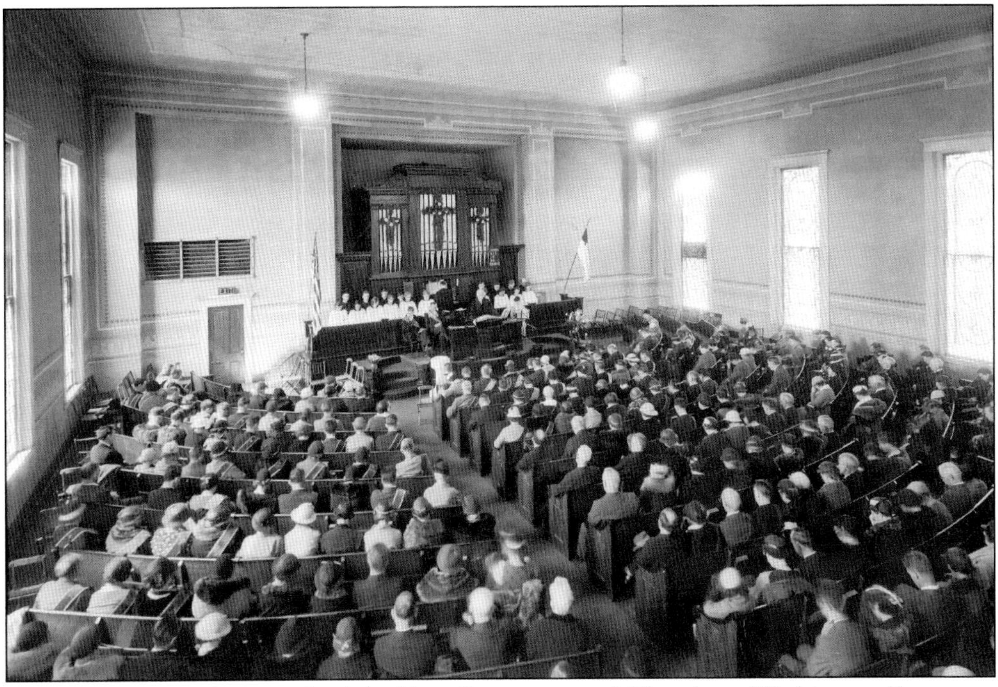

This rare interior photograph of the First Congregational Church on Washington Street was taken from the balcony on Grange Sunday, April 8, 1934. The minister at this service was Rev. Hugh P. Hughes, and the organist was Carl L. Smith.

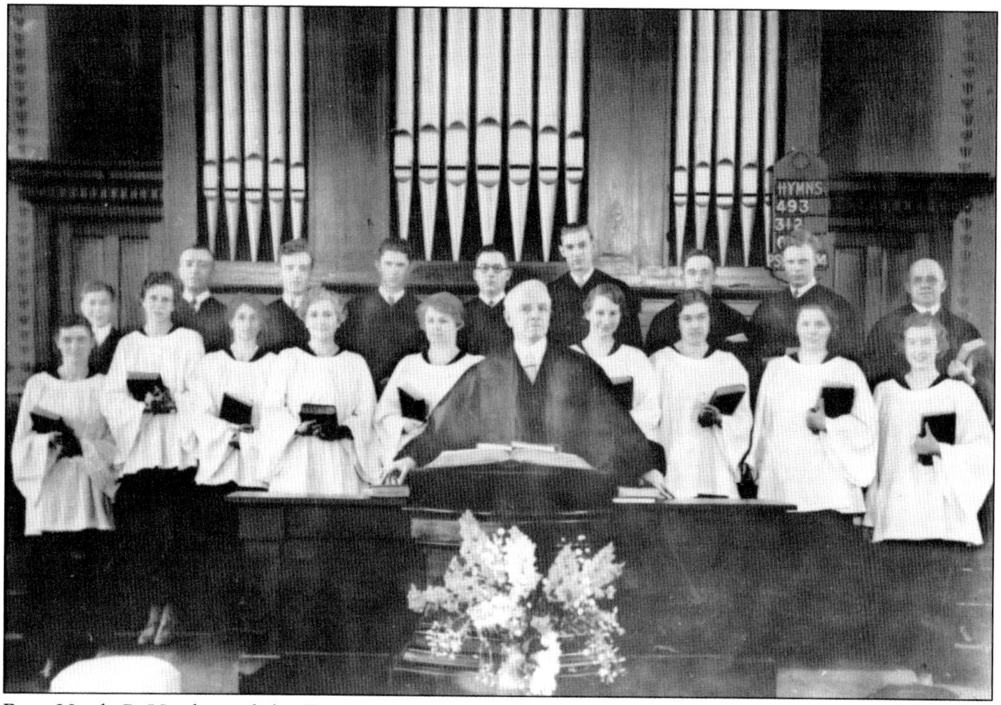

Rev. Hugh P. Hughes of the First Congregational Church and the church choir pose on May 13, 1934. With Hughes are, from left to right, (first row) Lillian Henry, Claire Cooper, Esther Snowdale, Olive Bisbee, Sylvia Evans, Esther (Kelle) Hughes, Constance Leonard, Mrs. Russell Estey, and Dorothy Bird; (second row) Robert Evans, William Gardner, Hugh I. Hughes, Charles Snowdale, Carl Smith, Russell Estey, Willard Emery, Fred Evans, and G. Lester Gay.

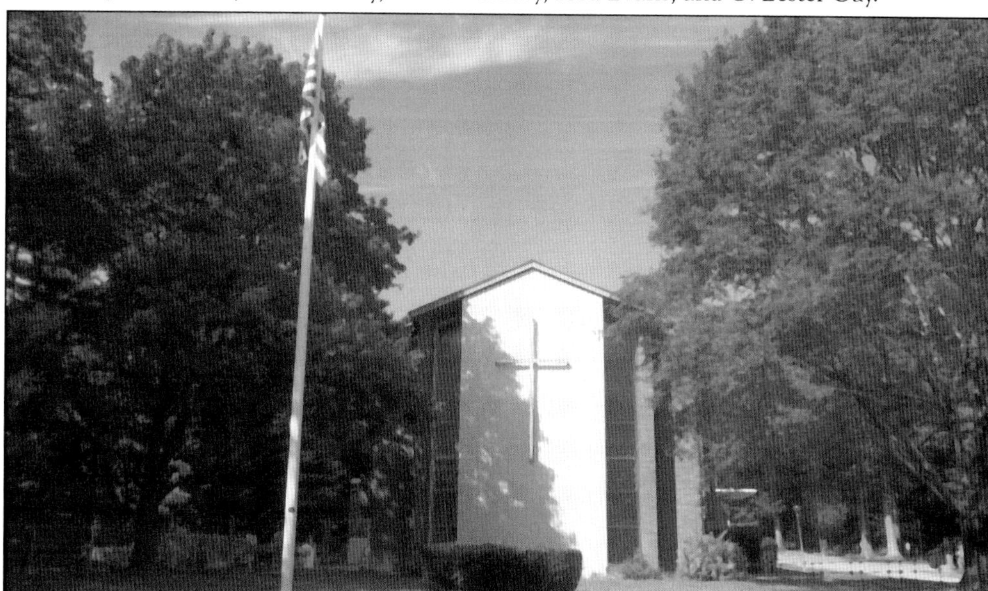

The present home of the First Congregational Church is at 76 Pierce Street in Stoughton. This structure was dedicated in 1959. Prior to being at this location, the church stood at 30 Pearl Street from 1949 until 1958, when it was sold to Ahavath Torah Congregation. (Authors' collection.)

This is the current home of the First United Methodist Church, at 103 Pleasant Street. Dedicated on December 5, 1866, it was built at a cost of $14,000 on the site of an earlier structure, which stood from 1835 to 1865. In 1896, a parsonage was built next to the church on Pleasant Street. The construction of the Tri Mu (Mind, Muscle and Morals) Gymnasium was started in 1928 on the Seaver Street side behind the church. The original church steeple and bell were removed due to rotted timbers on August 24, 1984. A fiberglass spire was added to the top of the church on May 6, 1987.

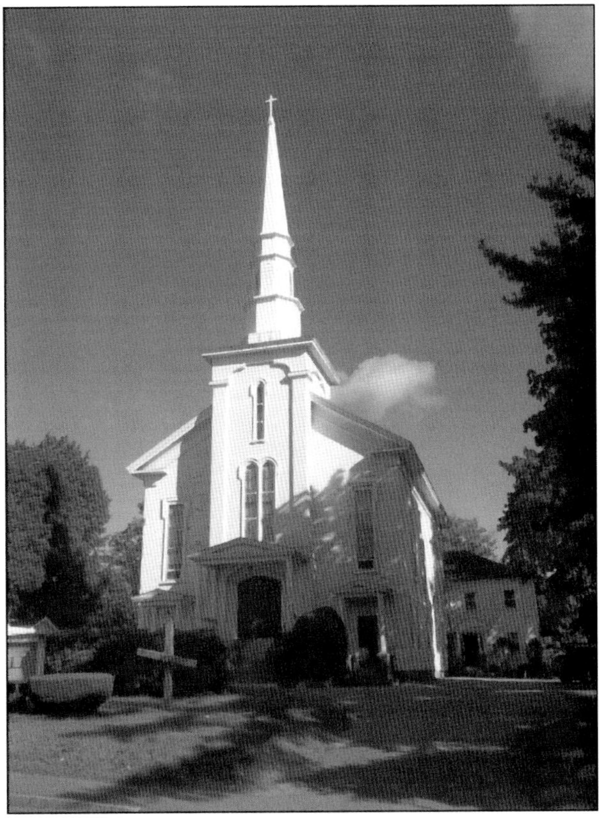

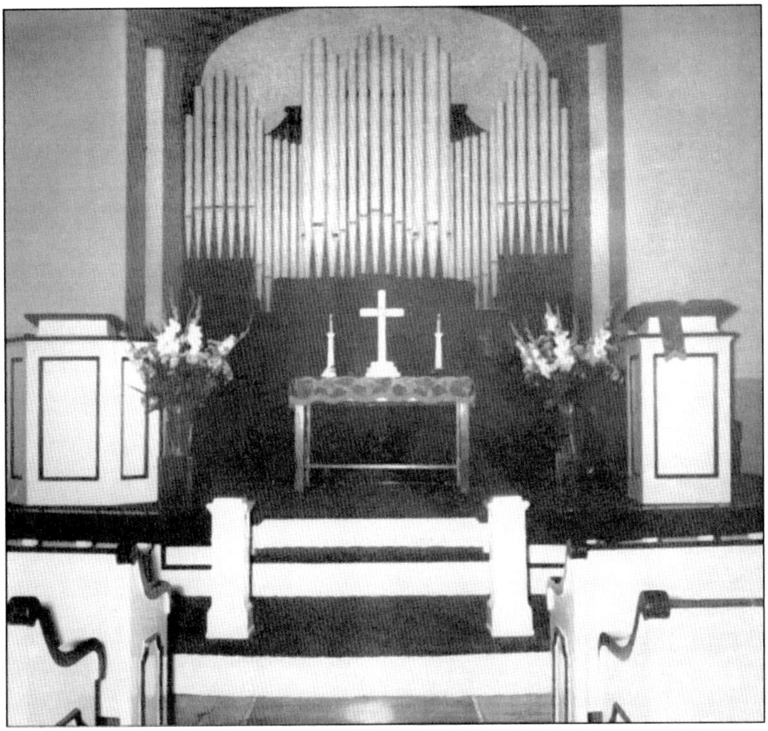

This interior photograph shows the First United Methodist Church's current organ. This Estey organ was installed in 1910 at a cost of $1,600 and is still used today. The wooden pews of the oldest church structure in present-day Stoughton still serve this parish.

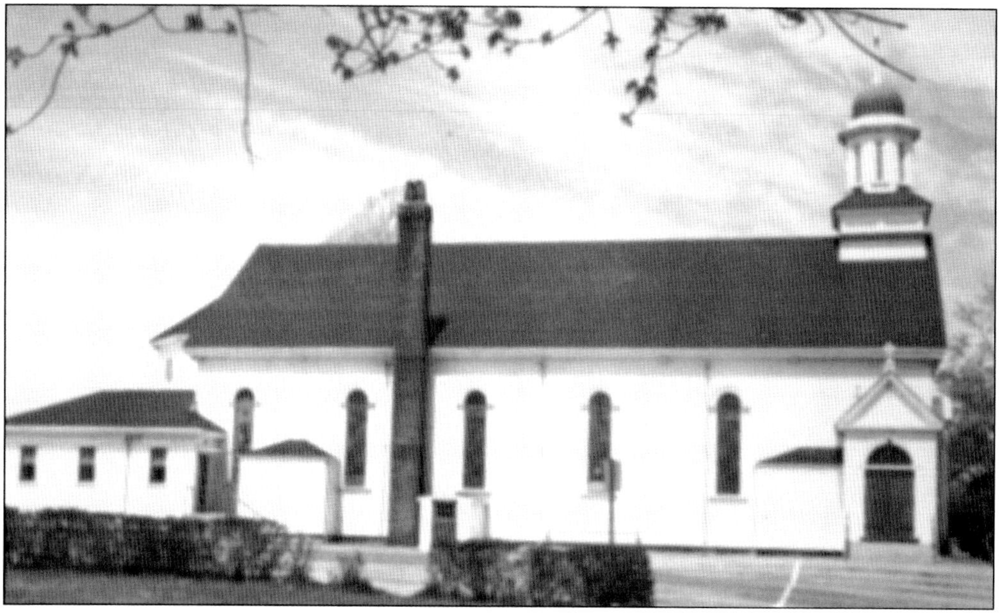

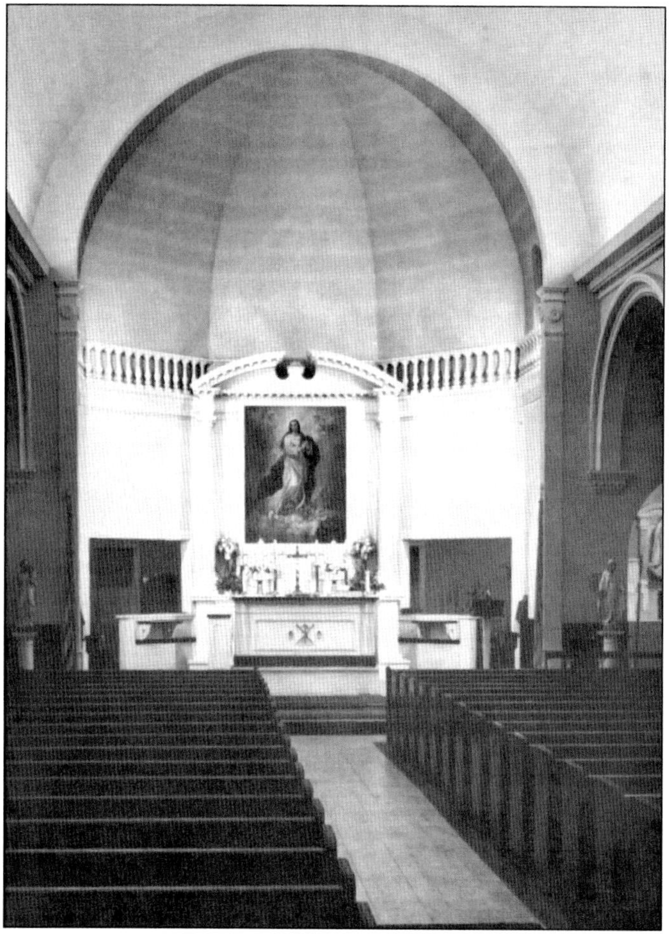

The Immaculate Conception Church at Canton and School Streets was dedicated on November 10, 1859. This church, formalized as a parish in 1872, was the home of many generations of Stoughton Catholics until it was razed in the early 1970s. (Authors' collection.)

This is an interior view of the Immaculate Conception Church. The altar portrait was painted by noted Stoughton artist Frederick Mortimer Lamb (1866–1936).

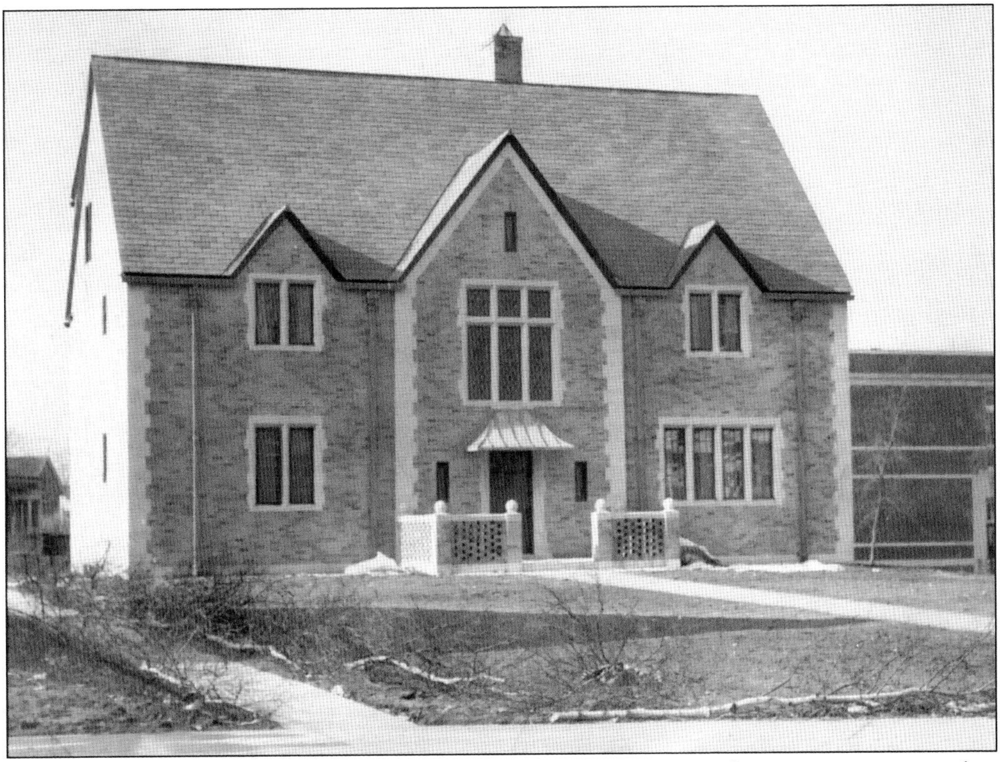

The rectory for the Immaculate Conception Church, at 122 Canton Street, was constructed in the early 1920s and still serves the parish today.

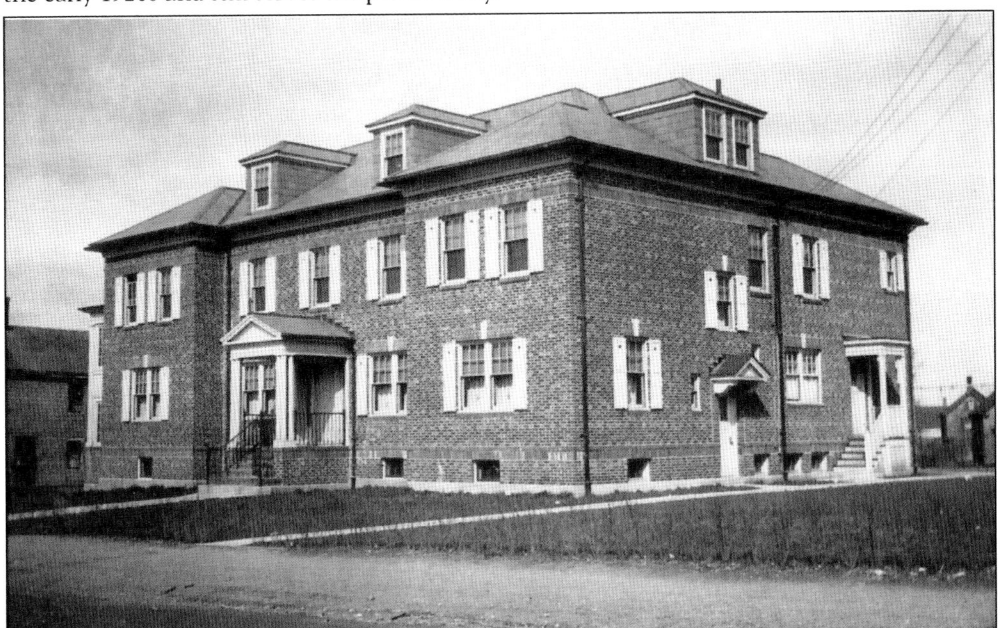

The brick convent for the teachers of the Sisters of St. Joseph was located on School Street. It was demolished in the early 1970s. This site is now part of the parking lot that has hosted many festivals and feasts associated with the church.

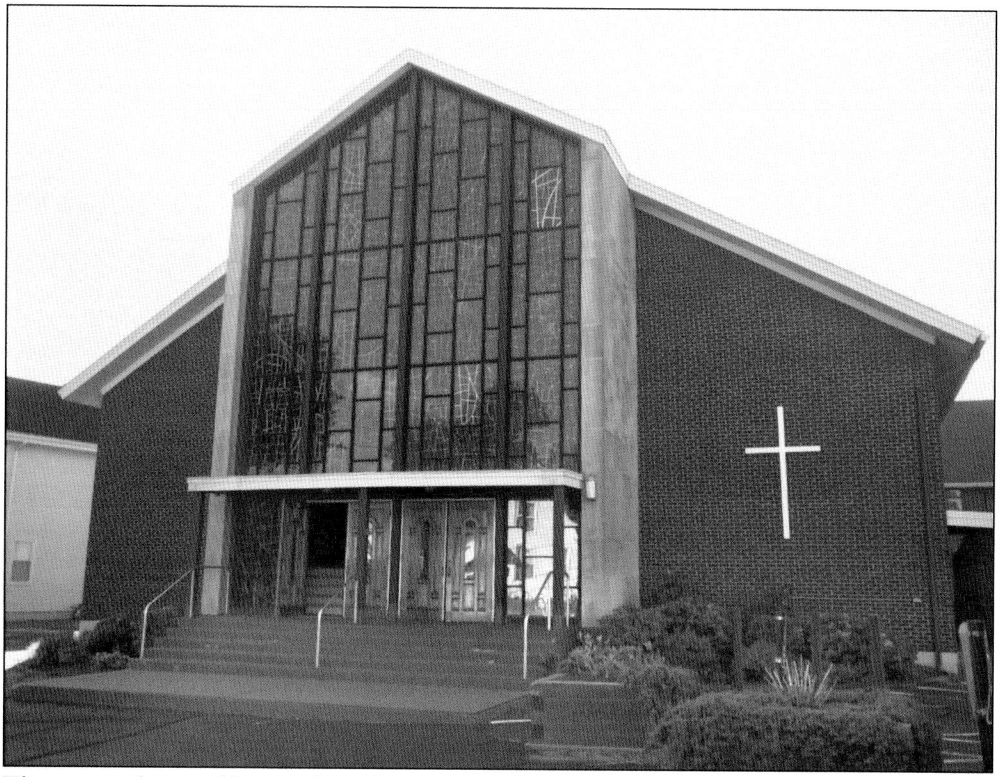
The current home of Immaculate Conception Church opened in 1979 on the location of the 19th-century church at School and Canton Streets. Before construction was completed, the parish met in the basement of this structure. (Authors' collection.)

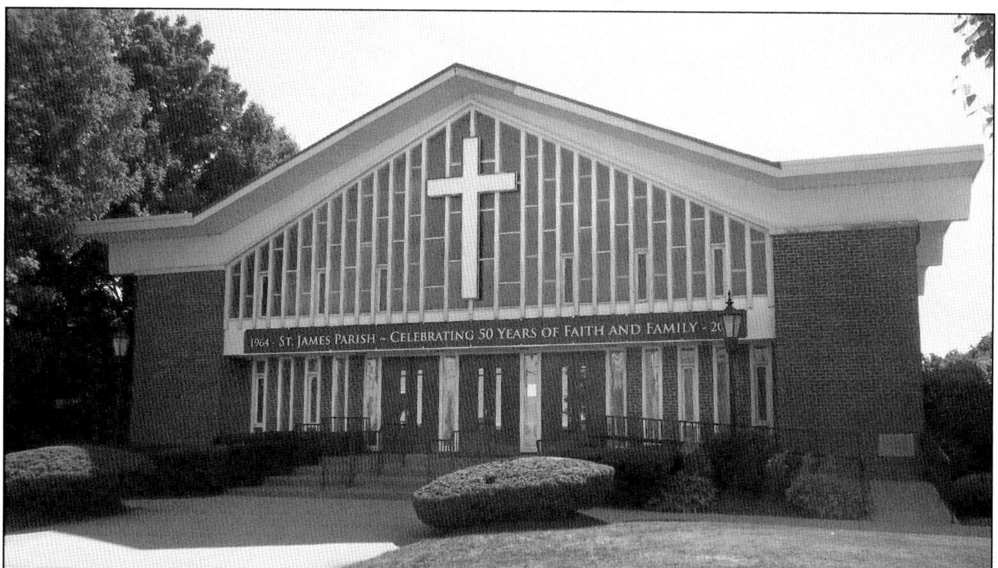

St. James Parish Church has served the Catholic parishioners of North Stoughton for 50 years. St. James opened this structure at 560 Page Street in 1964. The congregation had formerly met in the old Sullivan family barn across the street. (Authors' collection.)

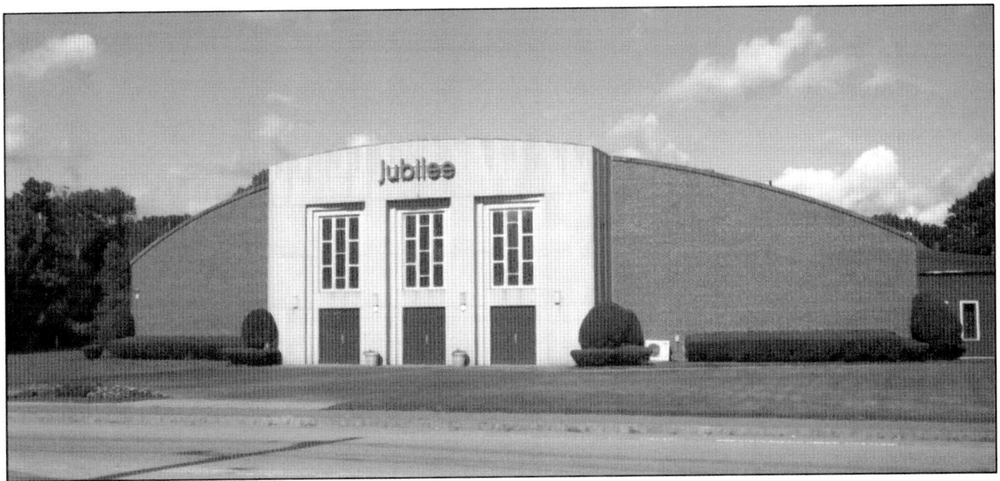

The Jubilee Christian Church purchased the former Our Lady of the Rosary Church at 1278 Park Street. This structure opened in 1958 and was sold by the Boston Catholic Archdiocese to the Jubilee Christian Church International in 2006. (Authors' collection.)

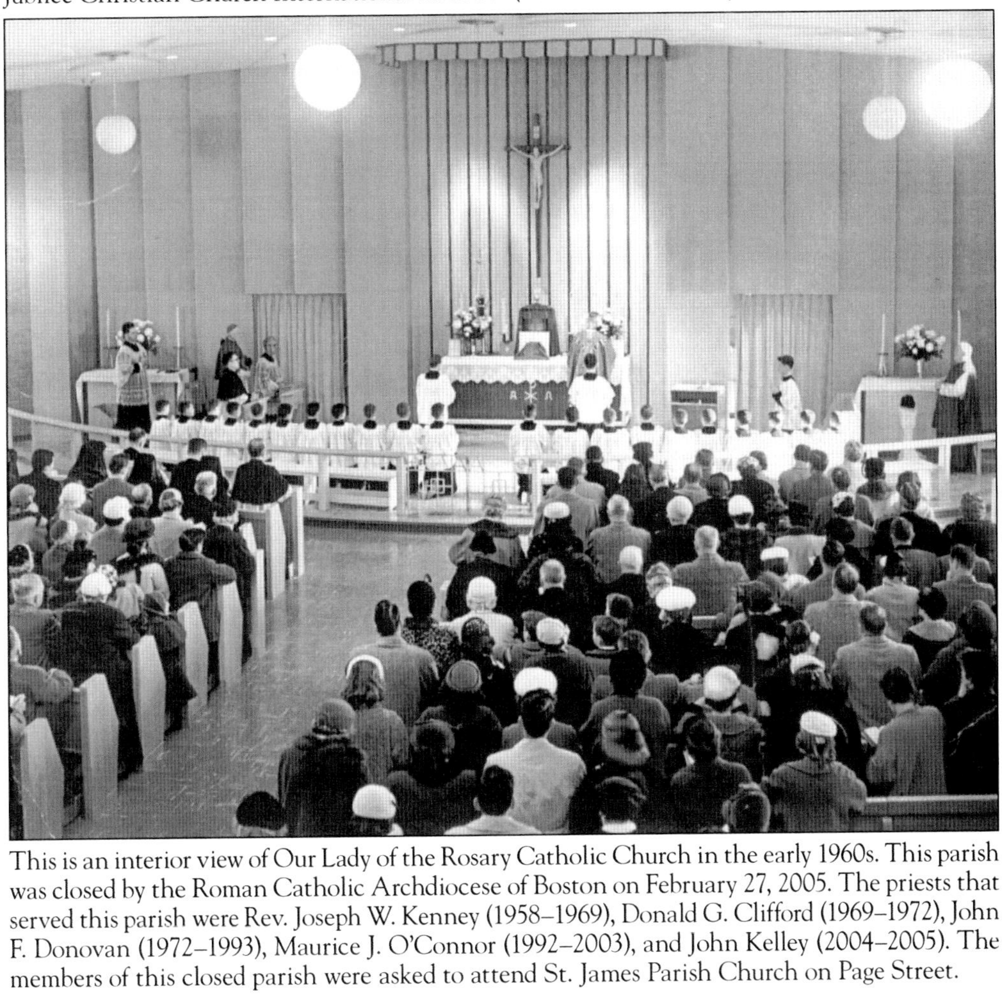
This is an interior view of Our Lady of the Rosary Catholic Church in the early 1960s. This parish was closed by the Roman Catholic Archdiocese of Boston on February 27, 2005. The priests that served this parish were Rev. Joseph W. Kenney (1958–1969), Donald G. Clifford (1969–1972), John F. Donovan (1972–1993), Maurice J. O'Connor (1992–2003), and John Kelley (2004–2005). The members of this closed parish were asked to attend St. James Parish Church on Page Street.

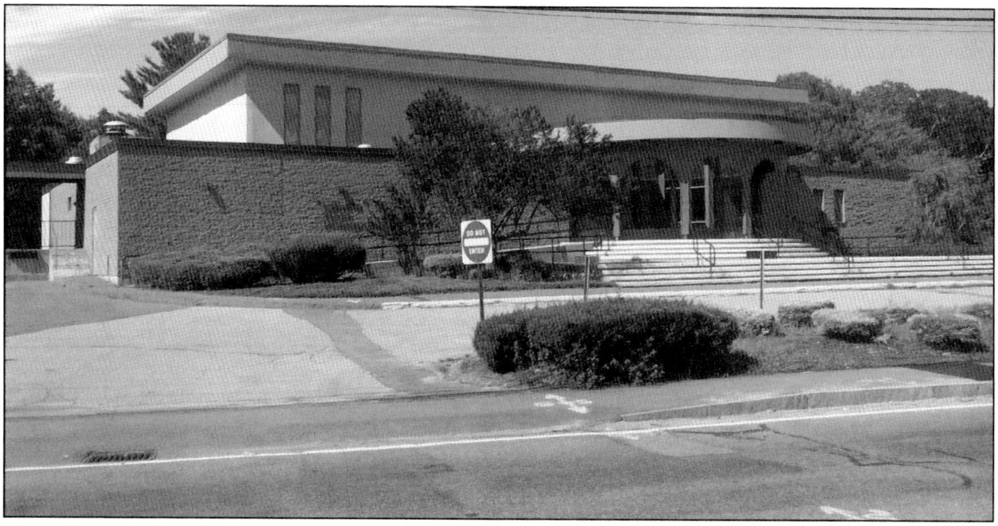

The Ahavath Torah Congregation synagogue, located at 1179 Central Street, was dedicated in June 1970. The congregation dedicated its first synagogue, on Porter Street, on October 14, 1919. It was relocated in 1958 to 30 Pearl Street, the former home of the First Congregational Church. (Authors' collection.)

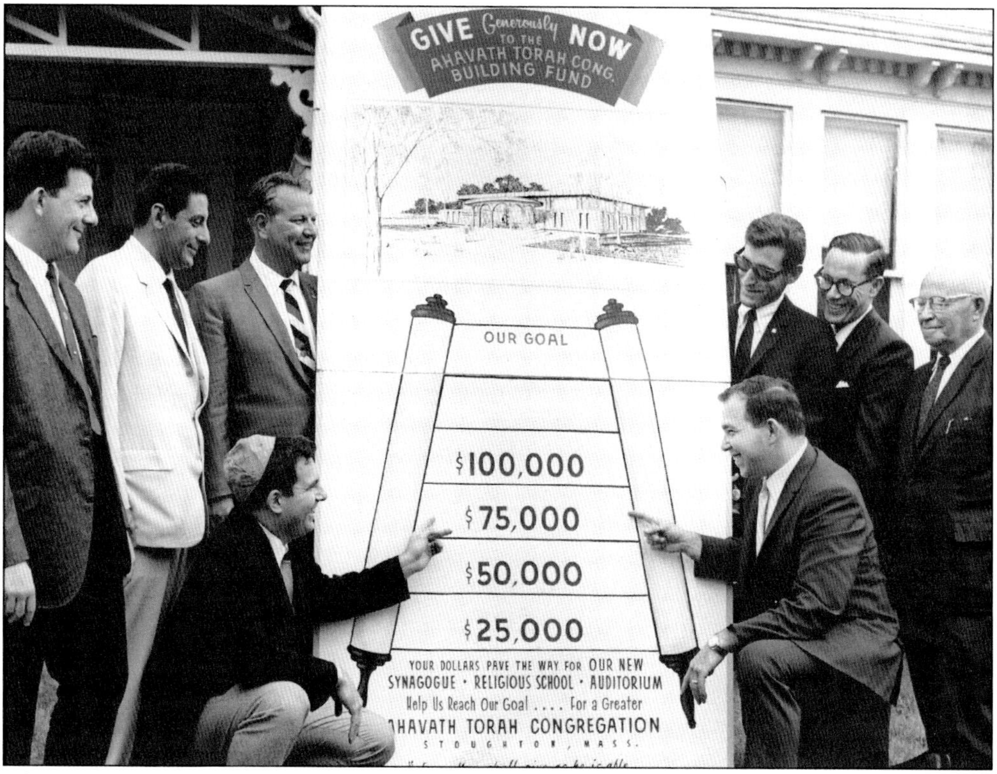

This poster was displayed outside of the 30 Pearl Street synagogue of the Ahavath Torah Congregation. Active fundraising to move to a modern structure appears to be at $75,000. The new temple would have a synagogue, an auditorium, and would house a Hebrew school in the basement. The temple was renovated and enlarged in 1987.

The Trinity Episcopal Church at 48 Freeman Street was dedicated in 1898 and served the parish until 1969. Trinity Church formed in Stoughton on October 1, 1893, and met originally at the old Masonic Block on Wyman Street. This photograph was taken by George A. Gerard in 1908.

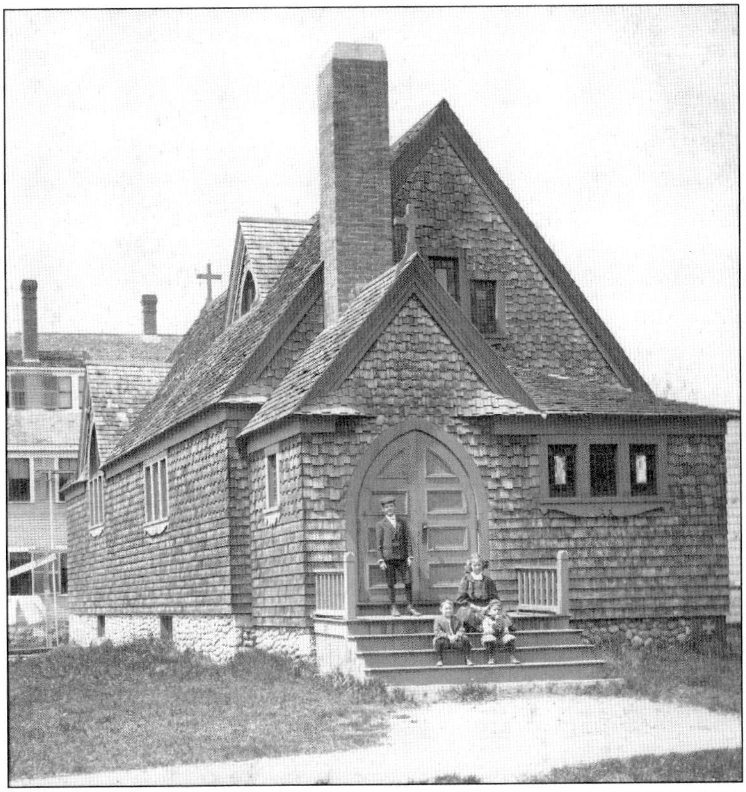

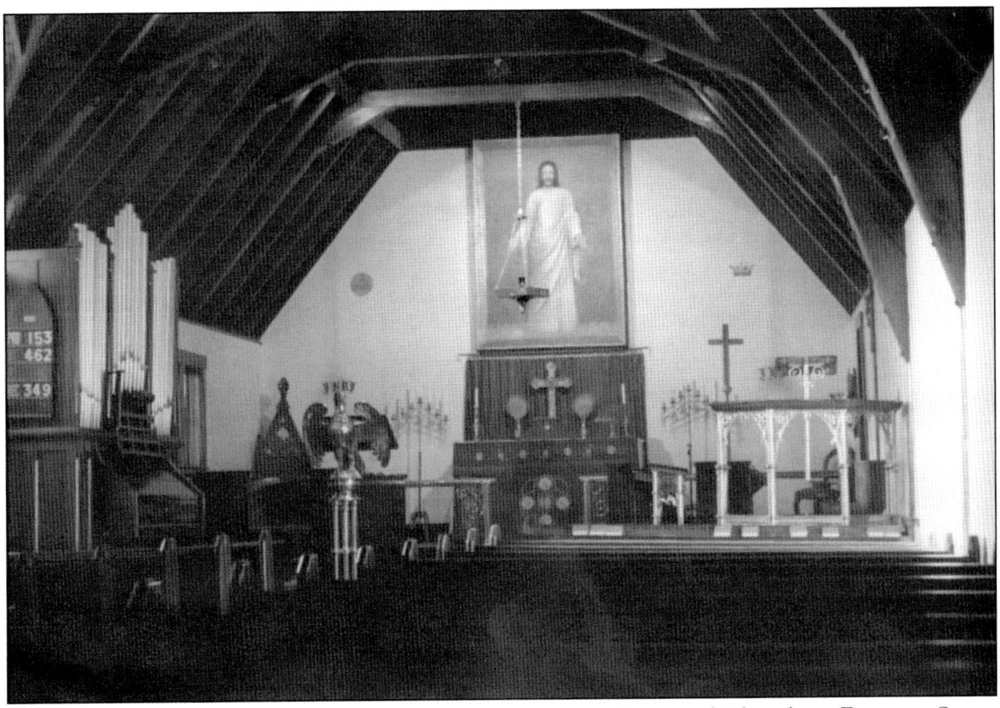

This interior view shows the timbered sanctuary of Trinity Episcopal Church on Freeman Street in 1949.

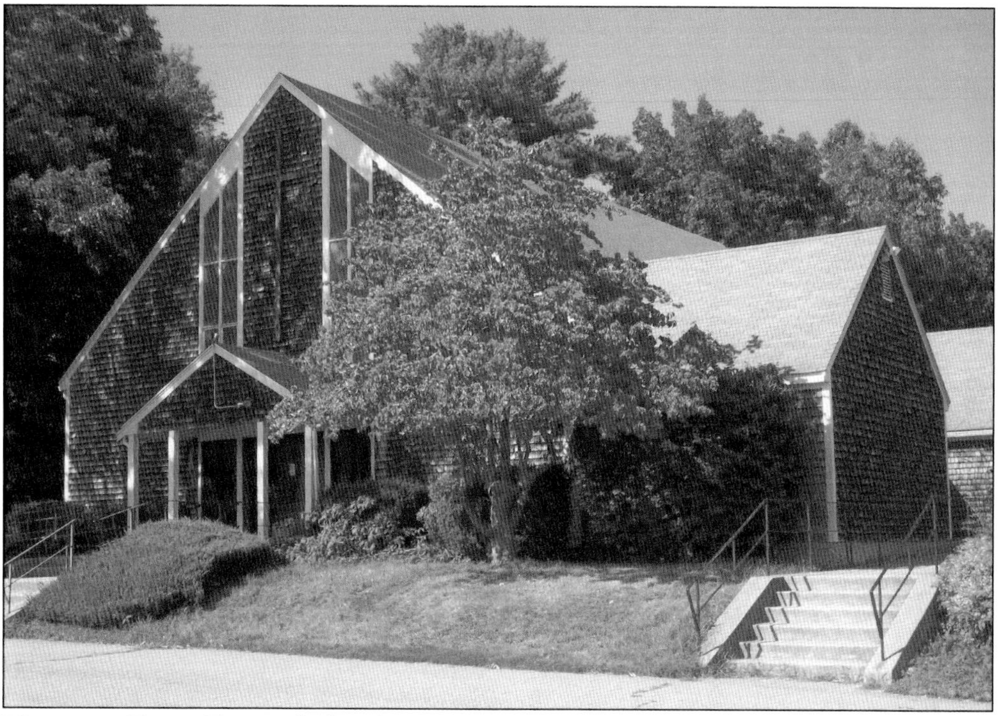

The present Trinity Episcopal Church, at 414 Sumner Street, was dedicated in 1969. This modern structure has also been home to a nursery school run by the parish. (Authors' collection.)

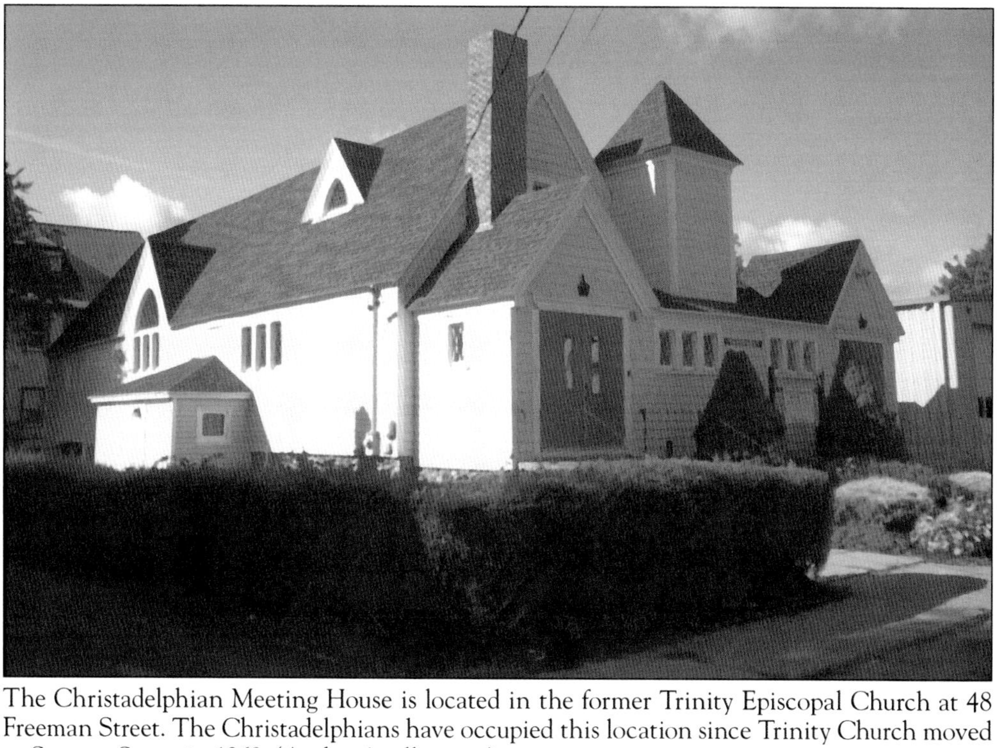

The Christadelphian Meeting House is located in the former Trinity Episcopal Church at 48 Freeman Street. The Christadelphians have occupied this location since Trinity Church moved to Sumner Street in 1969. (Authors' collection.)

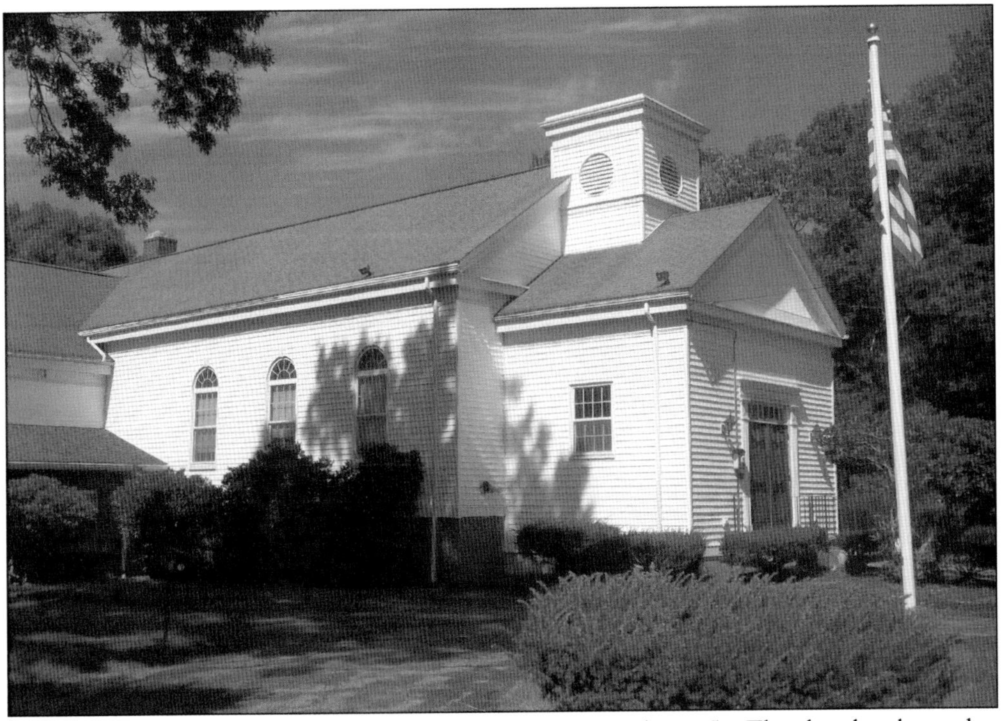

Faith Baptist Church was organized in Stoughton in September 1954. The church is located at 18 Stoughton Street. The congregation held its first services in the basement of this building on March 15, 1961. The new church at this location was dedicated on October 11, 1970, and a new sanctuary was dedicated on June 17, 1984. (Authors' collection.)

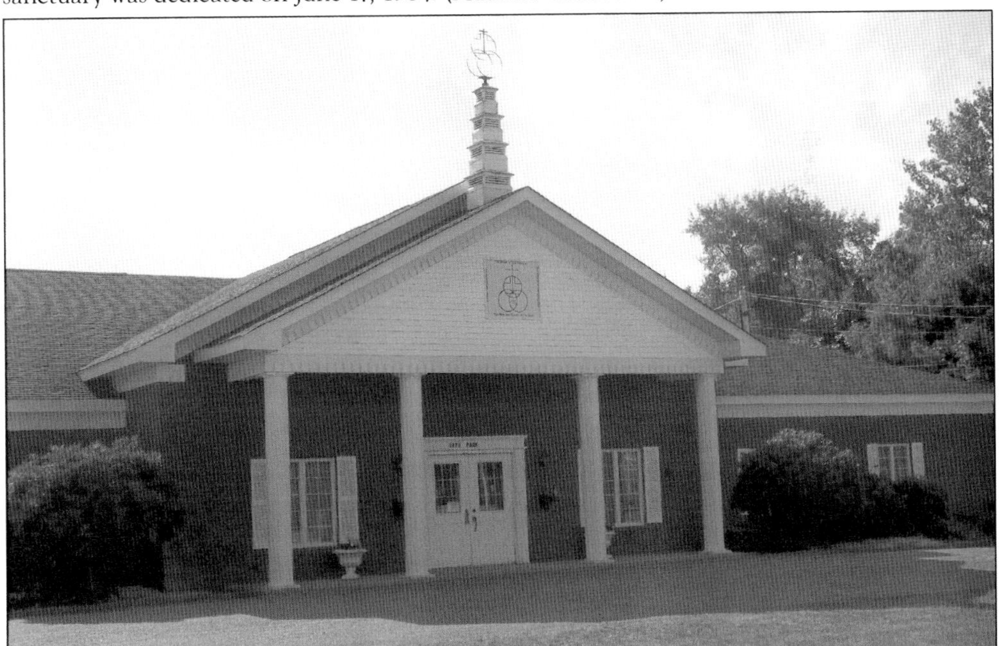

The House of God Church at 1271 Park Street was built in 1986. This church opened its doors in the former satellite location of Sheehan Funeral Home in 2005. (Authors' collection.)

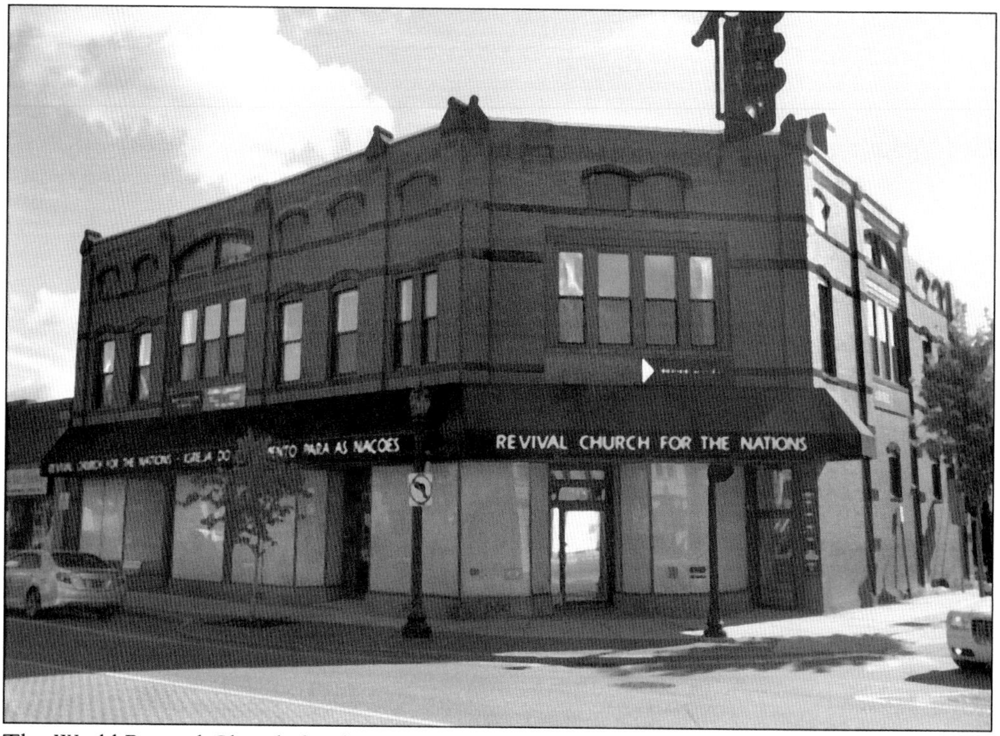

The World Revival Church for the Nations is located at 757 Washington Street in Stoughton Square. This church is located at the former site of Monk's Cash Store, J.J. Newberry Co., and the temporary home for Stoughton Town Hall in the late 1980s.

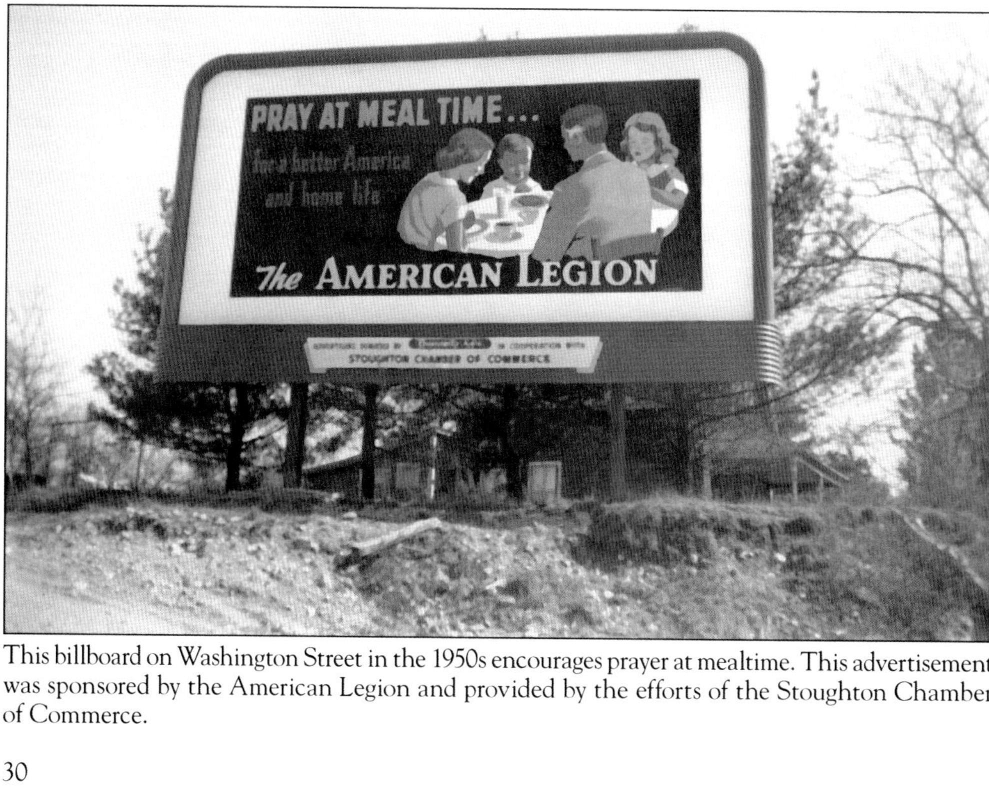

This billboard on Washington Street in the 1950s encourages prayer at mealtime. This advertisement was sponsored by the American Legion and provided by the efforts of the Stoughton Chamber of Commerce.

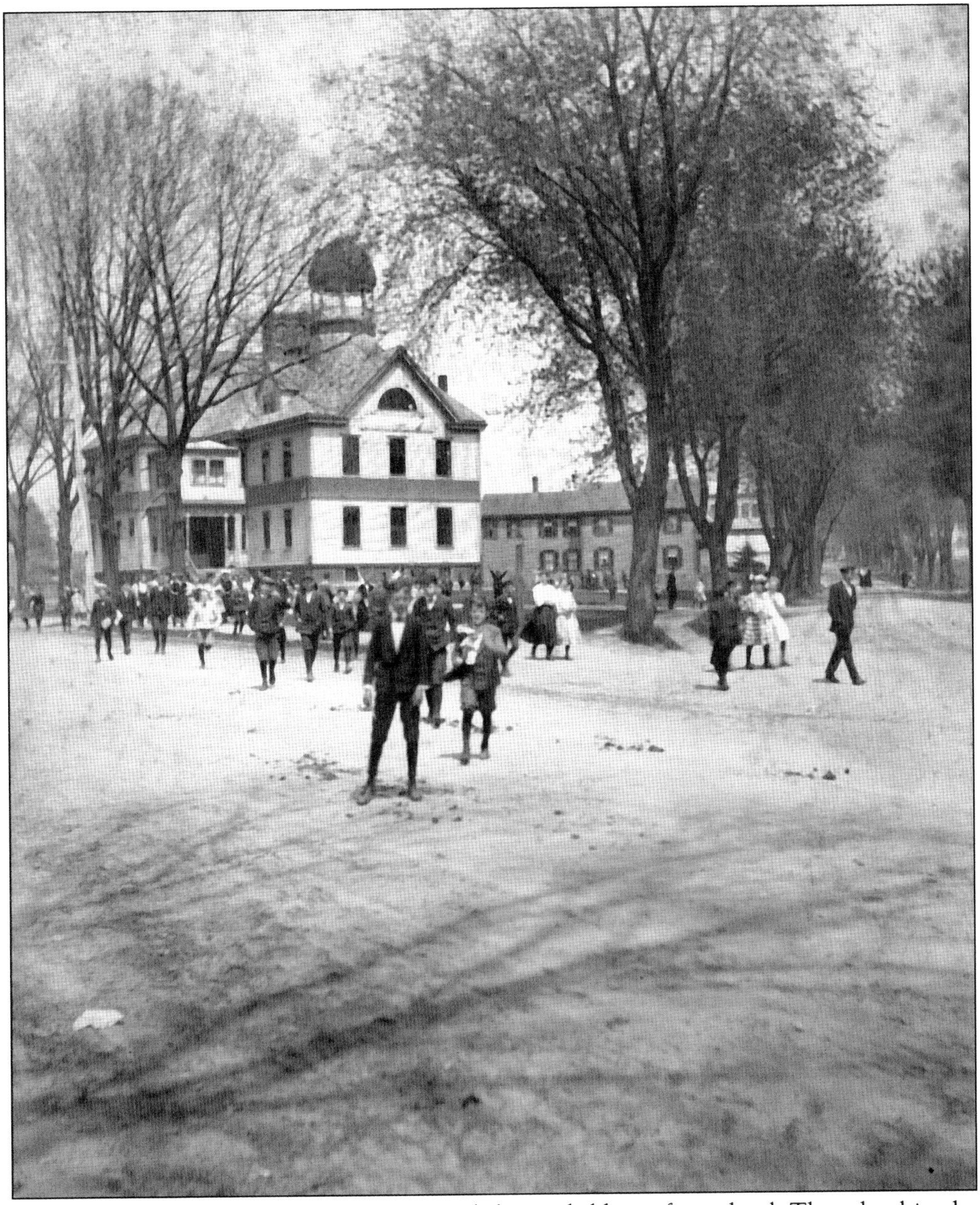

This 1908 photograph by George A. Gerard shows children after school. The school in the background is the former Drake School, at the intersection of Monk and Washington Streets. This site is now the location of Webster Bank, at 700 Washington Street.

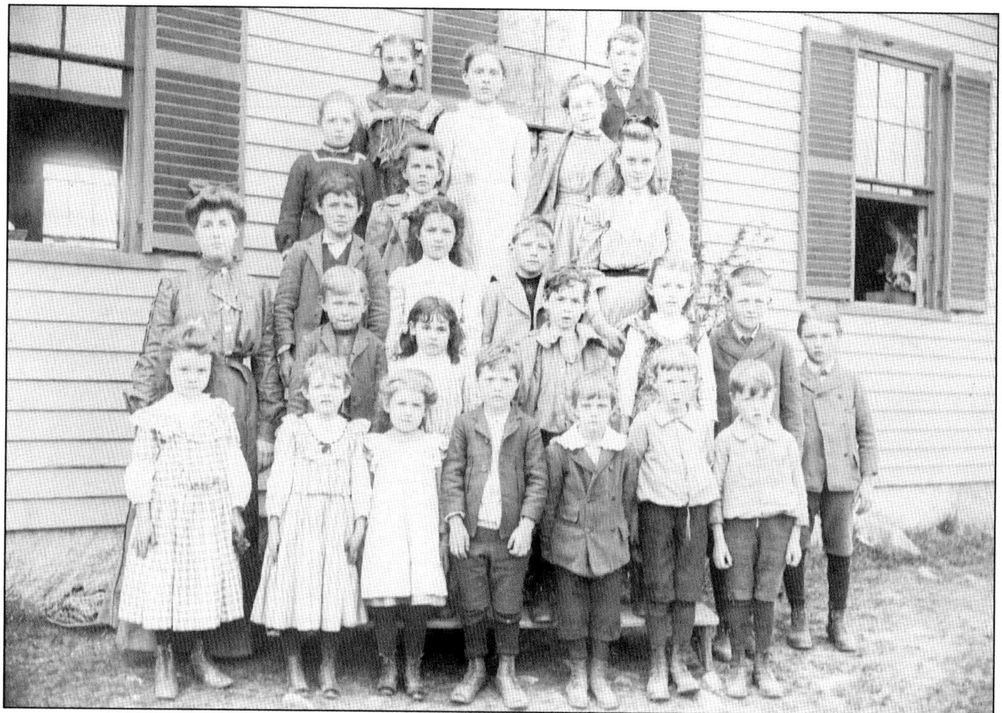

Students gather outside Adams Schoolhouse, located at 1575 Central Street, in the first decade of the 20th century. The schoolhouse, built in the 19th century, was later moved to the grounds of the Stoughton Department of Public Works. The school is behind the Charles H. Lane American Veterans Post No. 1977.

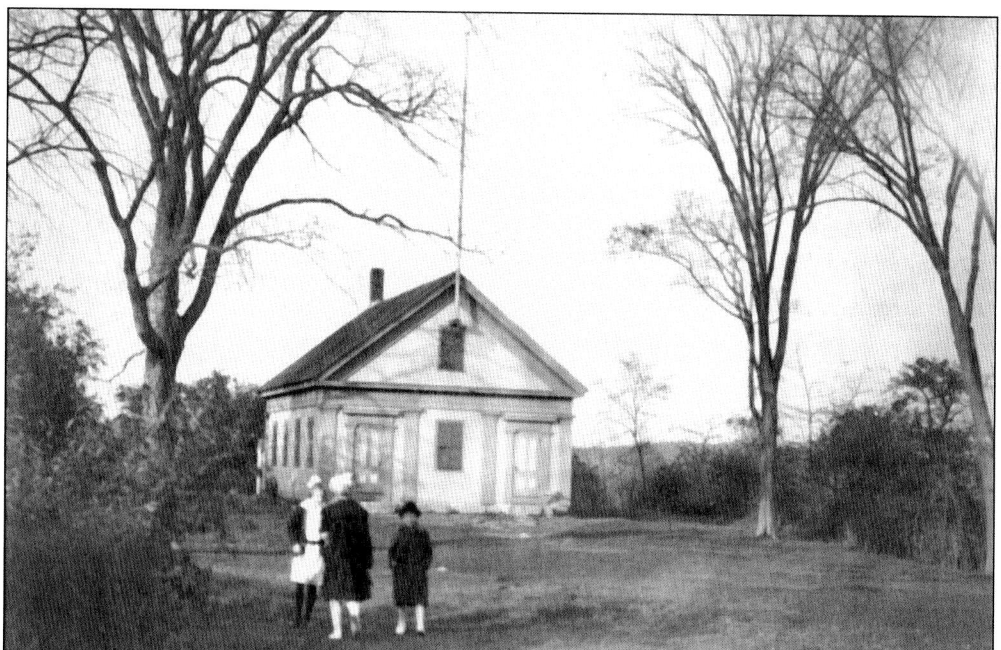

Atherton School at 365 Central Street in Stoughton is shown in 1915. This school opened in the 19th century and was used until 1933.

Capen School stood at the intersection of Page and Turnpike Streets in the 1920s. This school served the children of North Stoughton from 1892 until June 1969, when it closed. Its cost of $5,921.34 covered the land purchase and the school's construction, by Elisha S. Hawes. In 1924, a branch of the Stoughton Public Library was attempted here. (Authors' collection.)

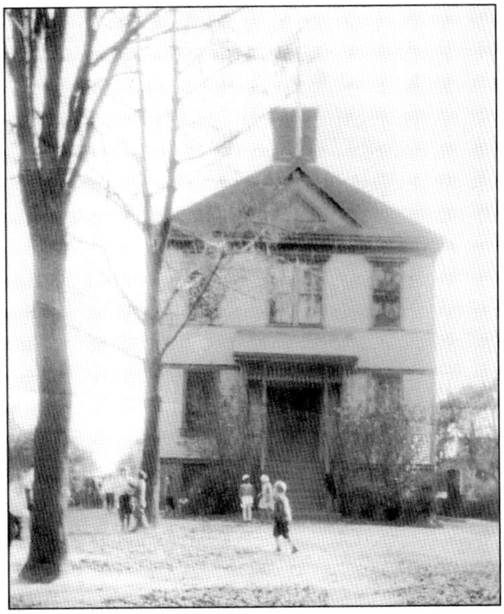

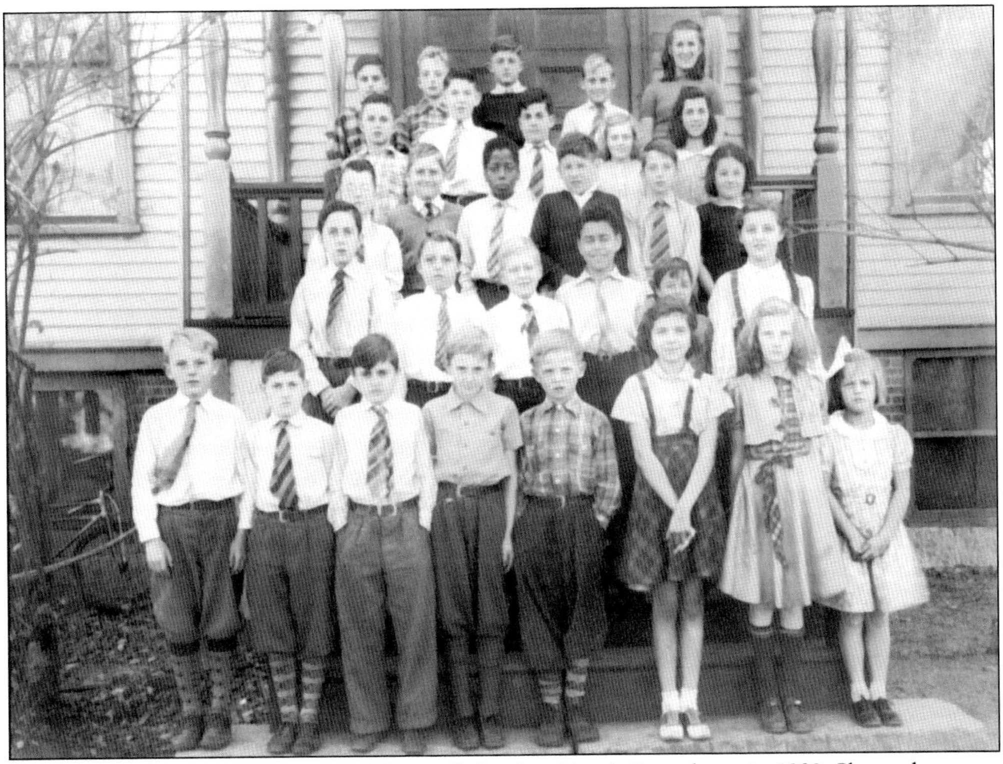

Students pose on the front steps of Capen School in North Stoughton in 1939. Shown here are, from left to right, (first row) unidentified, Chet Leathers, Edward Russo, Bob Davis, Paul Page, Violet Tukas, Shirley Laarhoven, and Paula Page; (second row) ? Lomar, Henry Sellars, Peter Leif, Sonny Fisher, Eddie Ambrosini, and Gladys Fisher; (third row) unidentified, Clarendon Cobb, Arthur Bryant, Donald Bissett, Walter Parr, and ? Bissett; (fourth row) Robert Page, Walter Cotter, Frank Vincent, Ruth Leathers, and Ella Ambrosini; (fifth row) unidentified, George Howland, two unidentified students, and Laura Barnes.

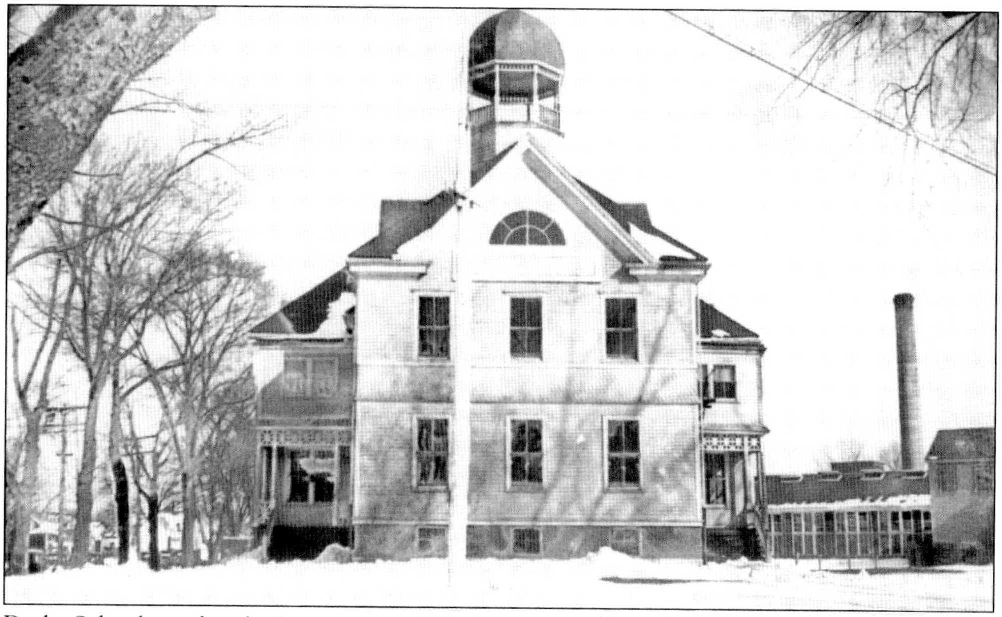

Drake School stood at the intersection of Washington and Monk Streets. The 1890 schoolhouse was designed by architect Fergus H. McKain. The school was closed, and it was razed in the summer of 1955. The Panther Panco Rubber Company factory can be seen behind the school.

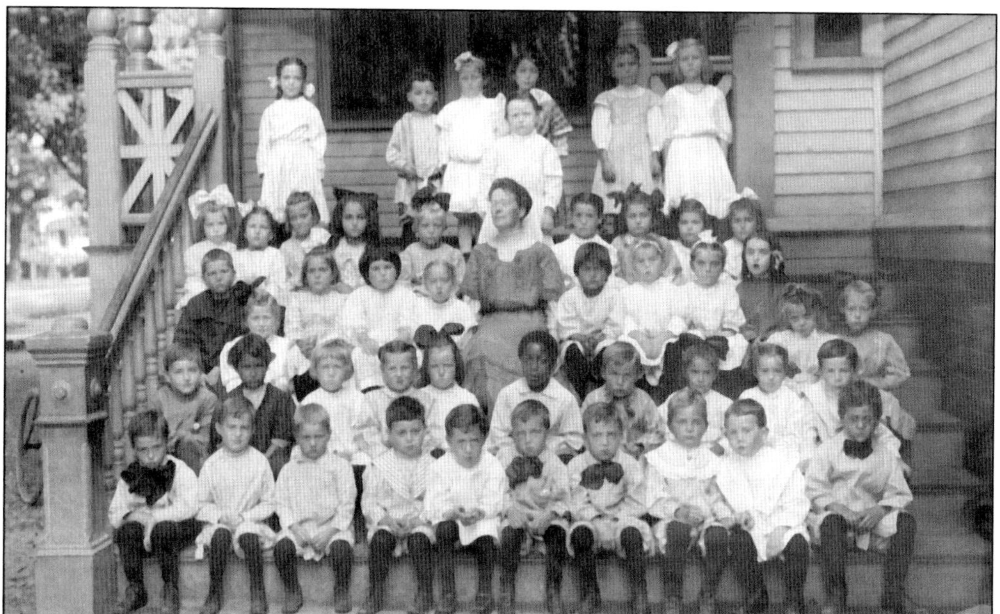

Hattie Tucker's first graders pose on the steps of Drake School in September 1910. The schoolhouse was built in 1890 and opened to the public for inspection on January 1, 1891. It was built for a cost of $15,815.55. The site is now the location of the Webster Bank at 700 Washington Street.

Clapp School, located on Walnut Street, was opened on November 30, 1896, to replace a structure destroyed by fire on January 7, 1896. The school was designed by architect C.L. Mitchell and built at a cost of $14,521.01. Equipment in the first school included horizontal bars, sets of dumbbells, Indian clubs, a springboard, mats, and chest weights. The first organized football team was established here. The school was torn down in August 1984 to make room for additional parking for Edwin A. Jones Elementary School.

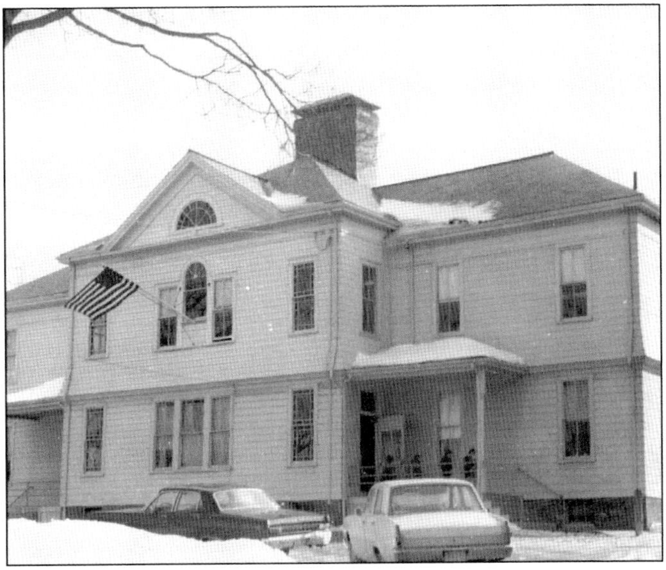

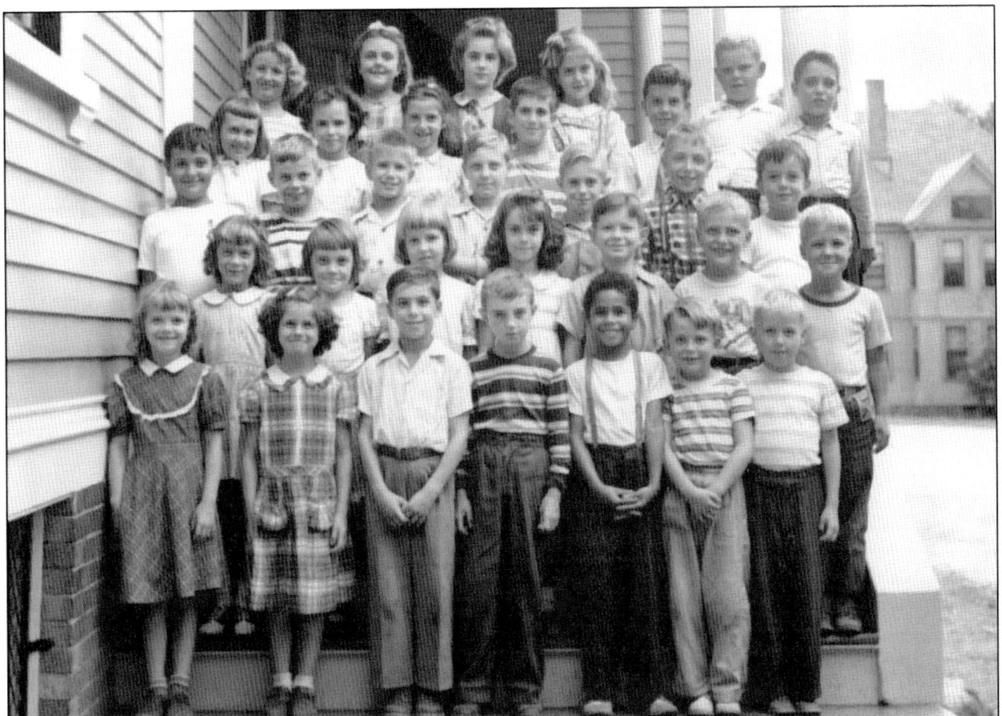

Second-grade students stand on the front steps of Clapp School in October 1949. They are, from left to right, (first row) Cynthia Larney, Mabel Mann, Marvin Wechsler, Charles Novick, Stephen Perry, Glenn DeCoster, and Paul Foster; (second row) Greta Baronisky, Janie Howland, Sally Esten, Karen McEwan, Wayne Robinson, Robert Kosiaski, and Harry Thomas; (third row) Paul Grannakowlis, Thomas Burbridge, Terrence Hinds, Francis Fenton, Thomas Caddell, Paul Johnannsen, and Teddy Morrill; (fourth row) Joanna Lindelof, Regina Jones, Mary Sperandio, Arthur Lesberg, Marc Heddy, and Robert Slade; (fifth row) Judith Lindelof, Deborah Bishop, Patricia Elliott, Virginia Murphy, and an unidentified student.

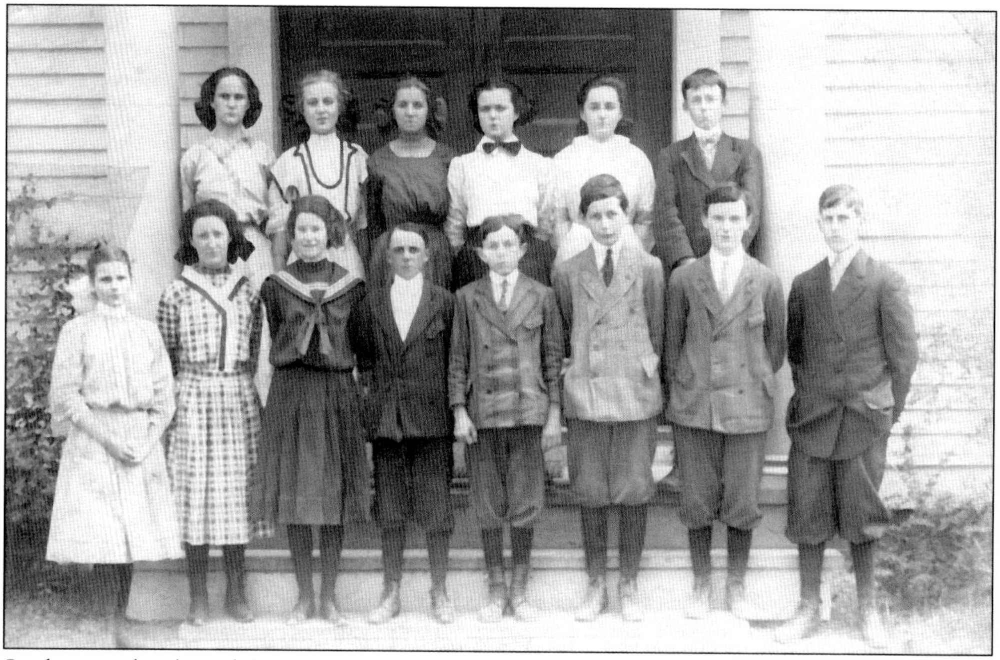

Students in the class of Sr. Mary Imelda of St. Mary's Catholic School gather in 1910. The original St. Mary's Catholic School was established in September 1883 on Canton Street. That structure was demolished to make room for the current church rectory. Posing here are, from left to right, (first row) Lauretta E. Leahy (Lord), Helen Feeley, unidentified, Frank Harns, Harry Willis, Frances Falvey, John Meers, and Timothy Roach; (second row) Mary Kelliher (Monahan), Mabel Hatch, Mary Rideout, Bernadette Finn, Kathleen Mahony Nally, and Frank Heelan.

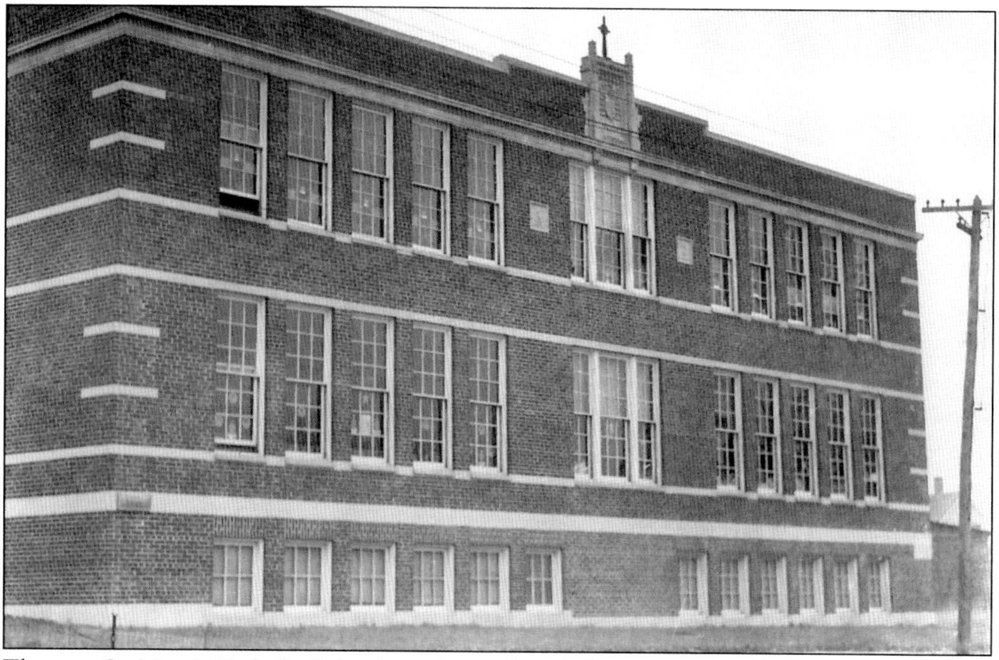

The new St. Mary's Catholic School was located on Atherton Street. It was built in 1931 at a cost of $160,000. This school was closed in 1972 and later demolished.

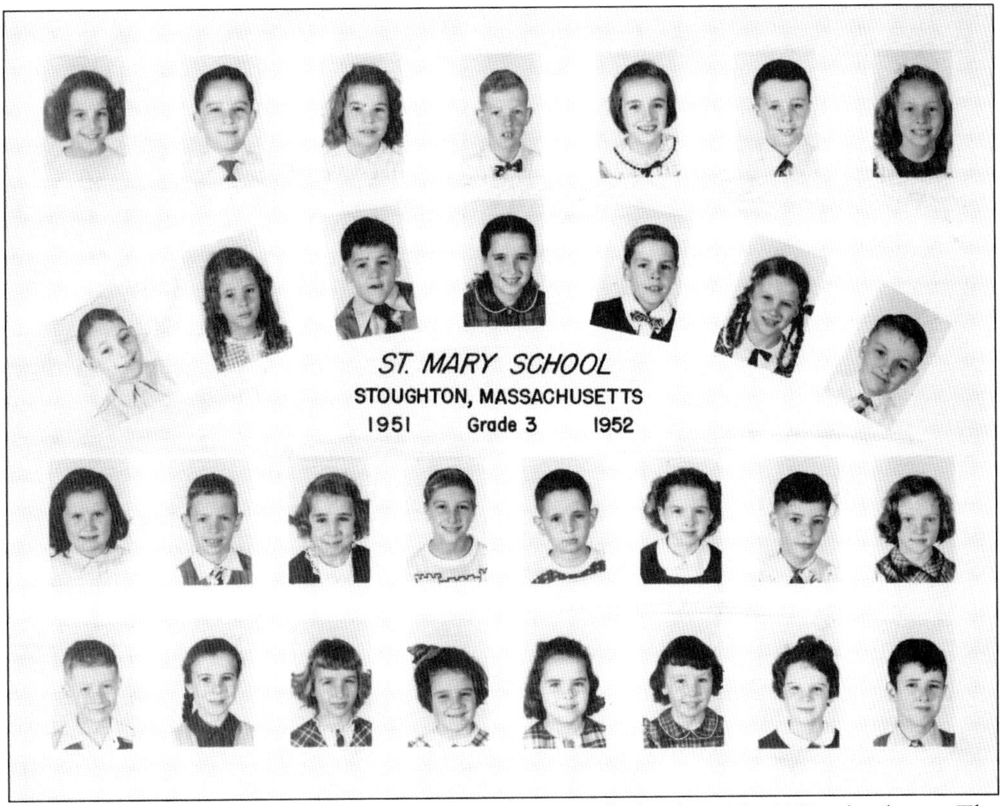

Shown here is the St. Mary's Catholic School third grade for the 1951–1952 school year. The school remained open for another two decades before children attended Stoughton public schools or Catholic schools in Canton. The school was taught by the Sisters of St. Joseph for the nearly 90 years it was open.

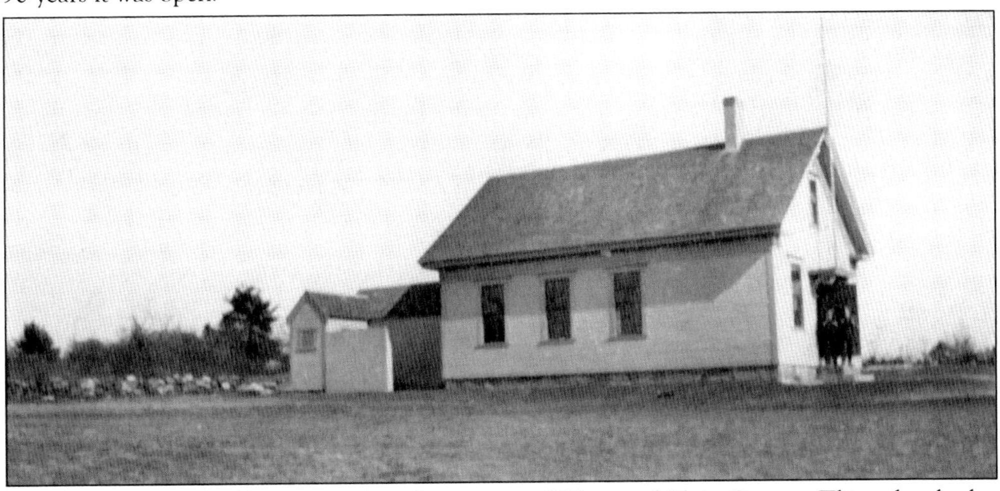

The Dry Pond Schoolhouse stood at the corner of West and Plain Streets. This school, also known as Smith School, was built in 1871. This was the third structure on this property, and it was closed as a school in 1933. The Dykeman family converted it into a residence, and it is still standing at 688 Plain Street as one of the few 19th-century schoolhouses in Stoughton. (Authors' collection.)

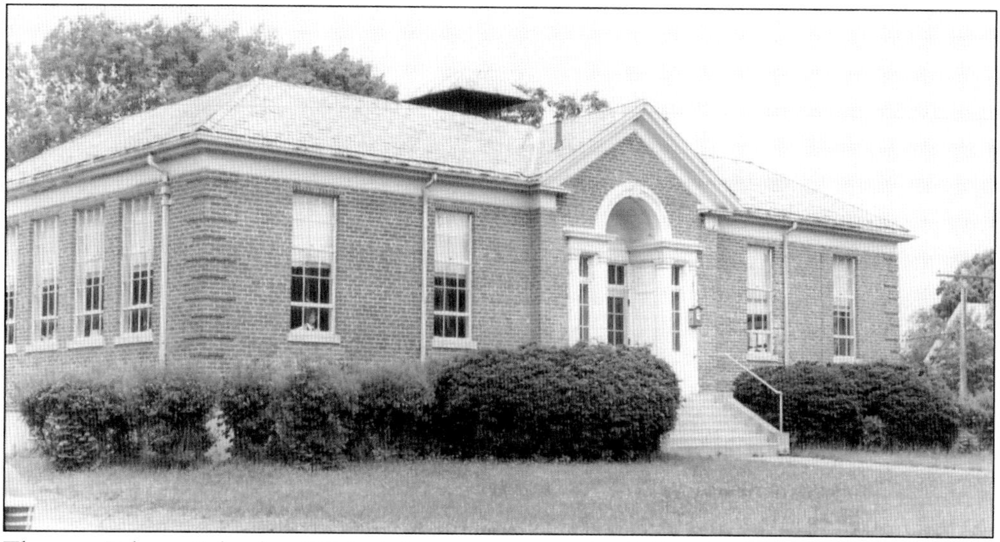

The new Tolman School at 882 Park Street is seen in the 1960s, photographed by Stoughton schoolteacher and photographer Frank Maioli. This school, now a private residence, served the children of South Stoughton from 1925 until June 1971. The school was built at a cost of $16,400. After it was closed, it served briefly as a school of nursing for the Southeastern Regional Vocational Technical High School.

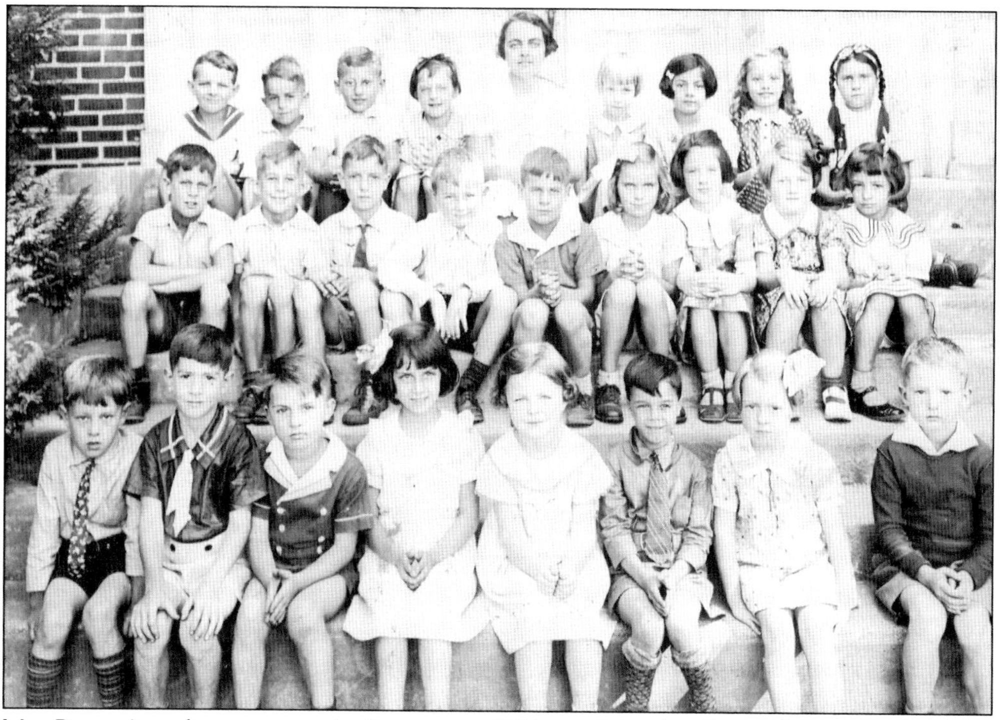

Mrs. Penney's students pose on the front steps of Tolman School in September 1937. This group comprises first, second, and third graders. The original Tolman School suffered a fire on November 27, 1923. After the fire, the children attended classes at the Three-K Shoe factory, where Nicola Sacco (1891–1927) had worked. Sacco is well known for the Sacco and Vanzetti murder case. He resided in South Stoughton.

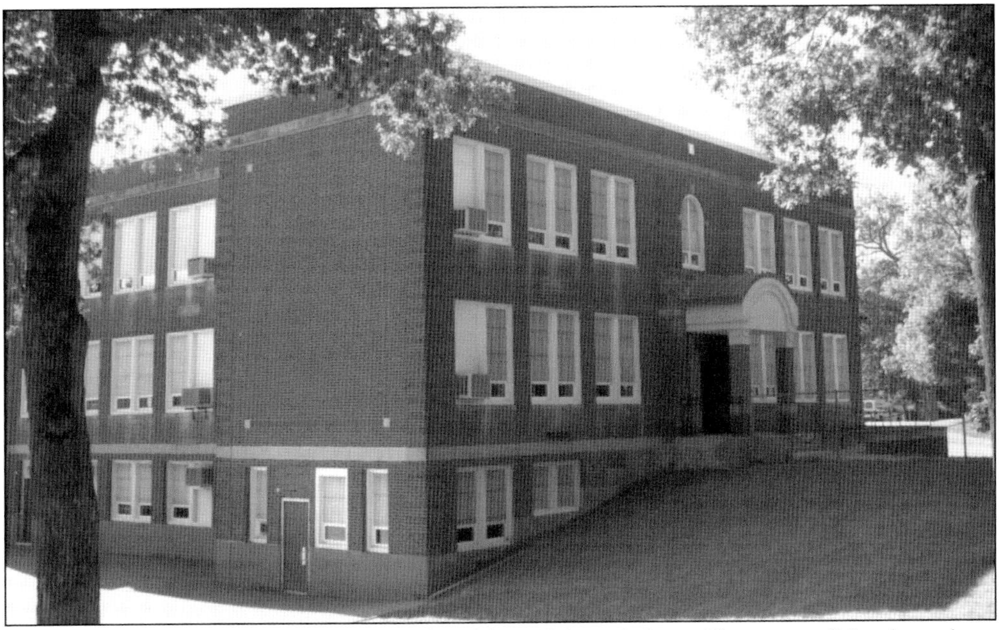

The former Stoughton Junior High School and, later, Edwin A. Jones Elementary School stands on Pierce Street. Built in 1930 at a cost of $118,000, this structure still serves students of Stoughton. The school was named in honor of composer and school committee member Edwin Arthur Jones (1853–1911). In 1954, an addition to the junior high school was built, designed by Collens, Willis & Beckonert. (Authors' collection.)

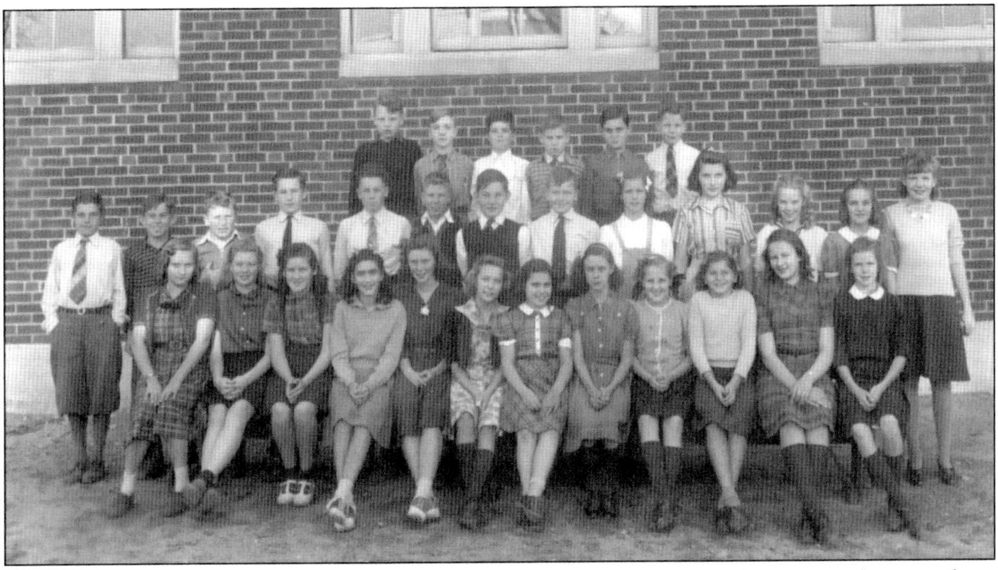

Junior high school students pose outside of the Edwin A. Jones School in 1941. They are, from left to right, (first row) Astrid Smith, Baily Harper, Babe Smith, Mary Sucian, Memie Tate, Pearl Schaaf, Barbara Savini, Barbara Smith, E. Lief, Beatie Green, Lydia Oldbach, and Joan Campbell; (second row) Al Green, Bruce Hawes, George Kirt, Dick Kelleher, Howard Holmes, Cliff Corbett, Ralph Mann, Billy Totman, Barbara Witham, Shirley Wry, "Pinky" Priest, Evelyn Backeldor, and Mabel Colcord; (third row) Billy Dykeman, Evan Shea, John Patton, Stanley Minkowski, Burton Gerson, and Bob Goward.

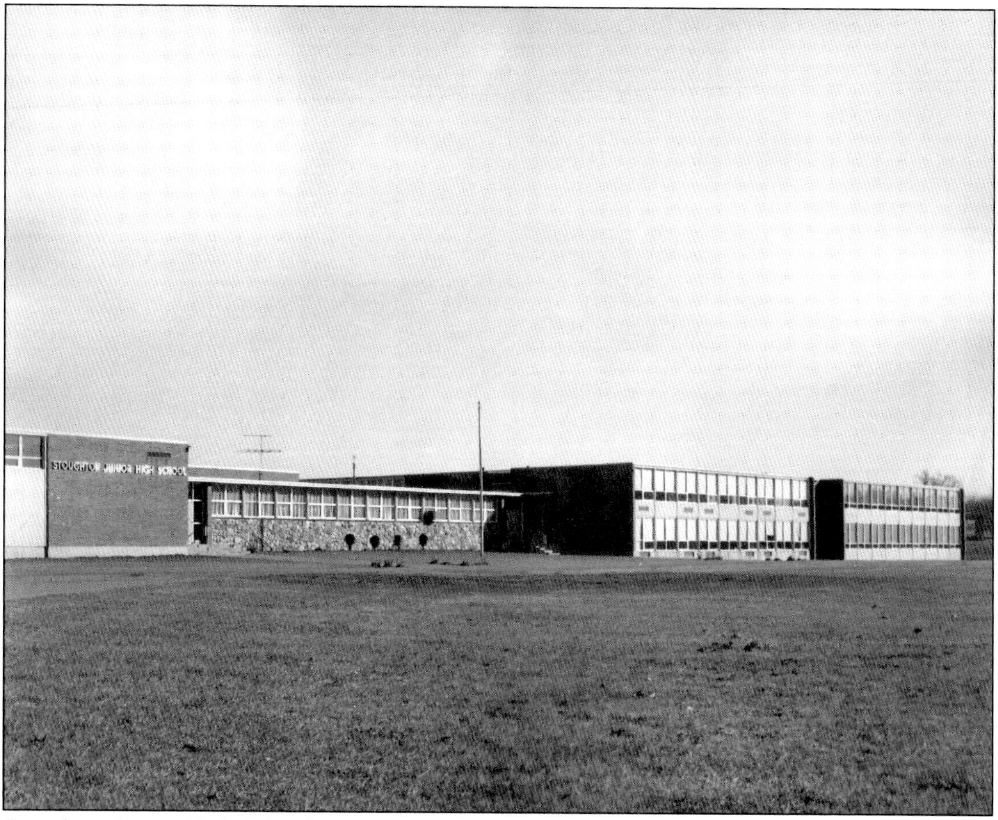

Stoughton Junior High School at 211 Cushing Street opened in early 1960. This school originally served seventh and eighth graders.

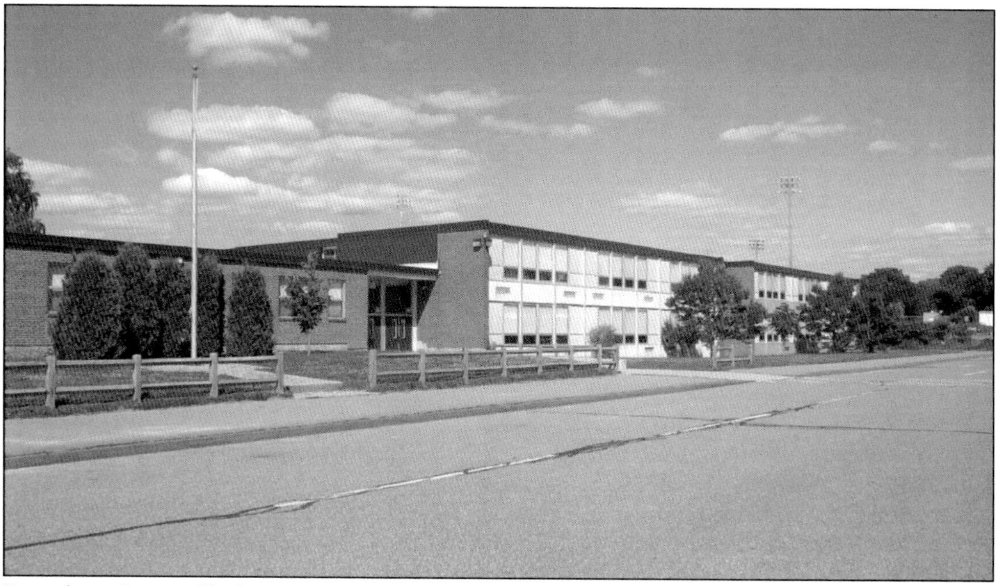

Stoughton Junior High was renamed in 1995 in honor of longtime principal Dr. Robert G. O'Donnell. In 1998, the school was enlarged and now accommodates students from sixth to eighth grades. (Authors' collection.)

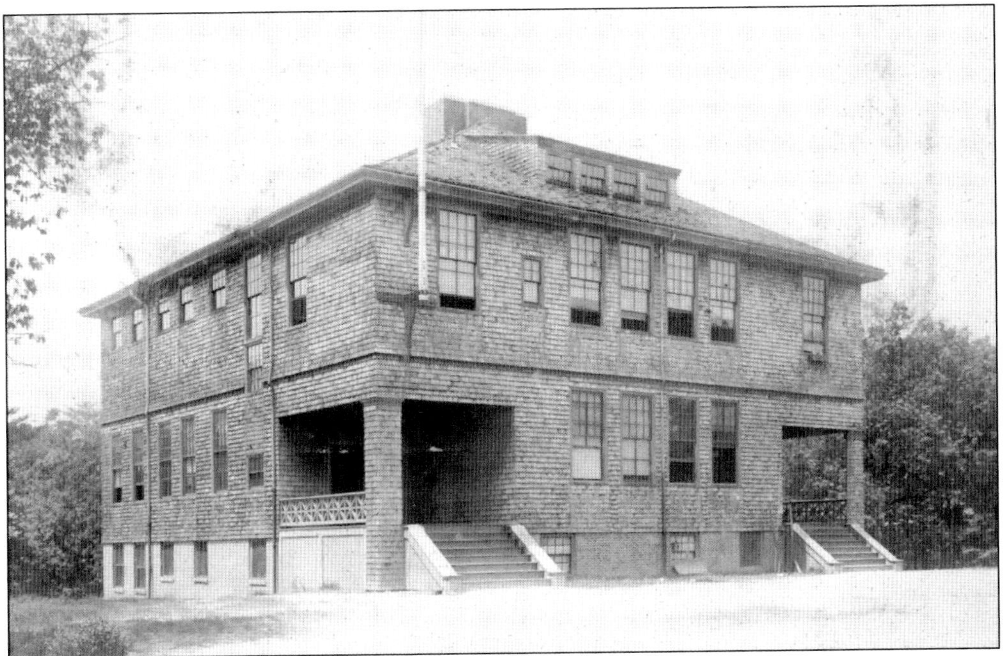

The Kimball School was opened on April 13, 1903, at 2 Park Avenue. It was named in honor of former Stoughton town clerk Henry Colman Kimball (1820–1894). It served as Stoughton High School until June 1923. Kimball School continued to serve the Stoughton community as a junior high and, later, an elementary school. (Authors' collection.)

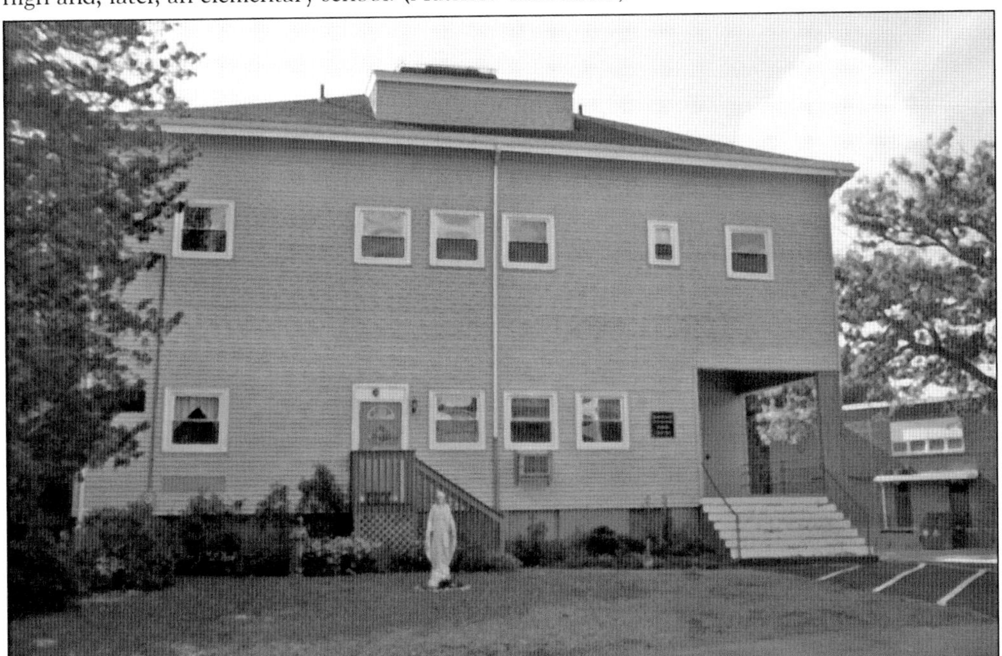

In recent decades, the former Kimball School has been home to Catholic CCD (Confraternity of Christian Doctrine) education classes. The structure is operated as the Immaculate Conception Parish Center, offering a food pantry to those in need. (Authors' collection.)

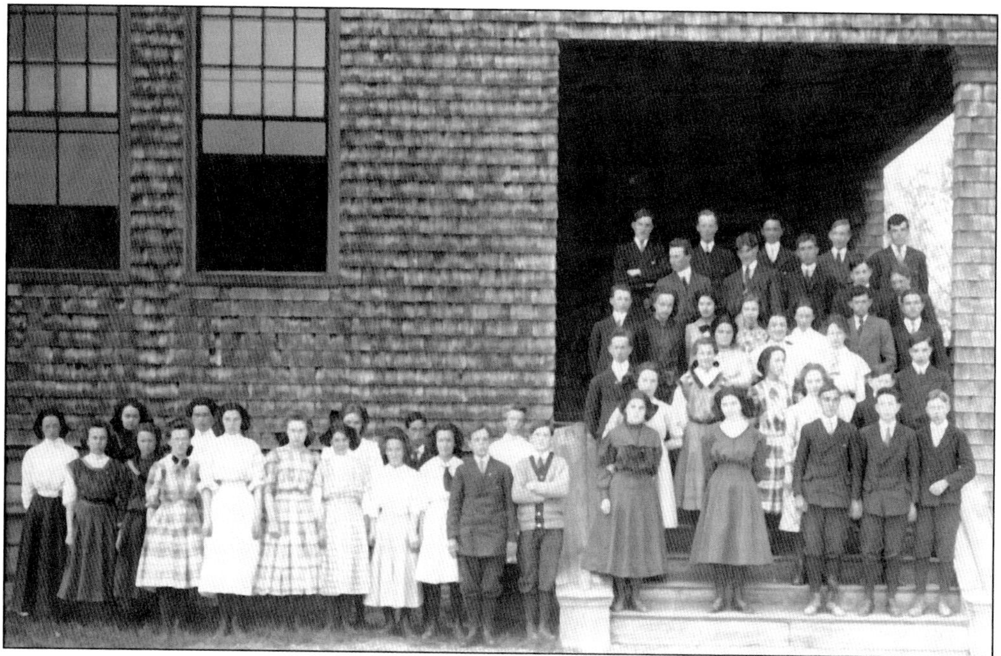

Students stand at the front steps of Kimball School around 1912. This structure on Park Avenue has been renovated, but it maintains many elements of the original building.

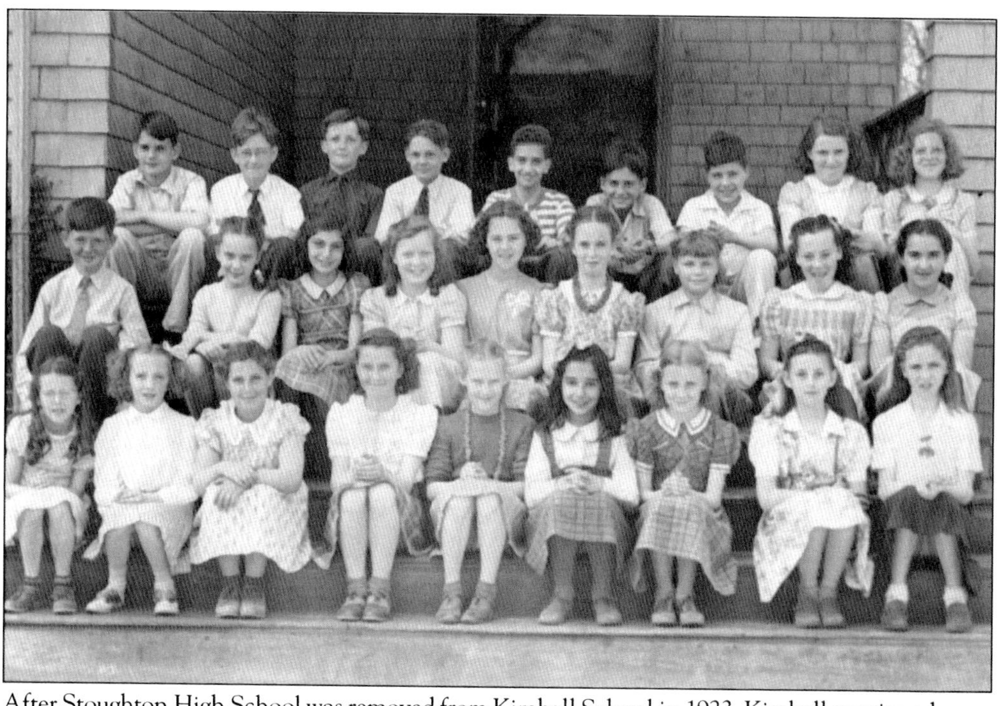

After Stoughton High School was removed from Kimball School in 1923, Kimball continued as an elementary school. This photograph shows members of the Kimball fifth-grade class in 1944.

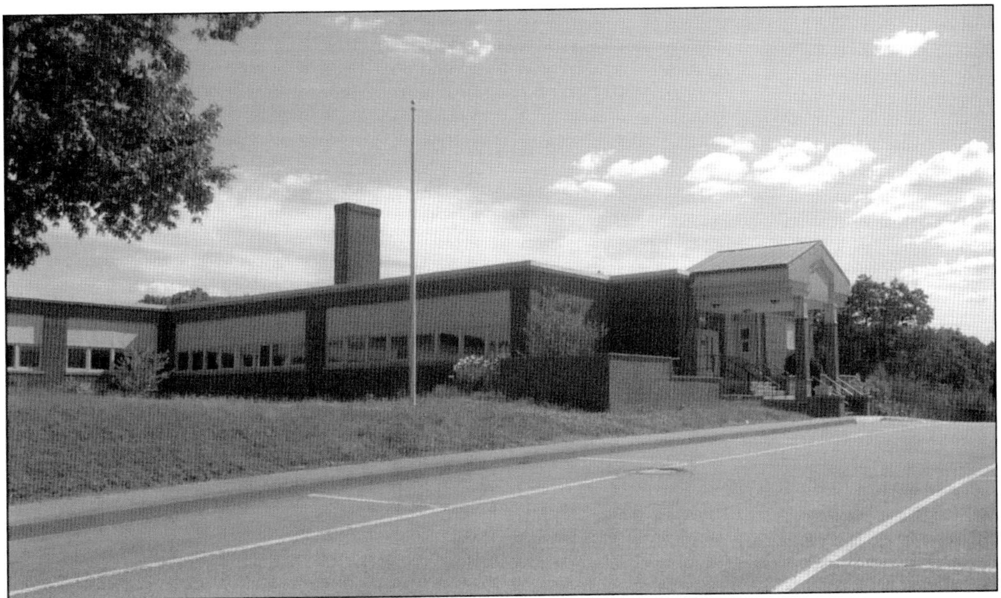

The West Elementary School at 1322 Central Street cost $601,755 and was designed by Collens, Willis & Beckonert. Construction of the school was completed on September 30, 1951. An addition by the same architect was completed on August 16, 1954. (Authors' collection.)

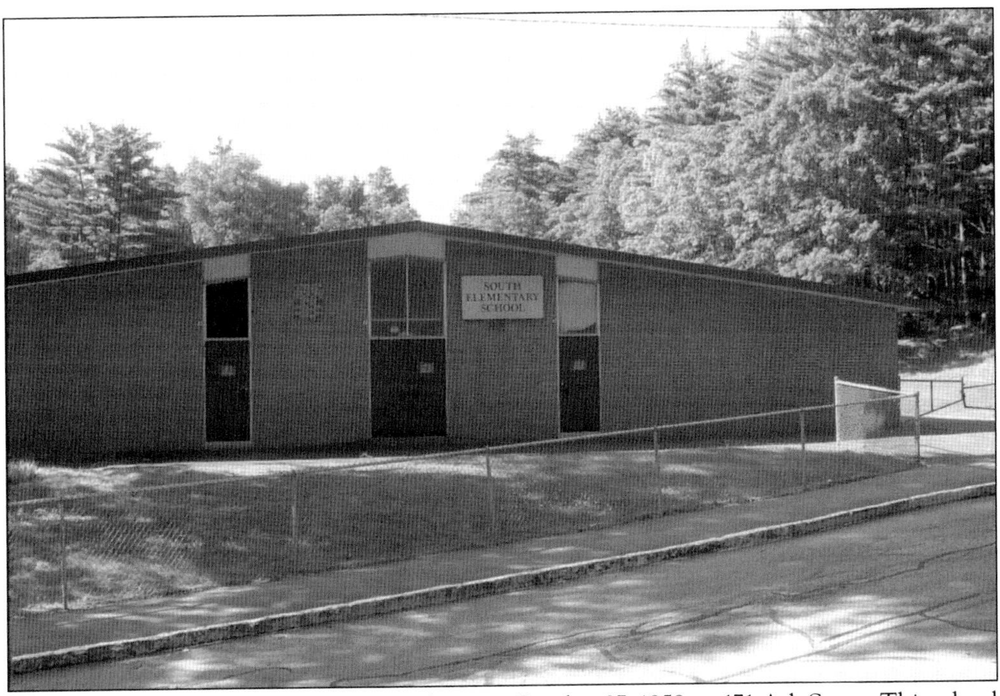

South Elementary School opened for students on October 27, 1958, at 171 Ash Street. This school would better accommodate the growing community in South Stoughton than the old Tolman School built three decades before. The school was designed by the Architects Collaborative. (Authors' collection.)

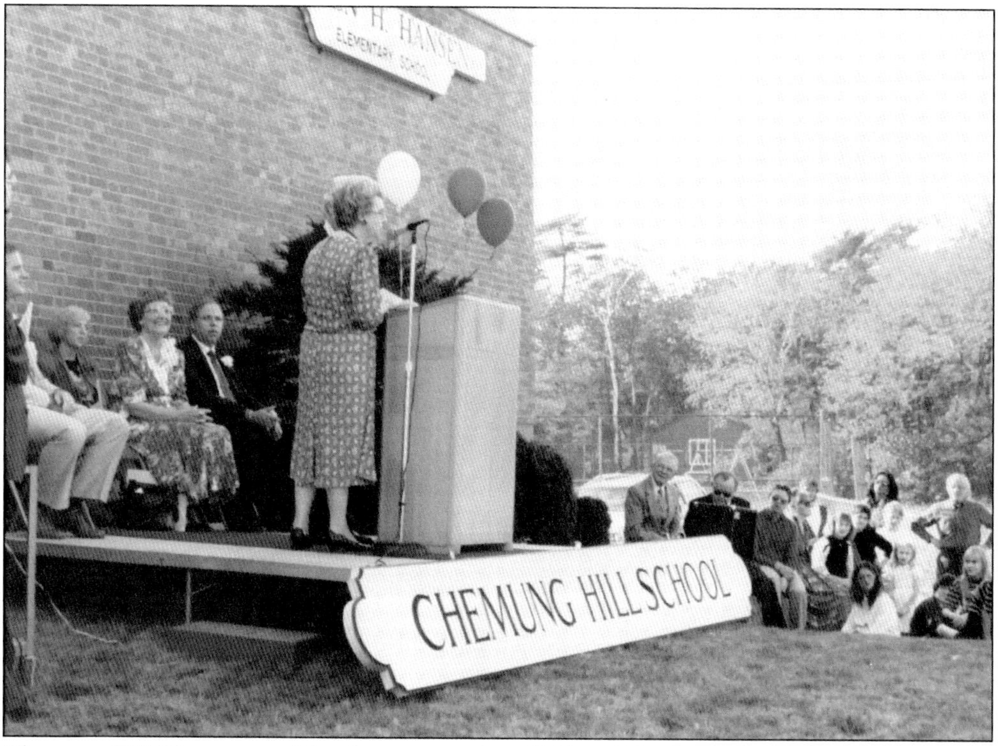

Chemung Hill Elementary School was opened in 1962 at 1800 Central Street. It was renamed on October 29, 1989, for longtime principal Helen H. Hansen. Shown here is the ceremony to official change the name to Helen H. Hansen Elementary School.

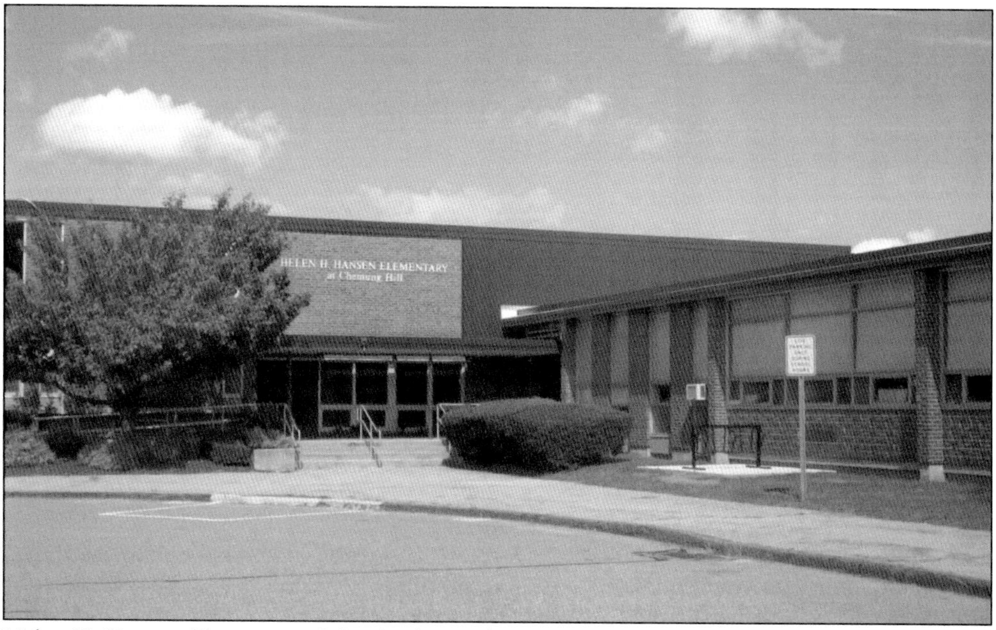

Helen H. Hansen Elementary School is located on Central Street at the base of Chemung Hill. The hill itself has been a popular sledding destination for generations of Stoughton residents. (Authors' collection.)

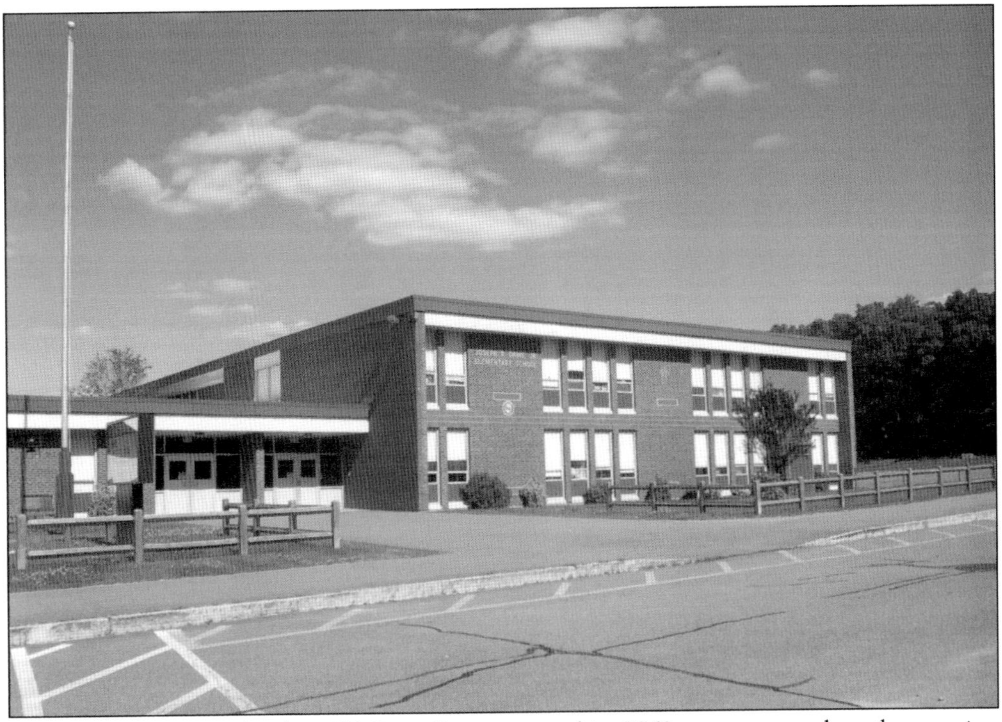

North Elementary School at 131 Pine Street opened in 1969 to accommodate the growing population in Stoughton. The school was recently renamed Joseph R. Dawe Jr. Elementary School, in honor of its longtime principal. (Authors' collection.)

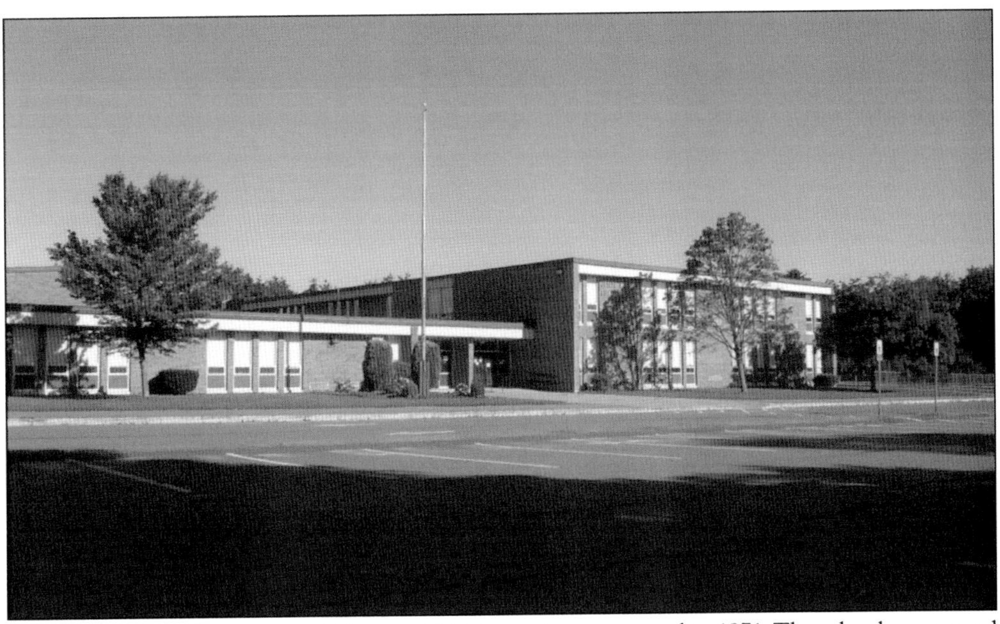

Joseph H. Gibbons Elementary School at 235 Morton Street opened in 1971. The school was named in honor of longtime Stoughton superintendent of schools Joe Gibbons. (Authors' collection.)

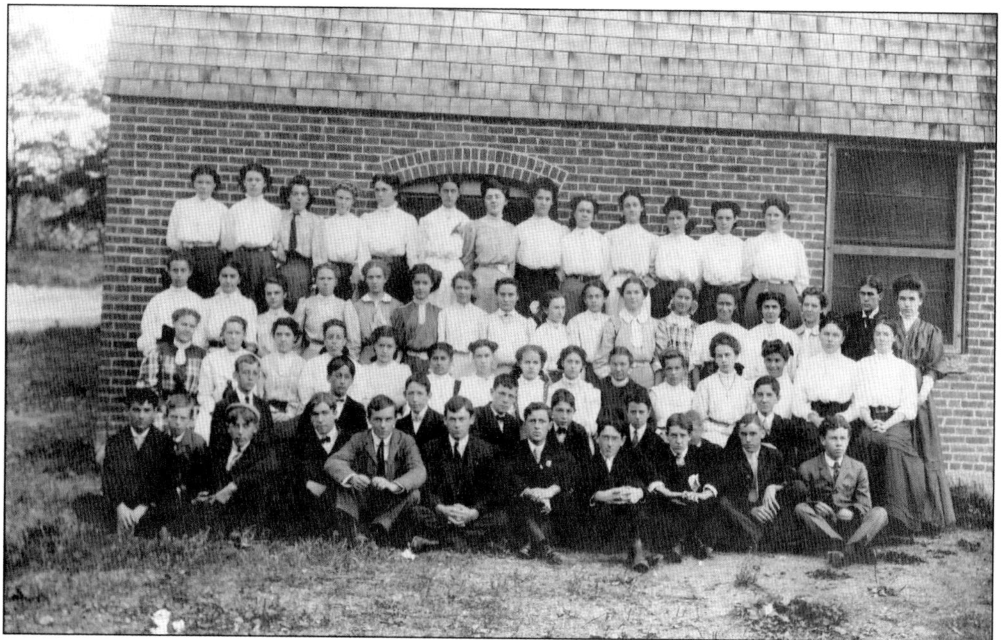

Students of Kimball School on Park Avenue are seen here in 1907. This photograph shows those in the high school class at Kimball School.

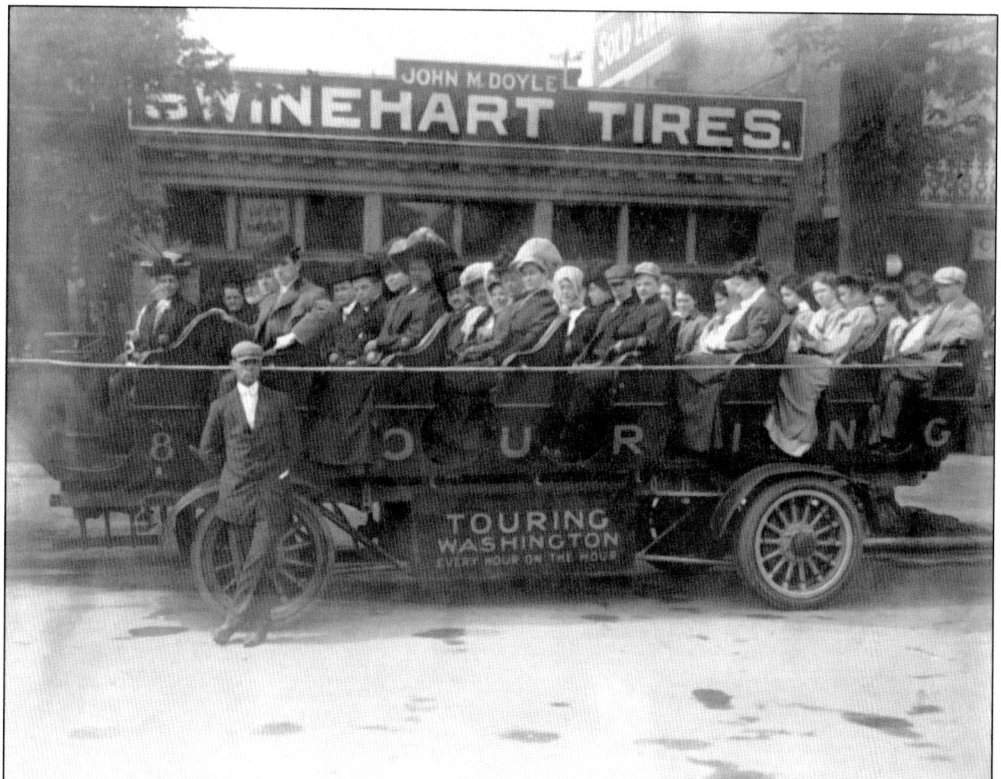

A long-standing tradition in Stoughton involved students visiting Washington, DC. The Stoughton High School class of 1910 is seen in a touring car about to explore the city.

This George A. Gerard photograph shows members of Stoughton High School's football team around 1915. The mascot in this photograph seems strange in light of the longtime rivalry between Stoughton High School's Black Knights and Canton High School's Bulldogs.

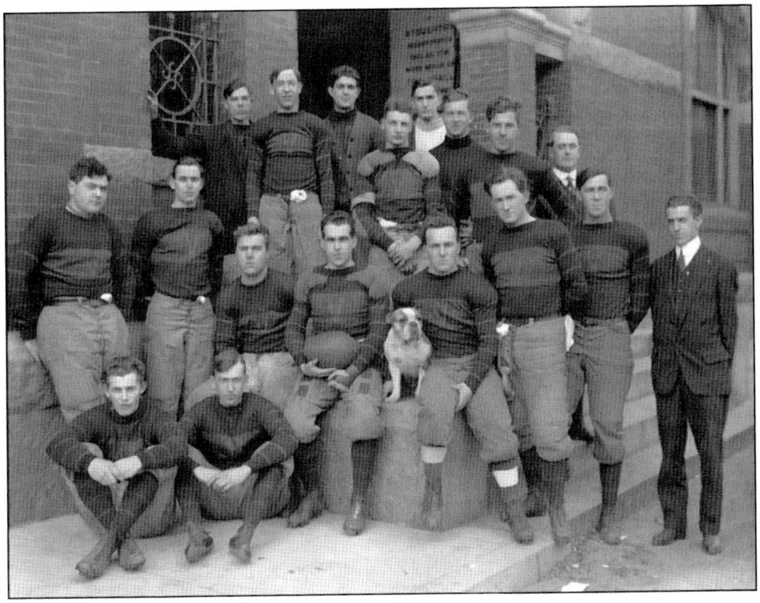

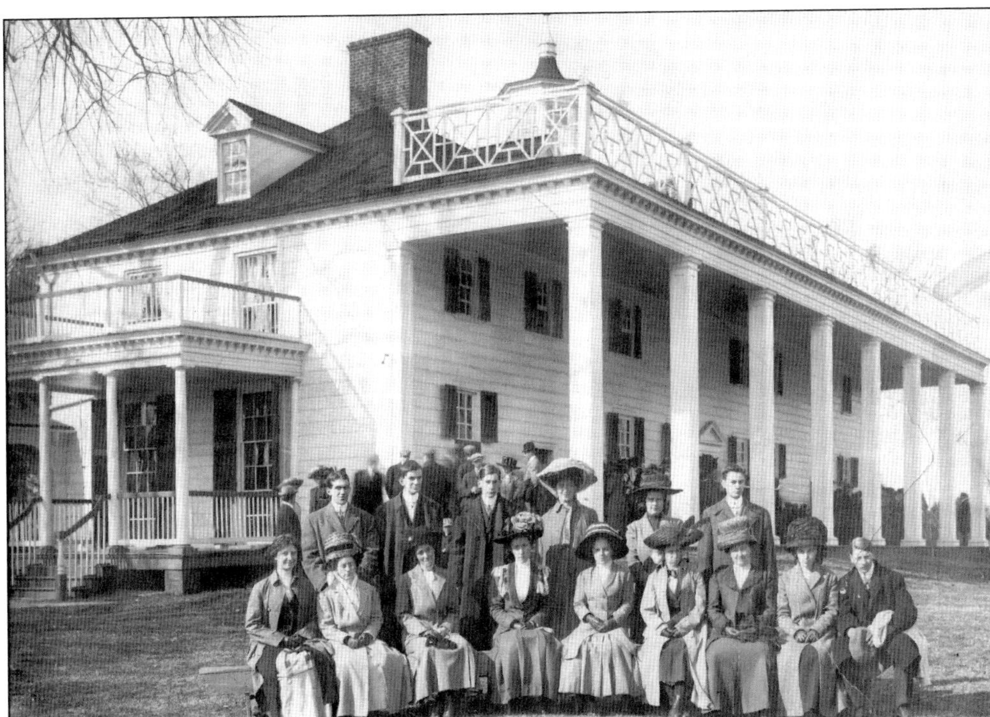

The Stoughton High School class of 1911 gathers at Mount Vernon, Virginia, on March 28, 1911. This field trip brought a Stoughton class to the home of George Washington. Shown here are, from left to right, (first row) Ruth Howard, Florence McCombie, Miss Fraser (teacher), Miss Holt (teacher), Celia Greenwald, Annie Rodman, Mrs. Howard, Grace McDermott, and Jack Dykeman; (second row) F. Burnham, F. Drake, Fred Snell, Alice Murphy, Alice Toomey, and Lewis Stoyle.

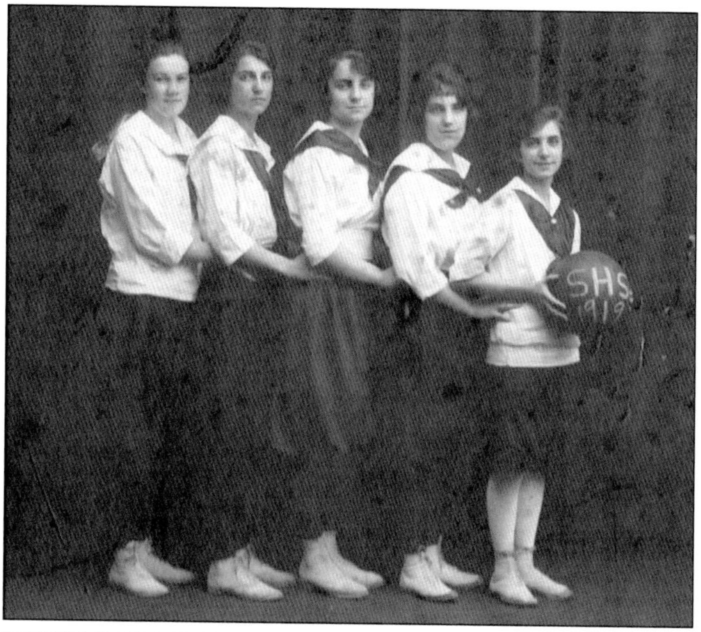

These unidentified members of the Stoughton High School girls' basketball team pose in 1919.

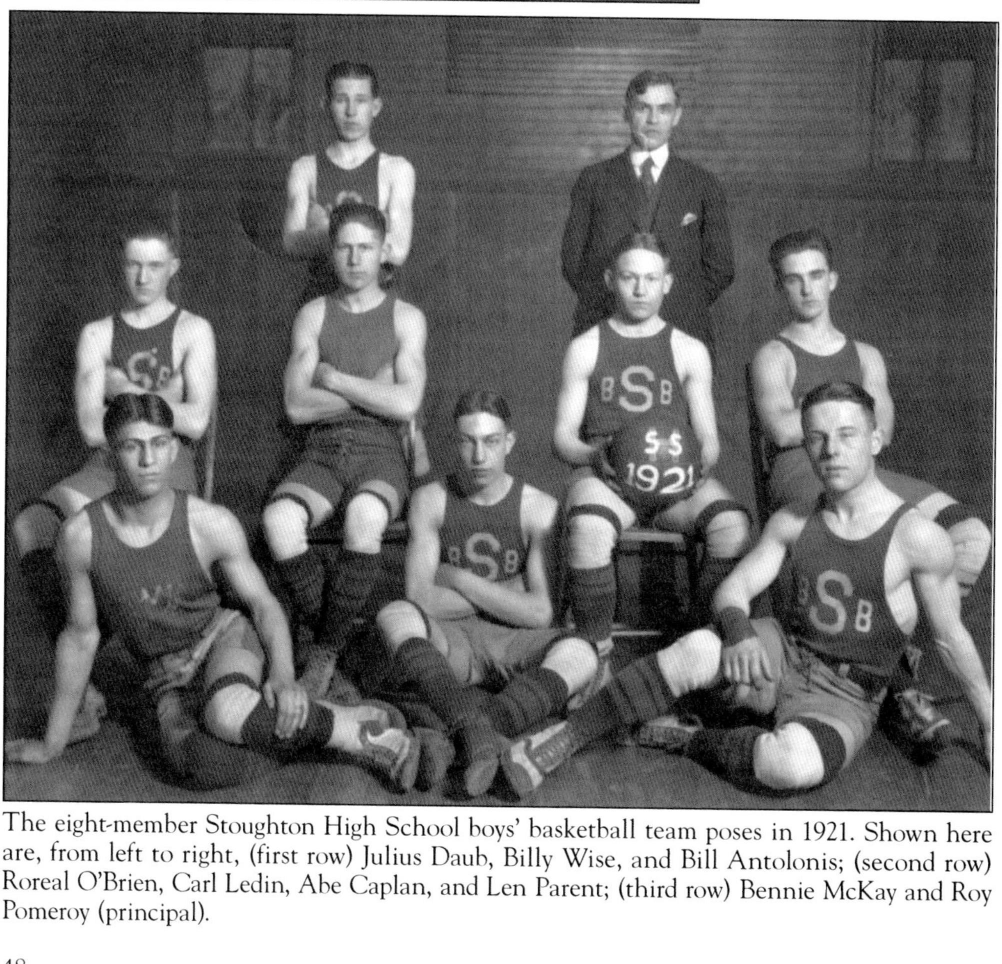

The eight-member Stoughton High School boys' basketball team poses in 1921. Shown here are, from left to right, (first row) Julius Daub, Billy Wise, and Bill Antolonis; (second row) Roreal O'Brien, Carl Ledin, Abe Caplan, and Len Parent; (third row) Bennie McKay and Roy Pomeroy (principal).

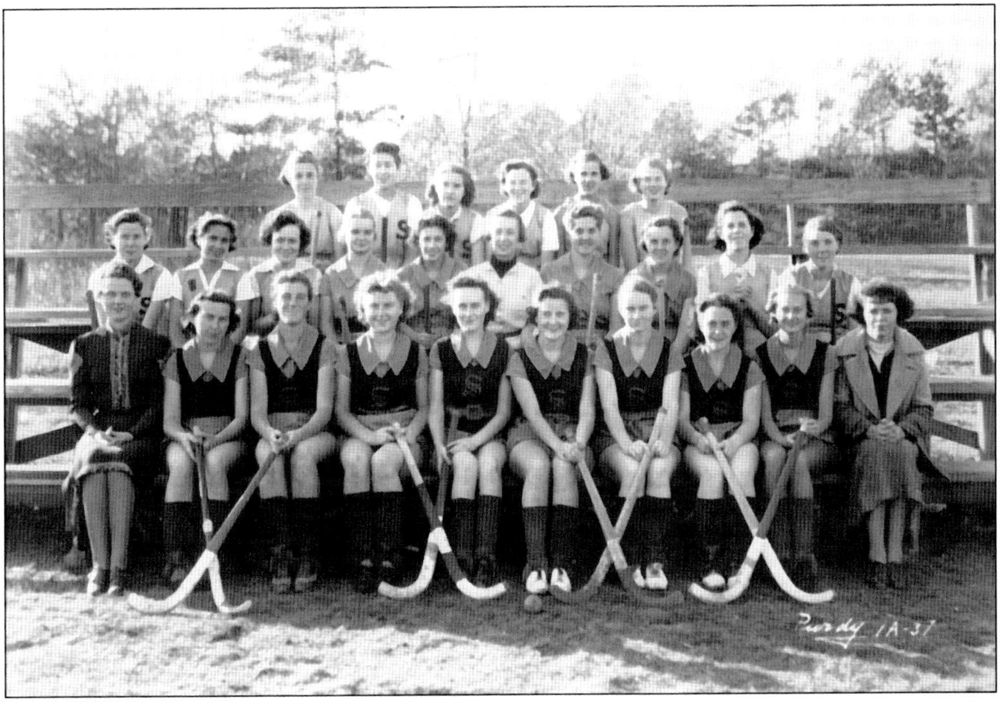

This is a 1930s Stoughton High School girls' field hockey team. Sports have been a part of the Stoughton school curriculum since the dawn of the 20th century.

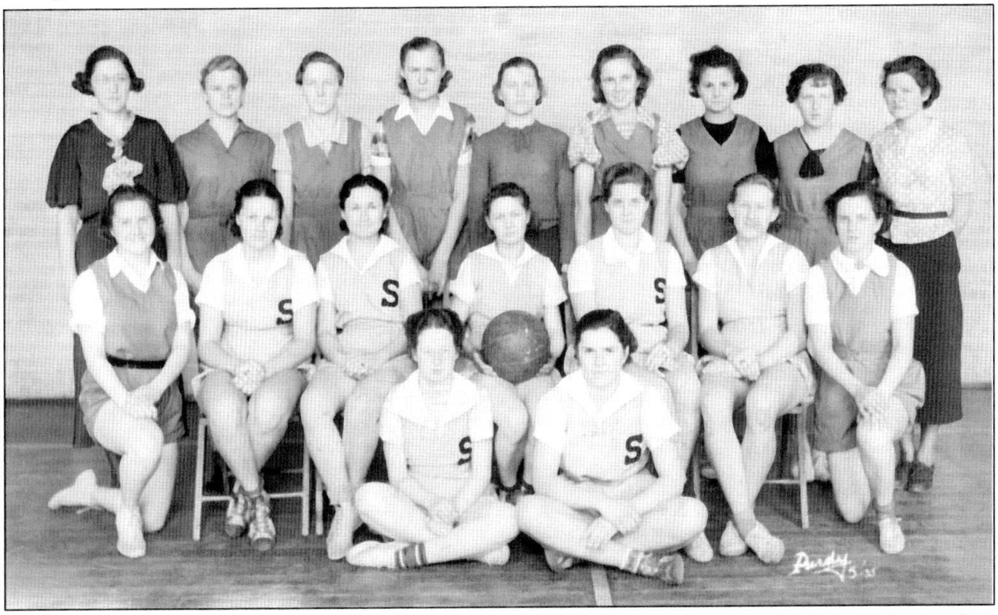

Stoughton High School's 1935 girls' basketball team is much larger than the team of 1919 (see page 48). Shown here are, from left to right, (first row) Jesselyn Innes and Leah Kell; (second row) Mary Rivella, Louise Wereska, Bronie Wasilewich, Hazel Burns (captain), Irene Tirelis, Anna Tumonis, and Kathleen Kell; (third row) Dorothy Zaiser (manager), Stella Alosevitch, Grace Tamulevich, Alice Stanwood, Isabel Murphy, Josephine Gill (coach), Josephine DeLuca, Ruth Raby, and Louis Cushing (manager).

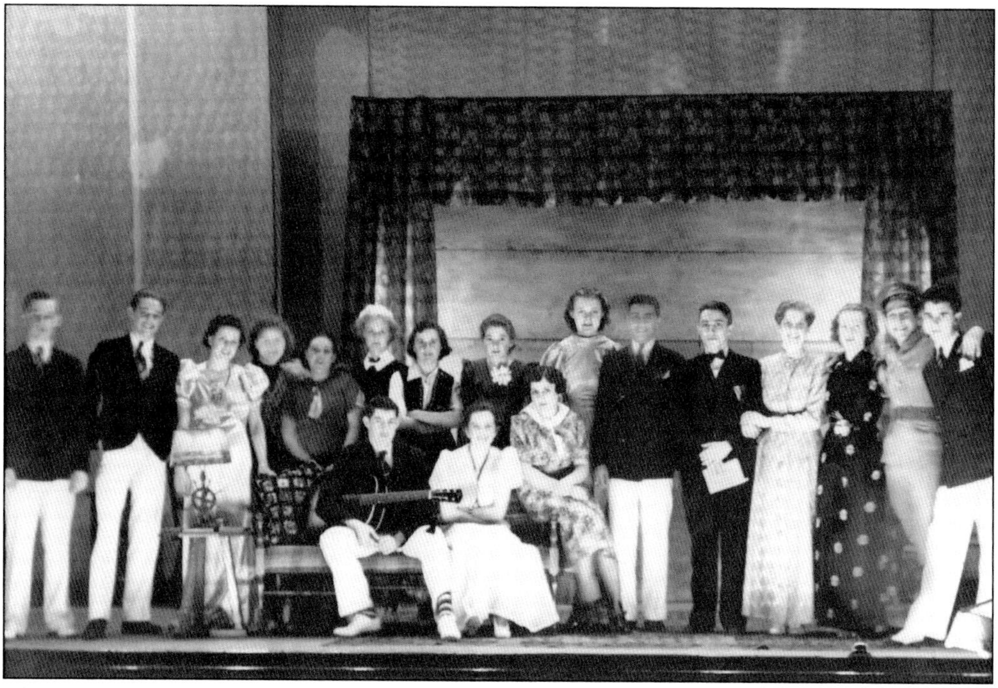

The Stoughton High School class of 1937 performs its class play, *Growing Pains*. Such productions, and many of the graduations, were held at the Stoughton State Theatre on Washington Street and Railroad Avenue. The high school did not have a stage until 1952.

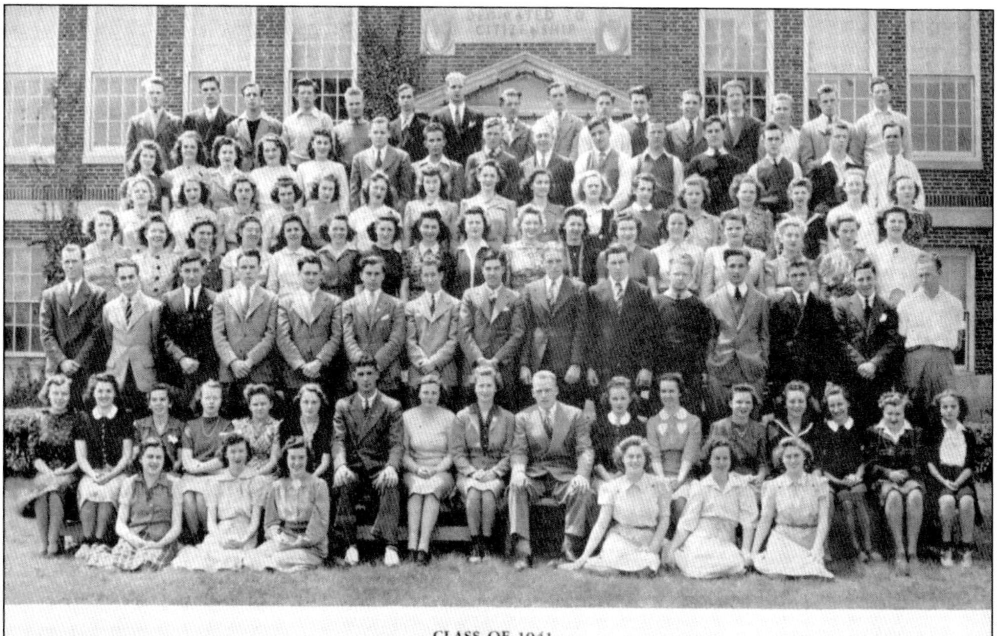

CLASS OF 1941
Class Motto: "Not for school but for life we learn."

The Stoughton High School class of 1941 poses in front of the doorway of the "A" building on Pearl Street. The old doorway still bears the inscription "Dedicated to Citizenship." Many members of this class, and others before and after, would participate in World War II.

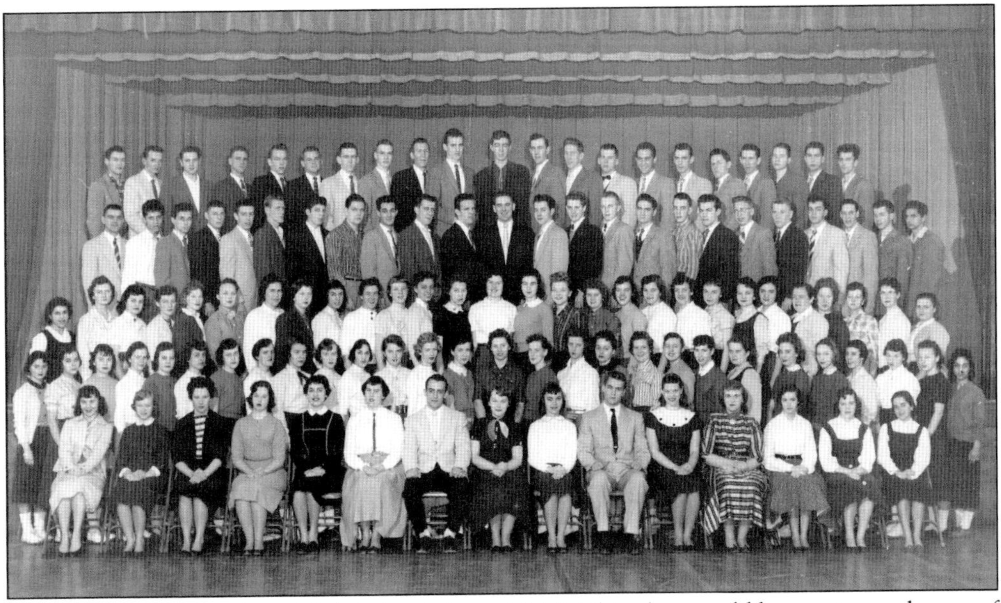

Seen here is the Stoughton High School class of 1956. This class would have witnessed some of the first physical changes to the high school in decades.

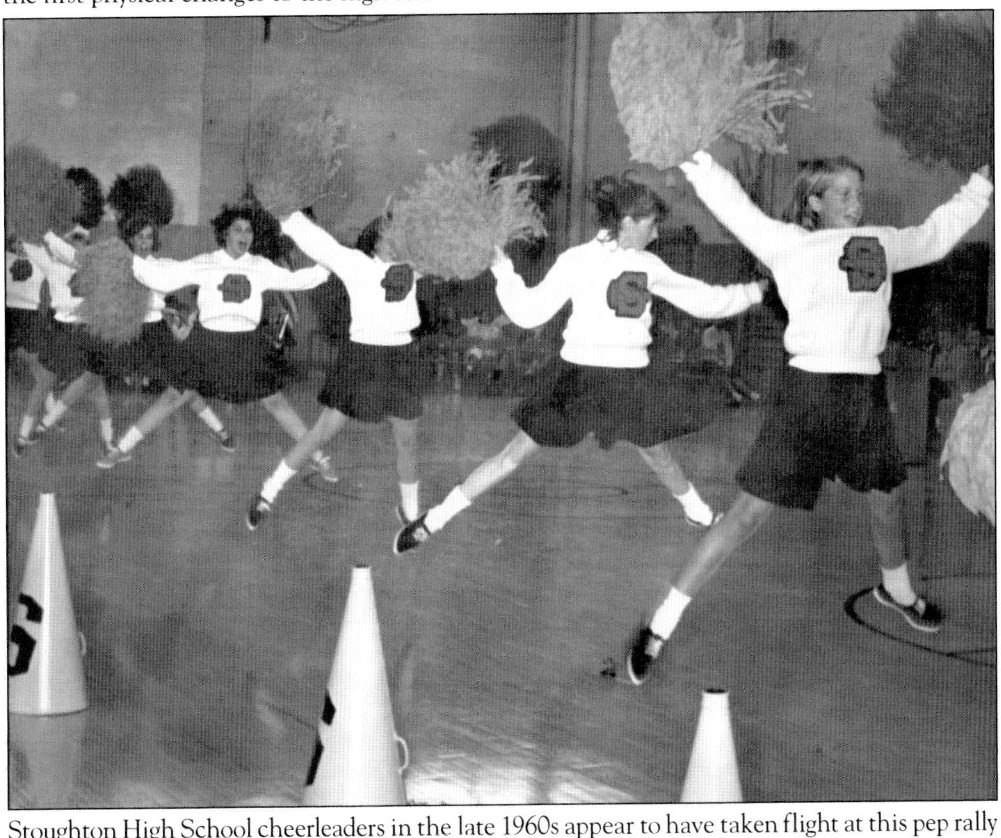

Stoughton High School cheerleaders in the late 1960s appear to have taken flight at this pep rally in the gymnasium. This is just one of countless photographs taken by Stoughton photographer and high school teacher Frank Maioli.

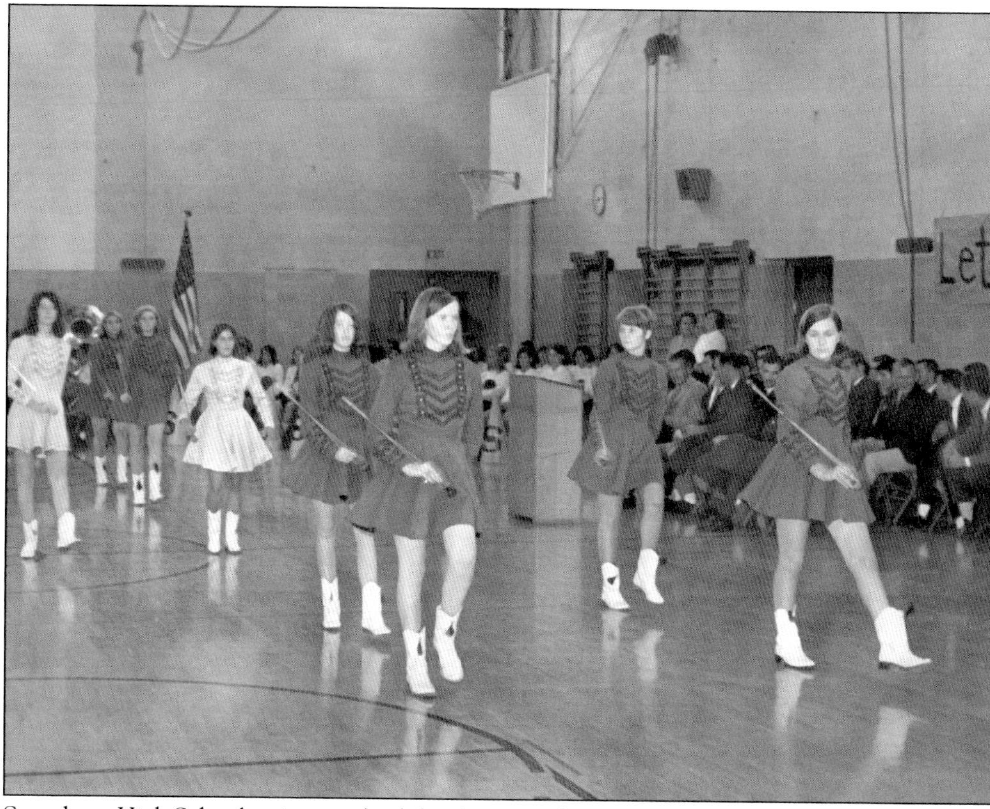

Stoughton High School majorettes lead the class into the gym before a pep rally in the late 1960s. The photograph was taken by Frank Maioli.

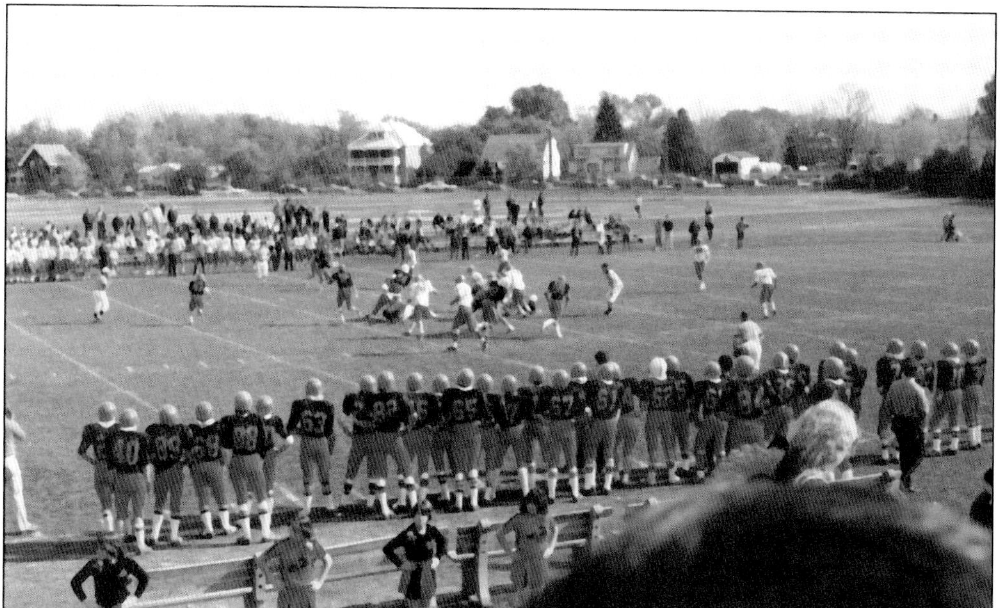

The Stoughton Black Knights play on the gridiron at the Stoughton High School field (now Anthony L. Sarno Field) in 1977. This photograph was taken by late Stoughton resident Bob Parsons.

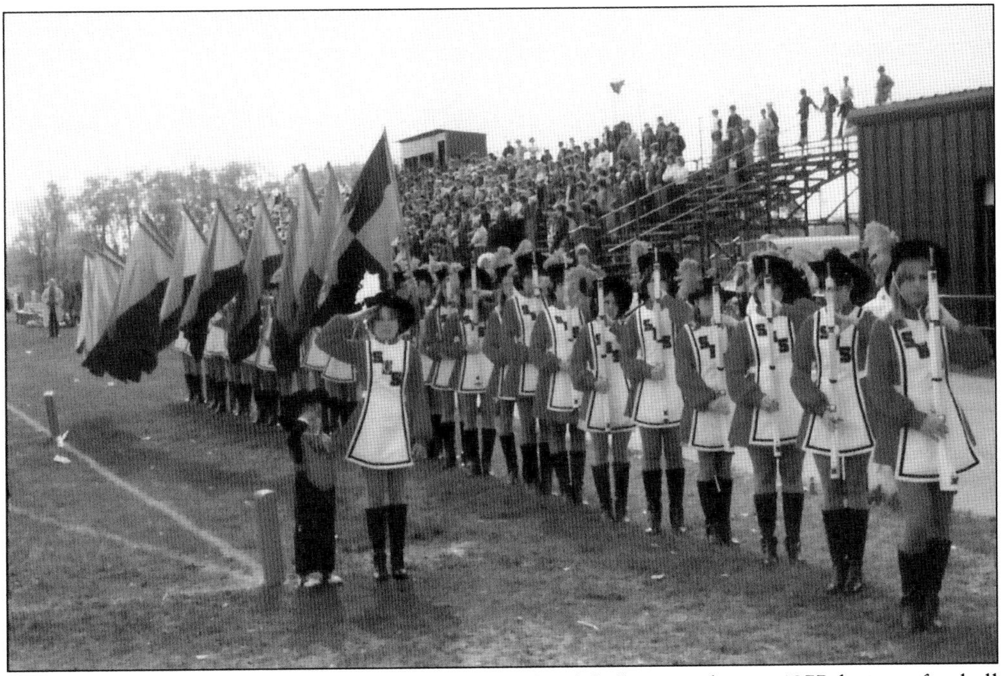

The mascot and members of the Stoughton High School drill team salute in 1977 during a football game. This photograph was taken by the late Bob Parsons.

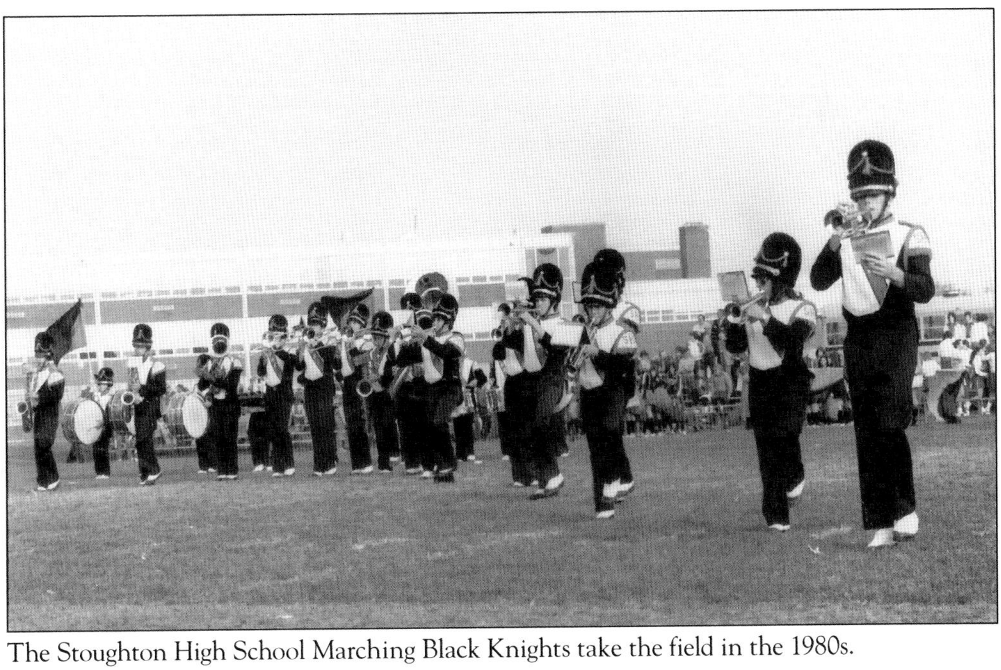

The Stoughton High School Marching Black Knights take the field in the 1980s.

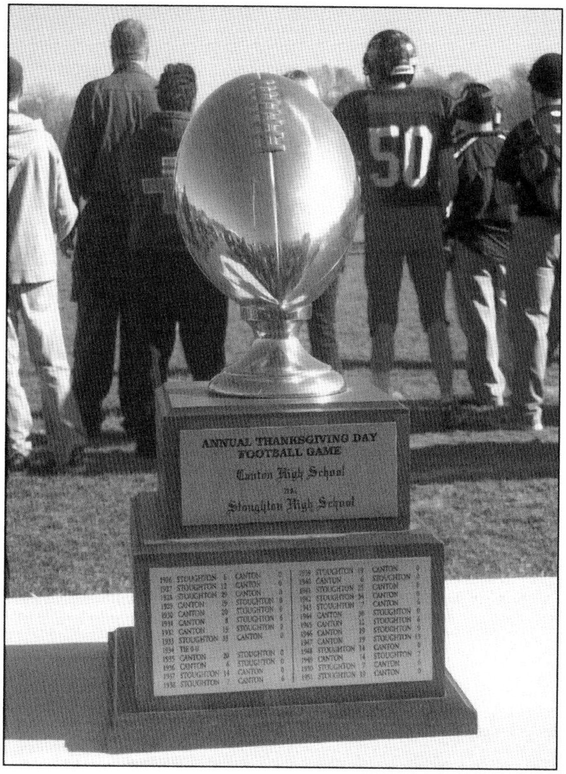

This is the beloved trophy awarded annually to the Stoughton Black Knights or Canton Bulldogs. These teams have battled it out every Thanksgiving Day since 1926. This photograph was taken in 2012, when the game was played on the Black Knights' home turf. (Authors' collection.)

Shown here are members of the award-winning Stoughton High School Marching Black Knights. This photograph, taken by coauthor David Allen Lambert, shows his coauthor and daughter Brenda Lambert (class of 2014) at center, playing the flute at the Thanksgiving Day game in 2012. (Authors' collection.)

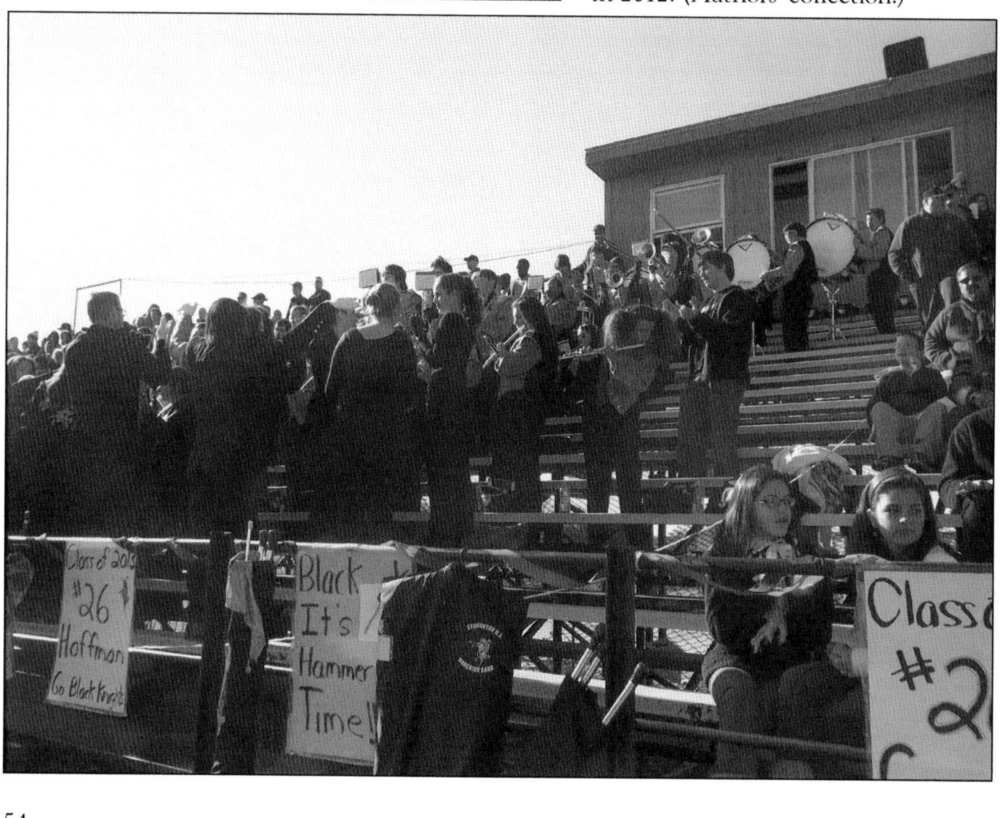

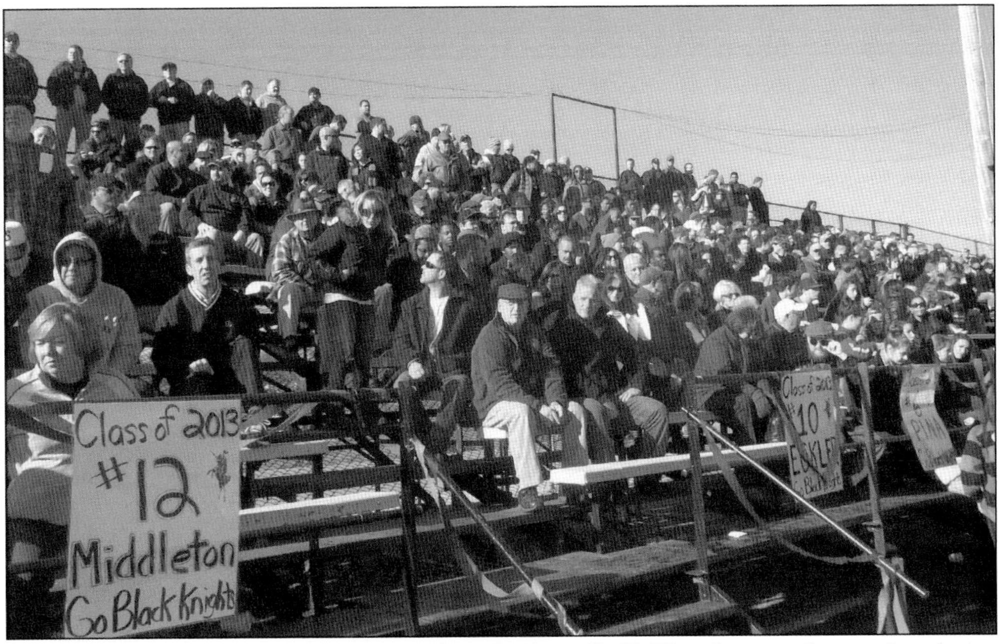

Stoughton fans crowd the bleachers at Anthony L. Sarno Field. This photograph was taken during the annual Thanksgiving Day game in 2012. (Authors' collection.)

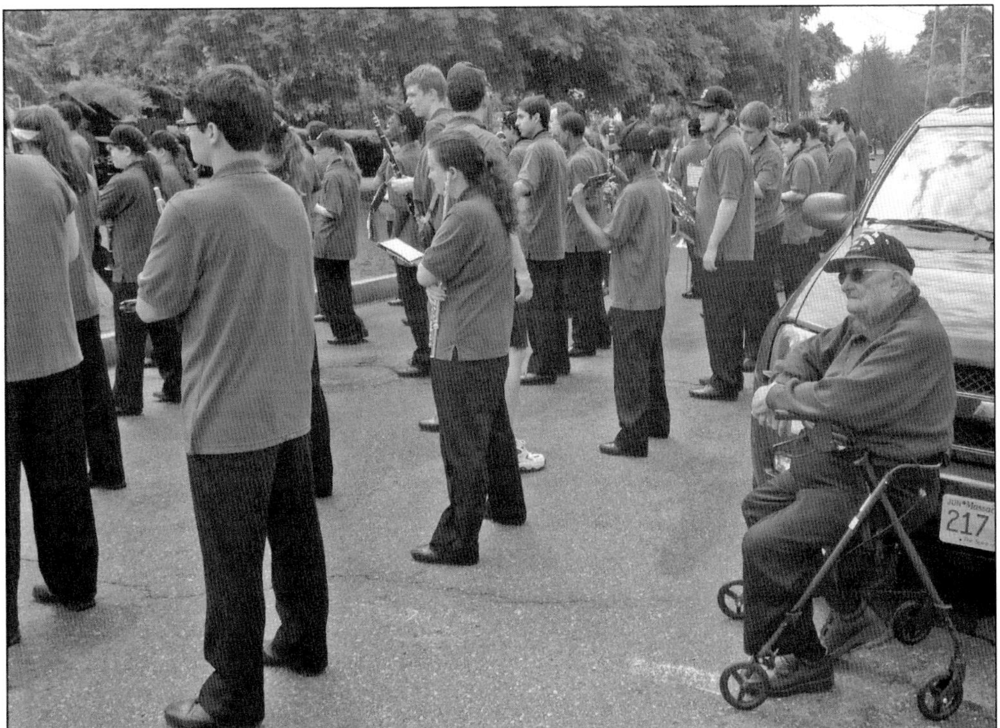

The SHS Marching Black Knights wear their casual summer uniforms during the Memorial Day Parade at Faxon Park on May 26, 2014. As the band prepares to play the national anthem, a Stoughton resident who served in World War II looks on. (Authors' collection.)

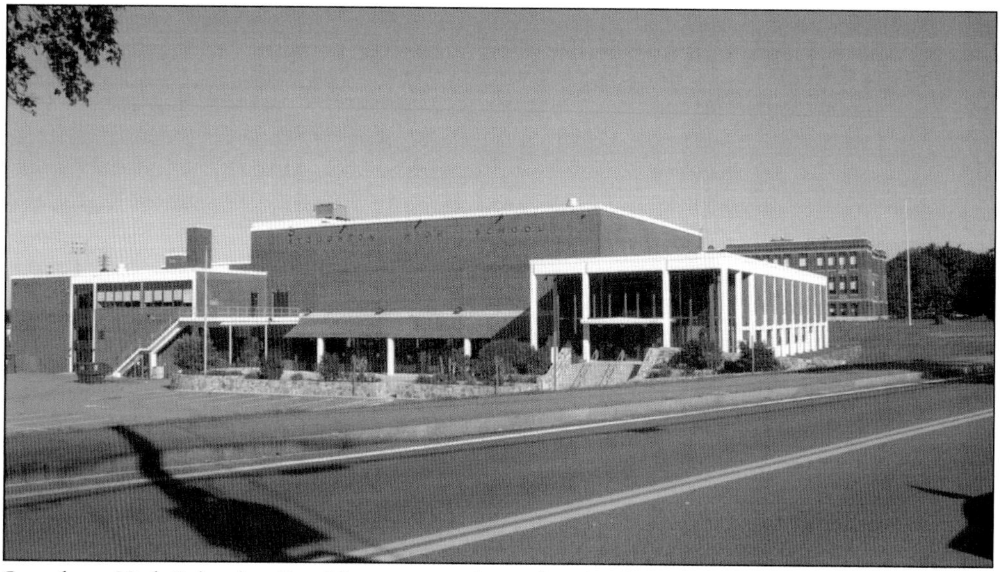

Stoughton High School on Pearl Street is seen here, shortly after it opened its doors on September 8, 1923. The "A" building has been serving the students of Stoughton for several decades, graduating its 90th high school class in 2014. Additions were made to the high school campus in 1952, 1955, and 1965.

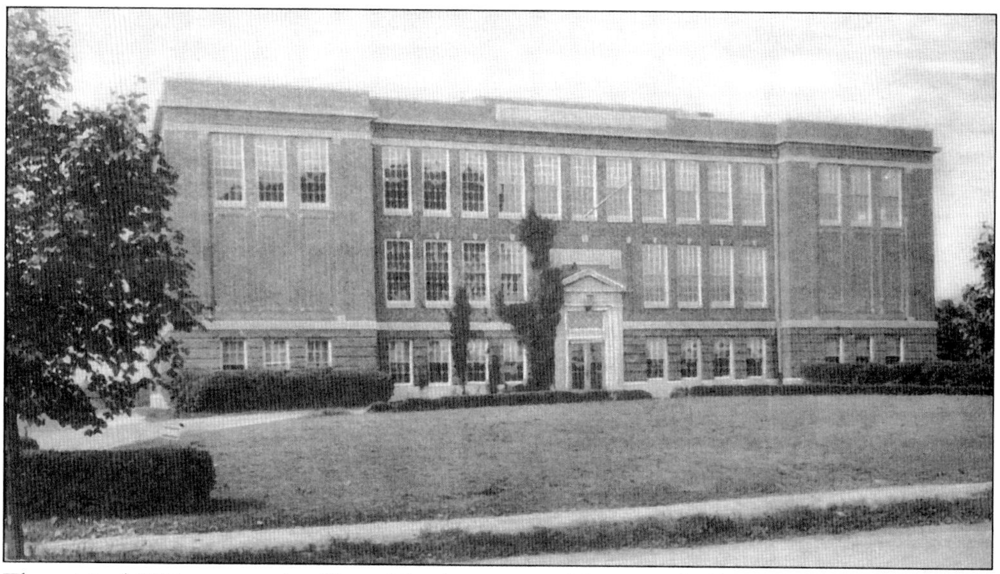

The original 1923 structure is still used for classrooms, a library, and offices. Later additions can be seen extending toward the intersection of Adams Street. The street was named for Rev. Jedediah Adams (1711–1799), whose parsonage stood directly across from the old "A" building until the late 1960s. (Authors' collection.)

Three

Touring around Stoughton Square

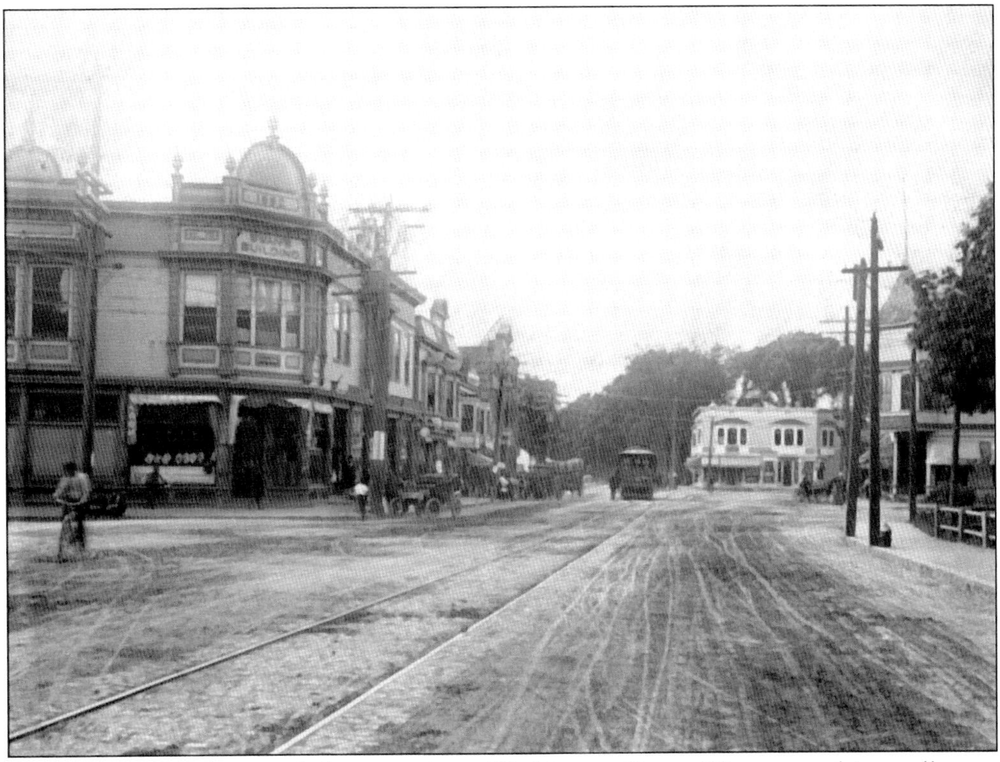

The view in this photograph faces north, up Washington Street. The approaching trolley car stops to pick up passengers after making the turn from Porter Street. The Brockton & Stoughton Street Railway Company operated in Stoughton from August 21, 1895, until August 25, 1933, when bus service replaced the trolleys.

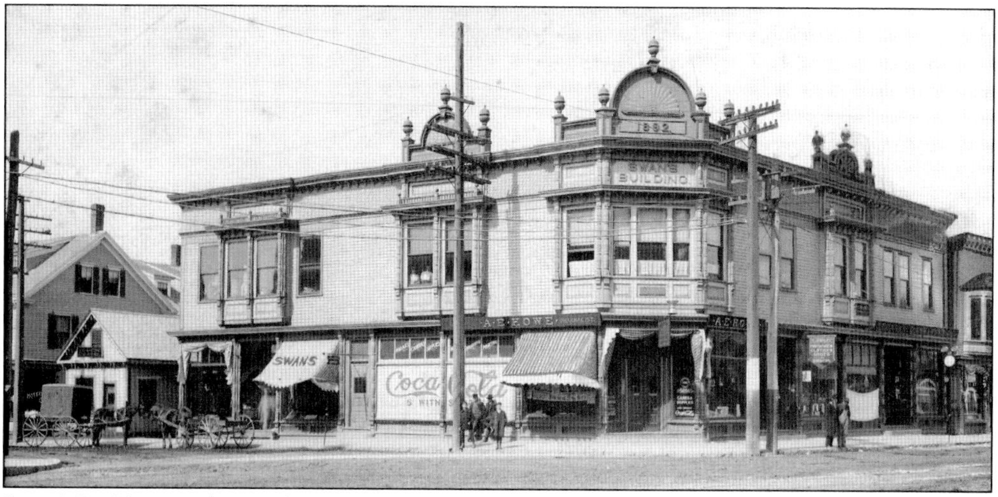

Swan's Building, at the northwest corner of Washington and Wyman Streets, is seen here around 1910. This building, constructed in 1892, was destroyed by fire on September 6, 1969. It served a variety of uses over the years, housing a bank, a candy store, a shorthand school, a liquor store, and a district court. Visible here are signs for A.E. Howe's Pharmacy; Dr. W.E. Chase, dentist; T.J. Farley, furnisher and clothier; attorney Oscar A. Marden's office (second floor); A.F. Capen's store; and W.L. Pierce, jeweler. To the left of the Swan's Building is Vanston's coal office before it was moved the first time, to make way for the Stoughton Post Office on Wyman Street. (Authors' collection.)

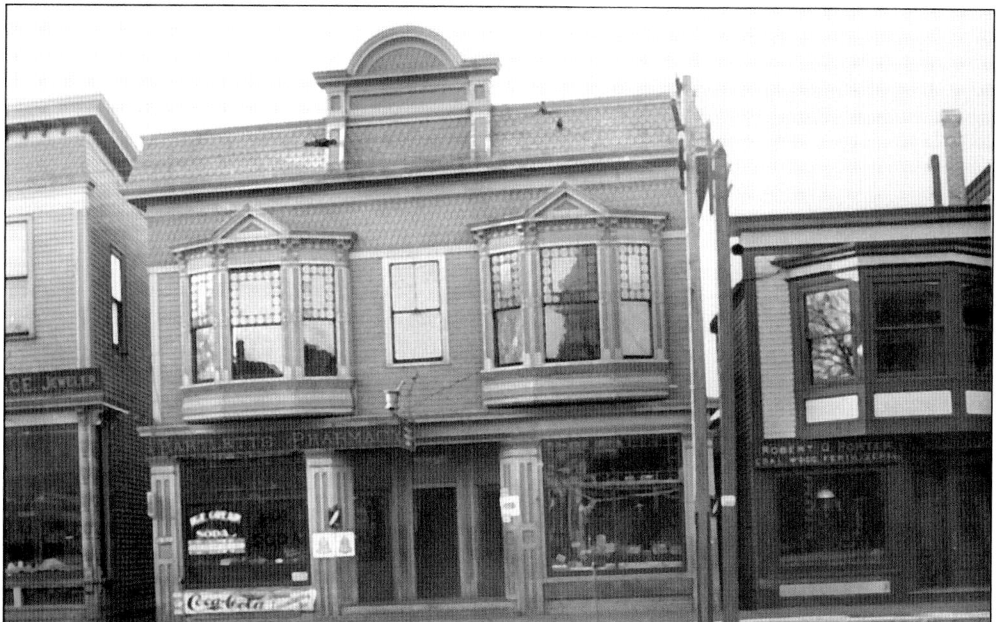

The Ellis Block, built in 1888 on Washington Street, is flanked by the Swan's Building (left) and James Lehan's bicycle shop. In this early photograph, Bartlett's Pharmacy offers ice cream sodas. This nearly century-old store was lost to fire in 1984. In recent years, Medical Pharmacy was located in the structure that replaced the old Ellis Block at 769 Washington Street.

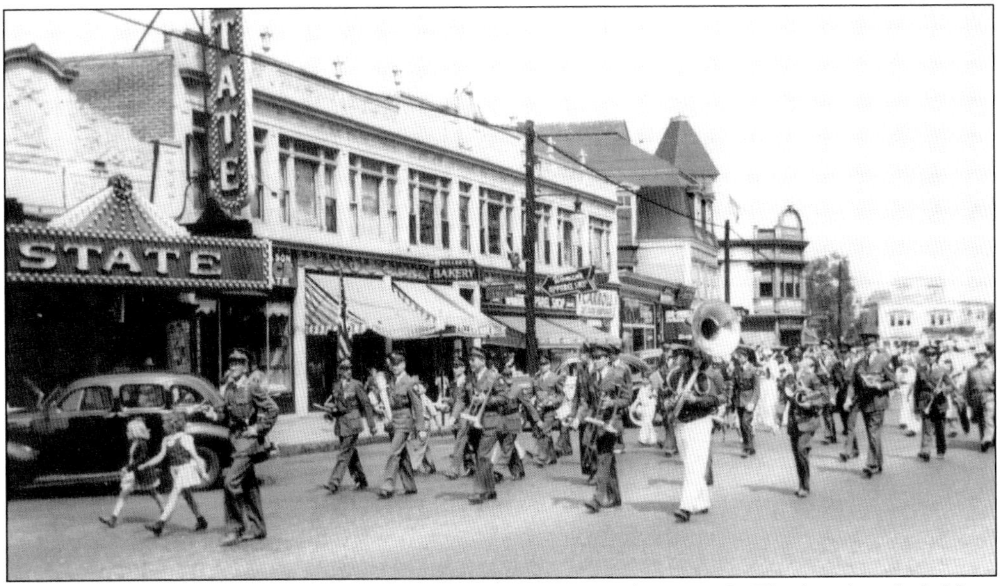

Washington Street is seen during the Memorial Day Parade in 1942. The band and children march past the State Theatre and the Stoughton Building.

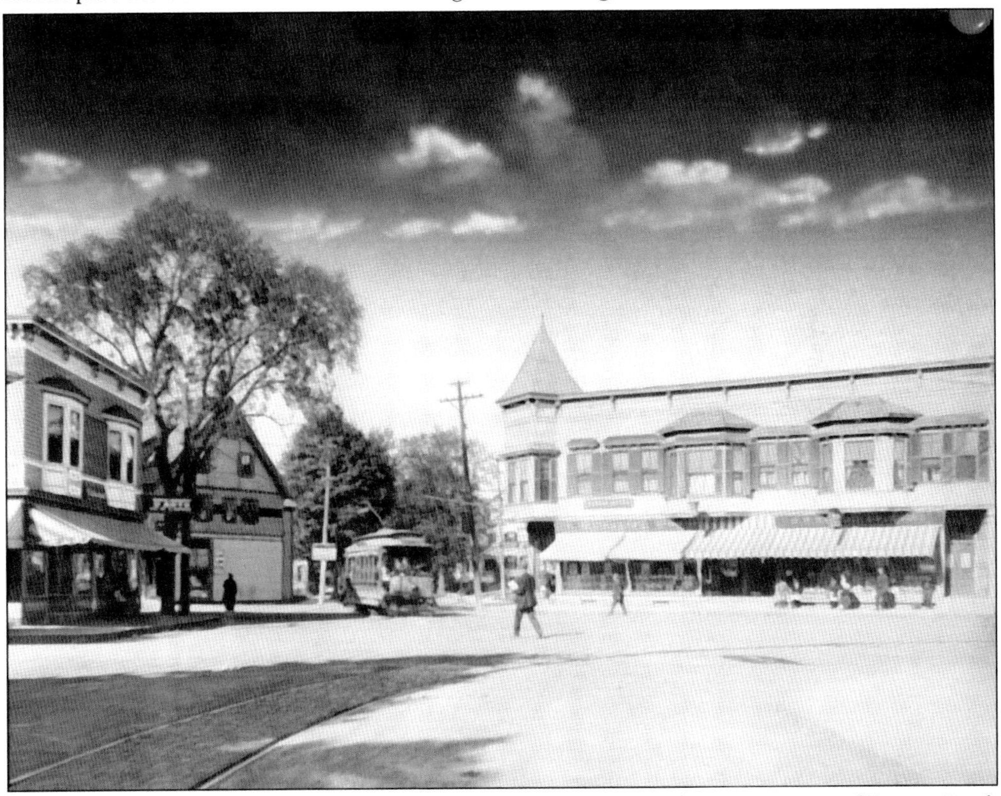

The view in this photograph of Stoughton Square looks east to the intersection of Porter, Pearl, and Washington Streets. The three buildings are practically unchanged since this photograph was taken around 1915. They are, from left to right, Britton's Block, Milliken's Block, and Swan's Block. Note the trolley car making the approach in the square, and the trolley tracks converging.

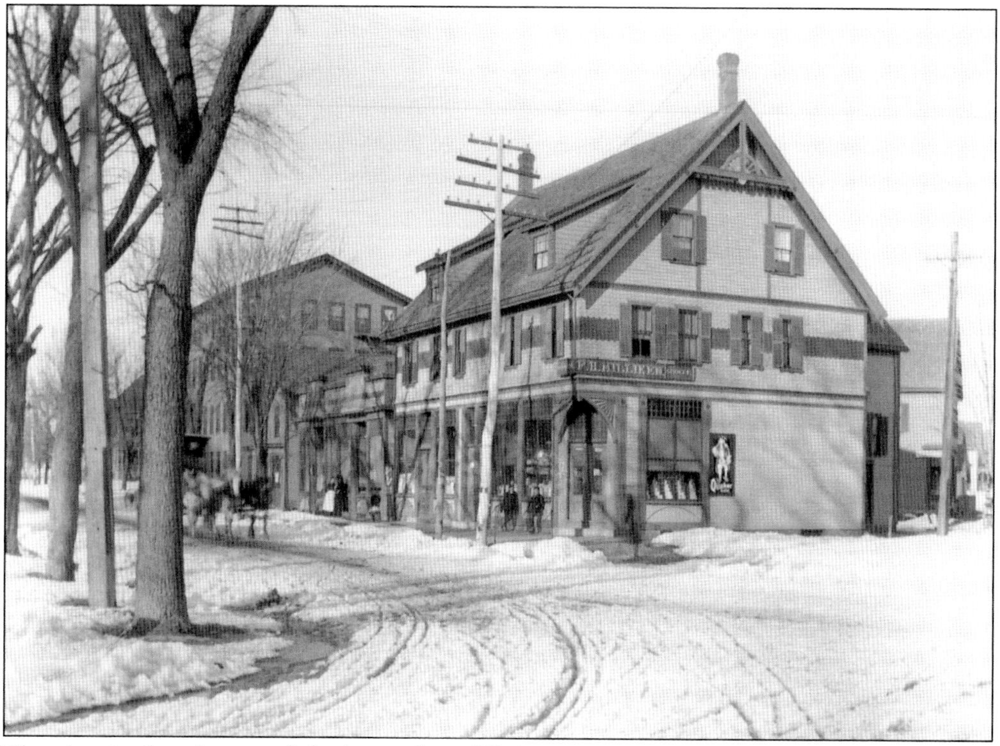

The view in this photograph looks north up Washington Street on a winter day. At left is the Fitzpatrick Shoe Factory. In the center is the Milliken Block, with the grocery shop of F.H. Milliken, now occupied by J&I Variety store at 742 Washington Street.

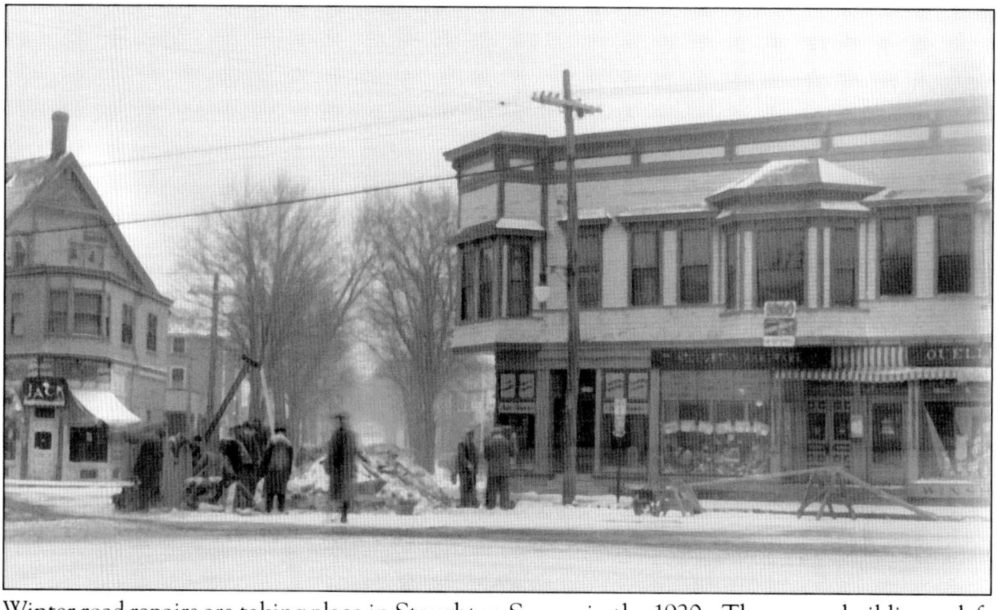

Winter road repairs are taking place in Stoughton Square in the 1920s. The corner building at left is today home to Jack the Haberdasher. To the right of the haberdashery is the snow-covered roof of the original Ahavath Torah Synagogue on Porter Street. Swan's Block has a Dutch Cleaners (now Olivio's restaurant), Stoughton Hardware, and Oulette's Pharmacy.

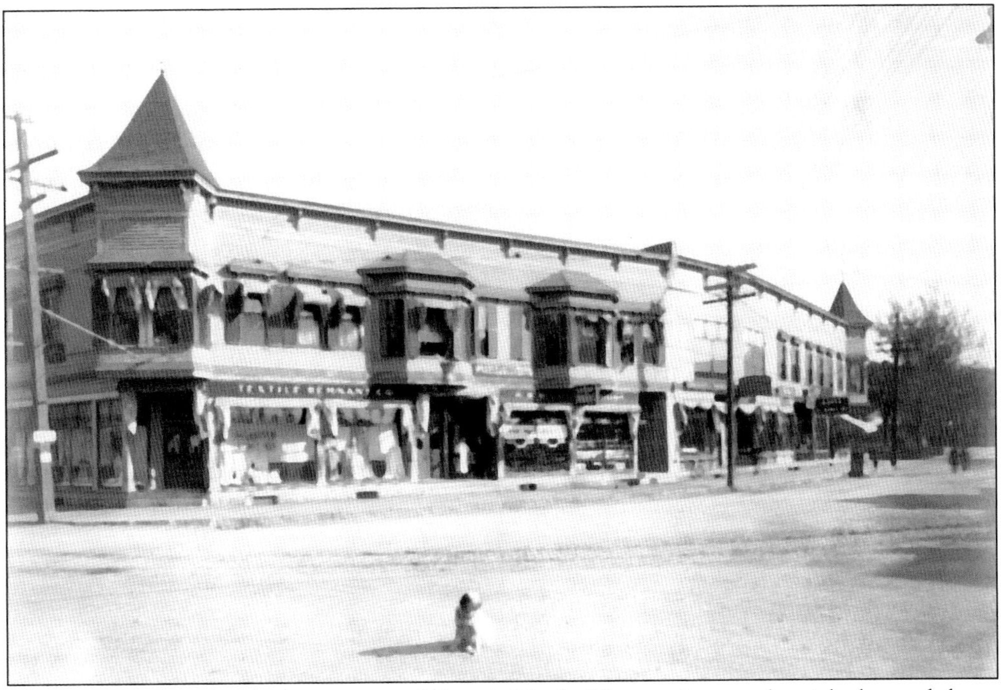

This c. 1910 photograph shows most of Swan's Block. The section on the right burned down in a fire in 1919. Located in the block are, from left to right, the Textile Remnant Co., H.W. Winship Drug Store, a store specializing in crockery and tinware, and the Auto Lunch restaurant. (Authors' collection.)

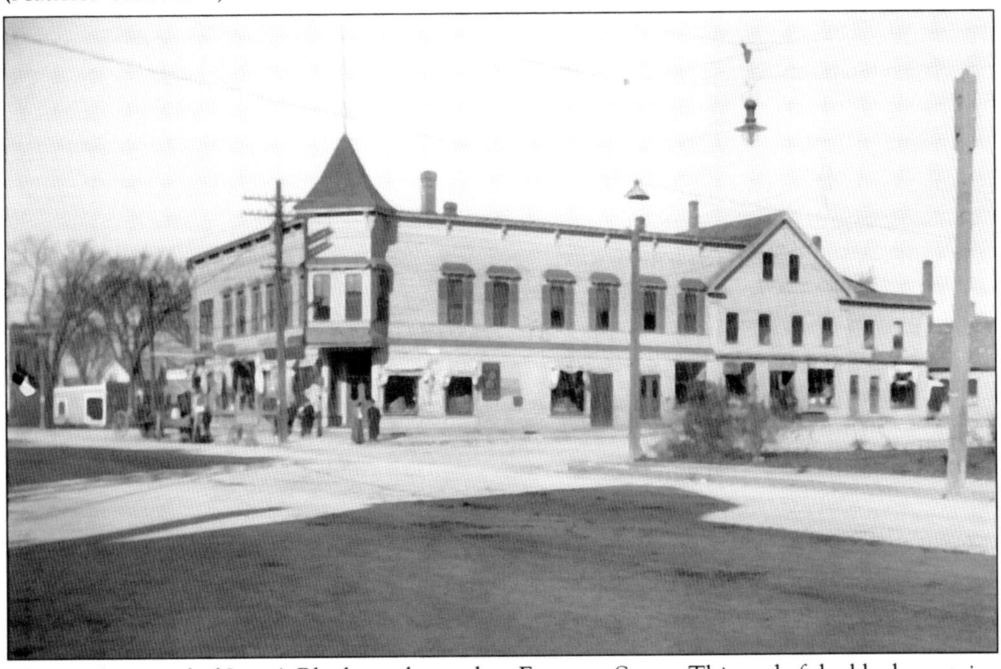

The northern end of Swan's Block was located on Freeman Street. This end of the block contains the old A-frame structure that once housed the Grand Army of the Republic (GAR) hall, now partly occupied by a bakery. This section of Swan's Block burned down in 1919.

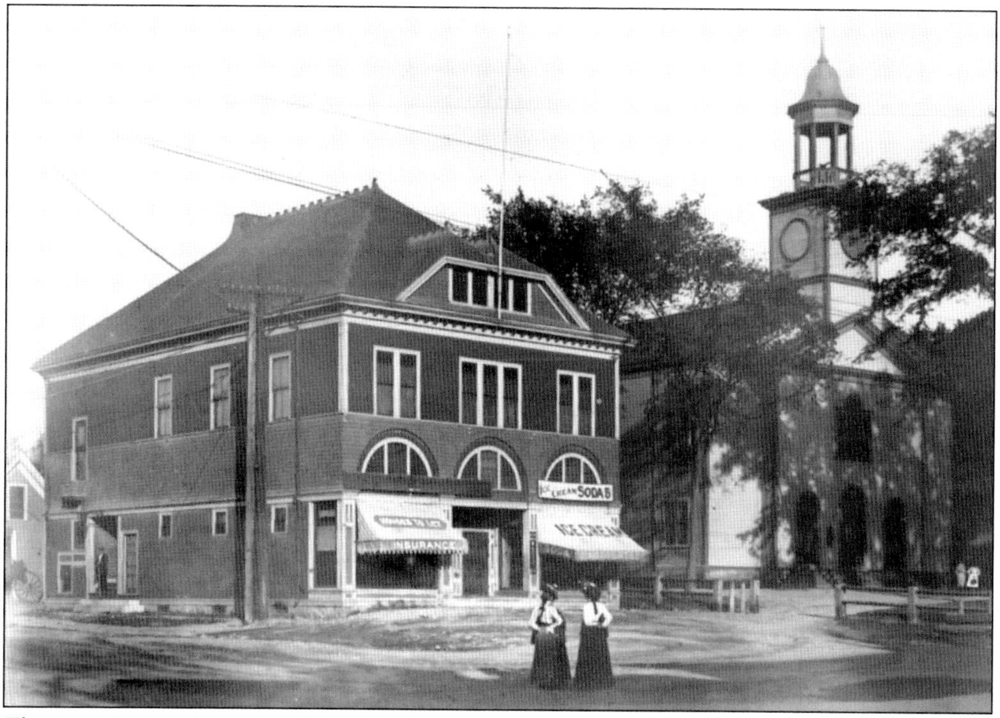

The Henry E. Holbrook Building, also known as the Odd Fellows Hall, was built in 1892 at 6 Freeman Street in Stoughton Square. At this point in time, the building housed an ice cream shop that advertised an ice cream soda for 5¢. To the right of this building is the edifice of the First Parish Universalist Church, built in 1808. In recent years, the Holbrook Building has had a driving school upstairs in the old Odd Fellows Hall. Manuel Pacheco's hardware store resided in the building from 1984 to 2010.

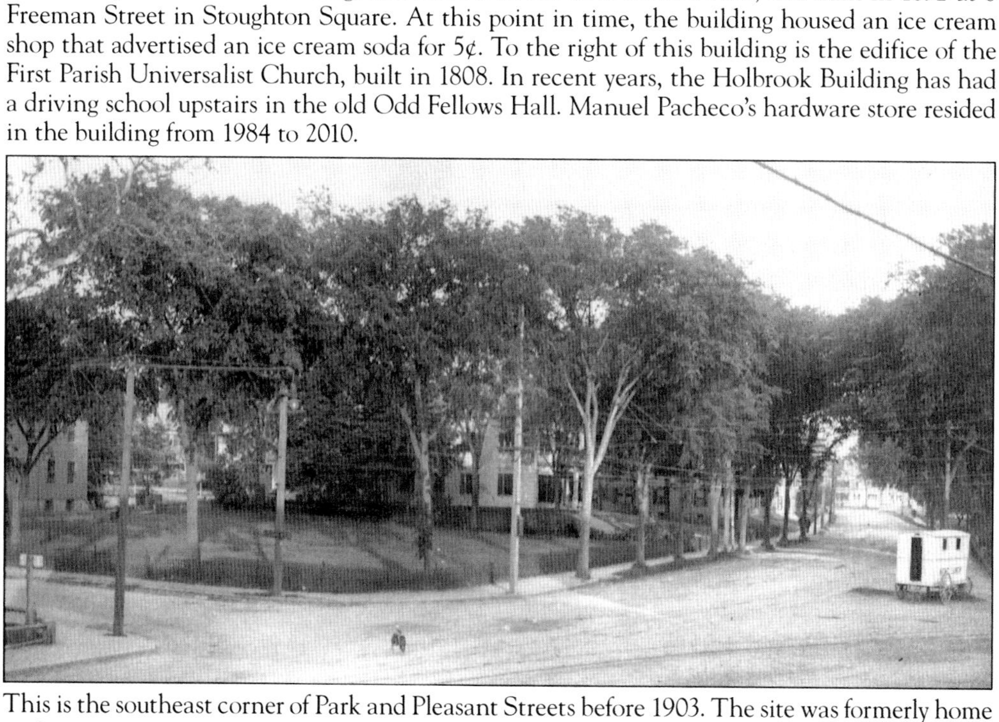

This is the southeast corner of Park and Pleasant Streets before 1903. The site was formerly home to Capen Tavern and would later be the location of the Stoughton Public Library. To the left of this lot is the factory for Atherton Boot Company (now Randolph Savings Bank), and to the right is the home of James Atherton (now the location of the Stoughton Co-operative Bank).

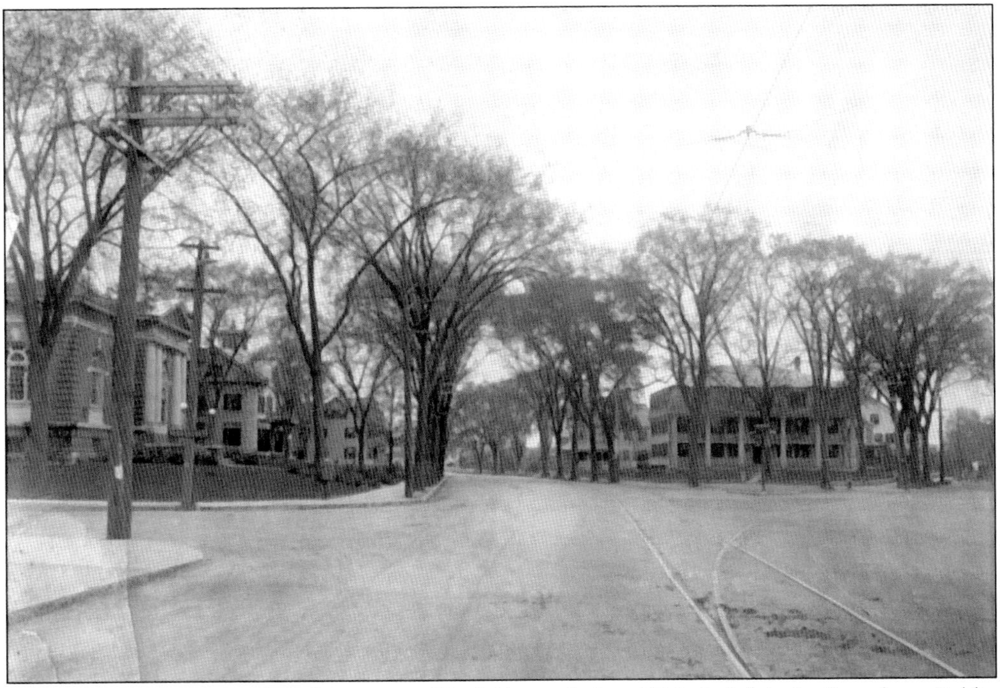

This is the intersection of Washington and Park Streets before 1916. At left is the Stoughton Public Library, and next to it is the Chicatabut Club. In the center is the former home of town clerk Martin Wales. It was demolished to start construction of the post office on Park Street in 1937.

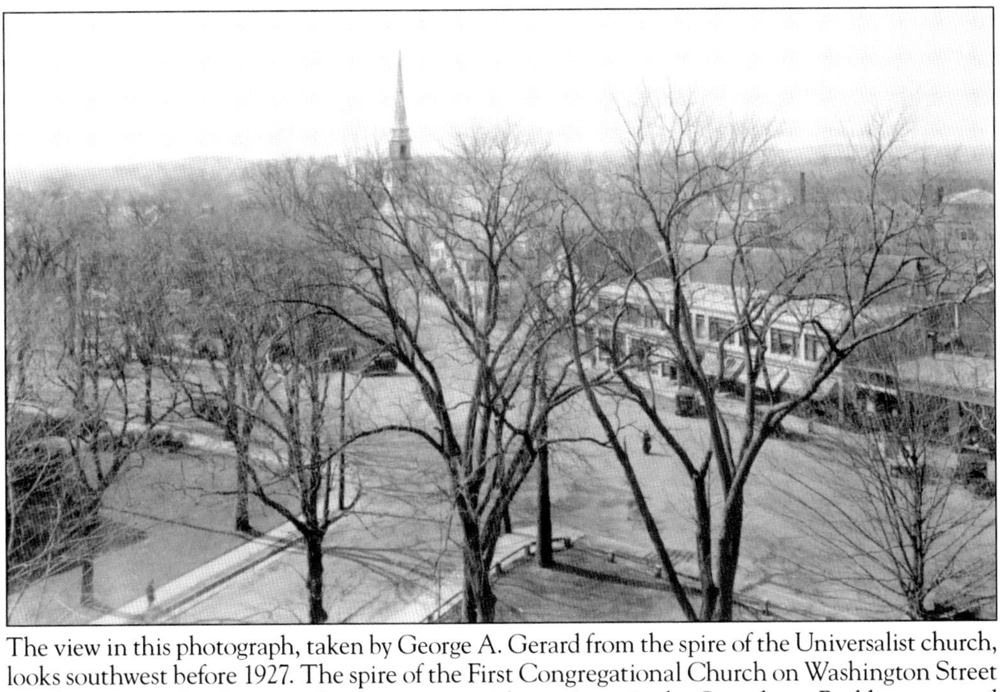

The view in this photograph, taken by George A. Gerard from the spire of the Universalist church, looks southwest before 1927. The spire of the First Congregational Church on Washington Street can be seen in the distance. In the center, with awnings, is the Stoughton Building, erected in 1923. To the left of the Stoughton Building is the A-frame known as Atwood's Market, on Washington Street and Railroad Avenue. It would be destroyed by fire in 1927.

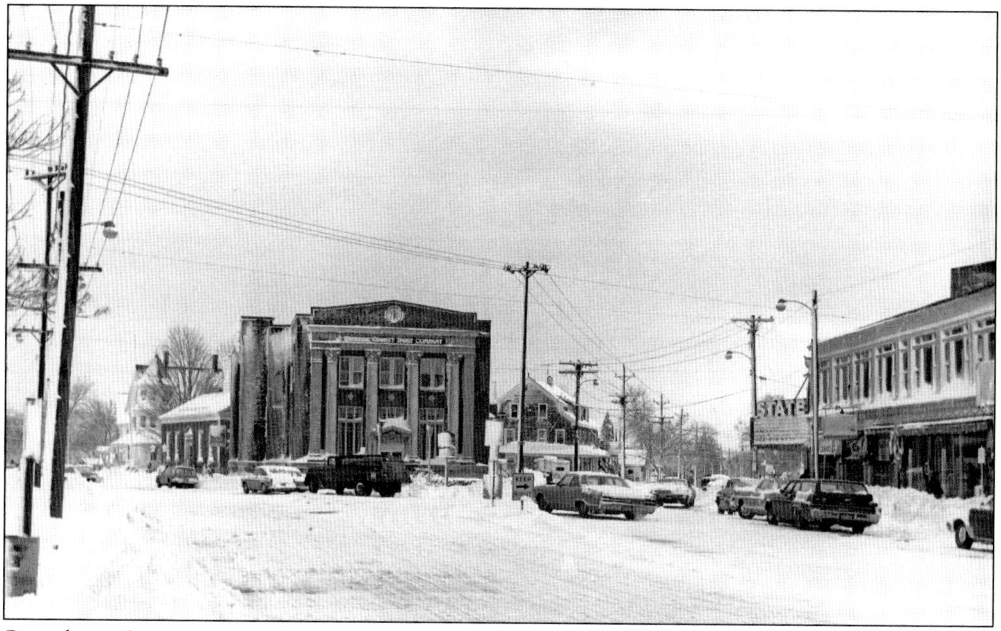

Stoughton Square is seen here in the late 1960s. The Norfolk County Trust Company is at center, flanked by the Stoughton Post Office on Park Street (left) and the Fieldbrook House on Washington Street (right). The last marquee attached to the State Theatre is at right, and next to it are the offices of photographer Chet Cohenno.

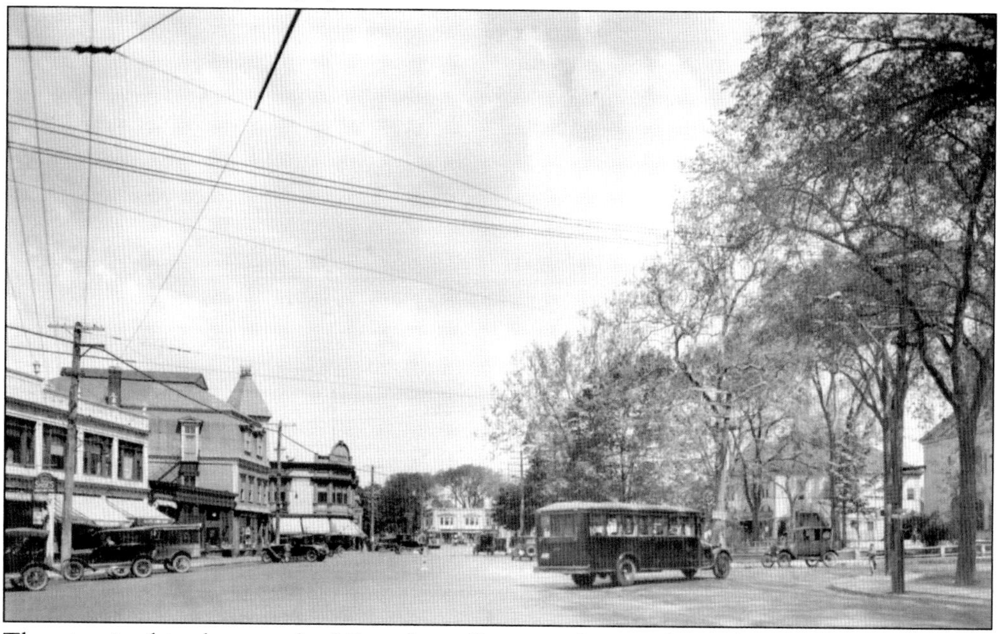

The view in this photograph of Stoughton Square, taken in the early 1930s, looks north up Washington Street. The newly erected Stoughton Building is on the far left. The small block next to it is the home of Murphy Coal & Oil. The spire of Darling's Block is visible, and next to it are the draped canopies of the Swan's Building. In the center distance is the white Britton's Block. The photograph shows three forms of motorized transportation: a trolley car approaching Stoughton center, cars, and a bus about to make the turn onto Pleasant Street.

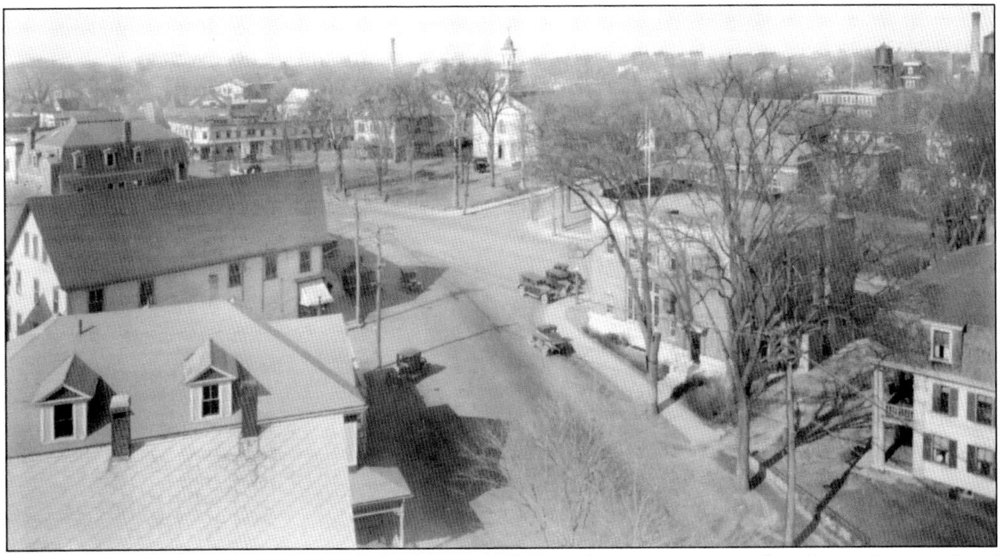

This 1920s photograph, with a view looking north into the square, was taken from the steeple of First Congregational Church. This view shows Washington Street on the way to the Universalist church at the corner of Pleasant Street. To the left of the church can be seen the smokestack of Panther Panco Rubber Co. on Washington and Monk Streets. At far right is the smokestack of George E. Belcher Last Co. on Pleasant Street.

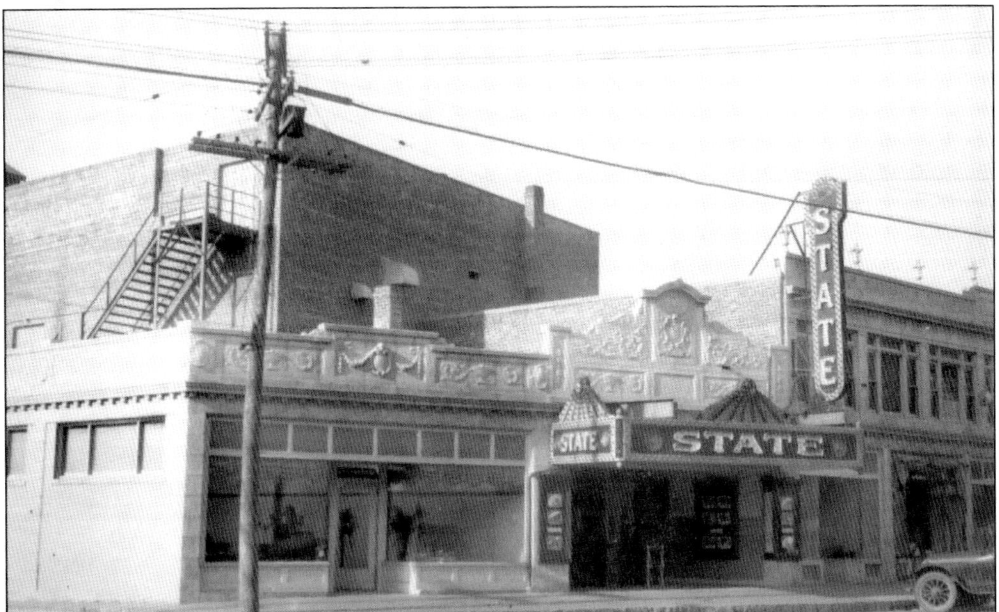

The State Theatre opened to the public on December 8, 1927, at 807 Washington Street, near the corner of Railroad Avenue. The venue was in use for nearly 80 years, as a movie theater and a vaudeville stage. It last operated as Stoughton Cinema Pub, and it housed the performances of the Stoughton Little Theatre, the Independent Theatre Co., and Stars. High school graduations and church services were also held in this building over the years. Current efforts led by former Stoughton selectman John Stagnone and others are being made to reopen and restore this historic landmark.

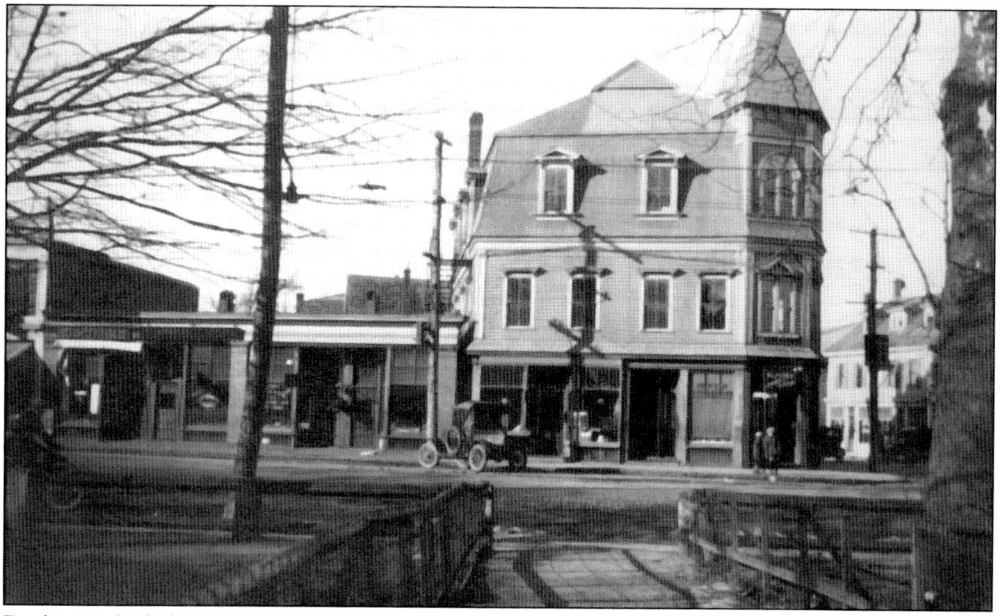

Darling's Block, built in 1885, occupied the northwest corner of Washington and Wyman Streets until March 1951. This 1920s photograph shows the newly built Stoughton Block on the far left and the offices of Murphy Coal & Oil left of center. Before Darling's Block was built, this was the site of the 18th-century home of Joseph Withington and Luther Johnson. The home was destroyed in the great Stoughton fire of February 27, 1880.

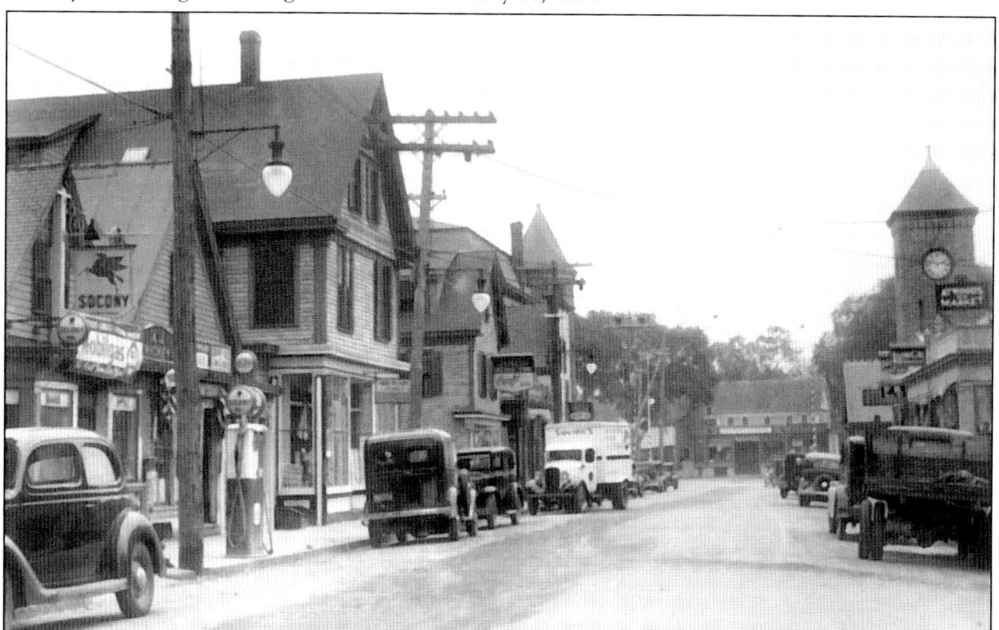

A glance down Wyman Street shows a bustling thoroughfare in the 1930s. Gas for automobiles could be obtained at A.J. Hickey's (left). To the right of the gas station is the Independent Lumber Co., which in recent years was Wyman's Jewelry store. Farther down the street are the Stoughton Package Store and the Busy-B Café. Across Wyman Street are the offices of Vanston Coal Co. and a lunch counter at Atwood's New Market.

Four

WINTERTIME IN STOUGHTON

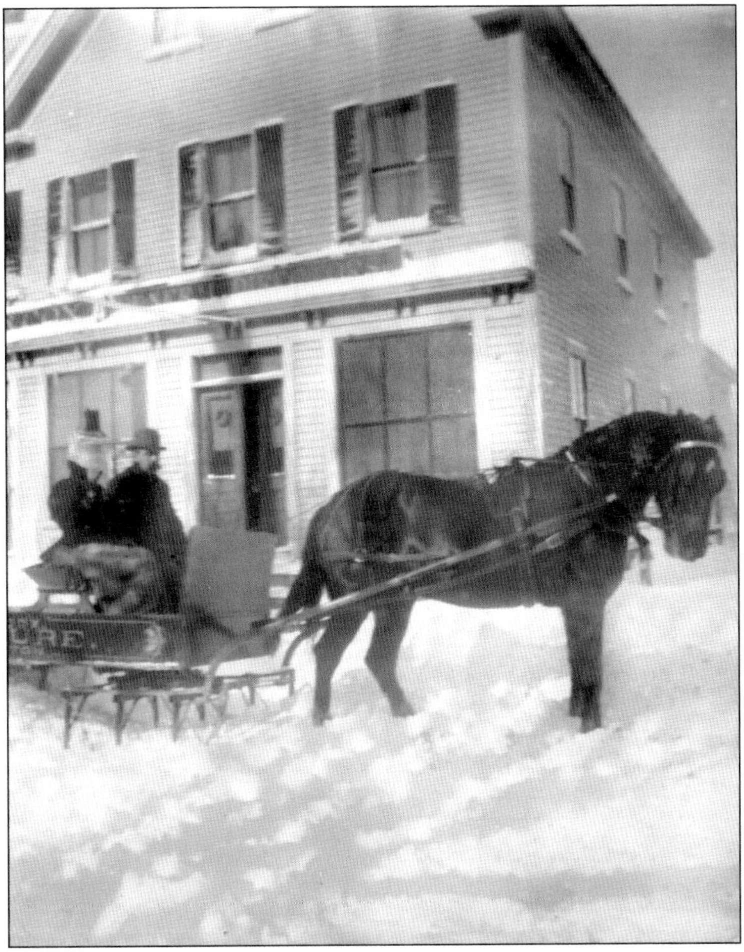

This view of Porter Street shows the Smith & Cox Furniture Store wagon in front of the business. Webster Smith built this structure in 1882, and the company competed in the funeral-director business with Withington & Lowe's next door. Note that the gentleman in the wagon is the only human passenger; the figure at his side is made of snow and is wrapped in a jacket and fur. This building, at the corner of Porter and Rose Streets, became the home to Stoughton's well-known Town Spa from 1955 to 1986. The structure was razed on February 15, 2006. (Authors' collection.)

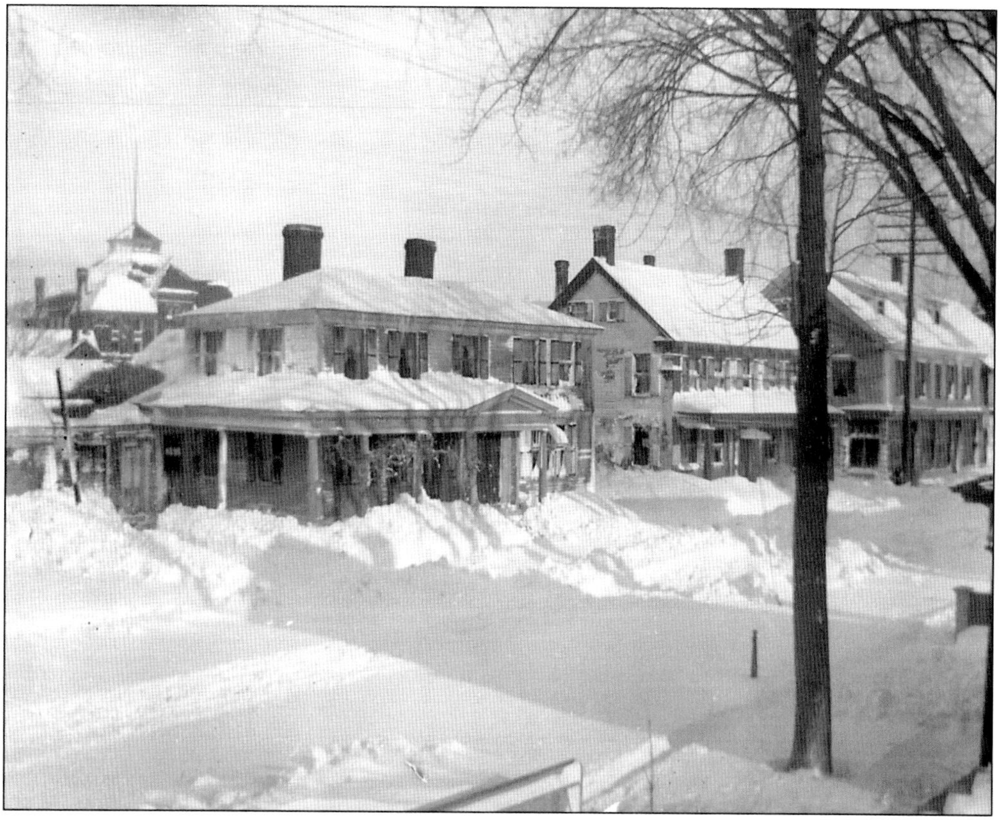

Wyman Street is covered in snow in the early 1900s. In the left background is the Stoughton Town Hall, with its flagpole on top. The house on the far left is the home of Dr. Charles S. Young, originally the home of Abraham Capen. Capen kept a tavern at the corner of Pleasant and Park Streets in 1799. The next structure still stands today as a multifamily residence, as it was previously a boardinghouse. The structure on the far right, destroyed by fire in the early 1960s, stood where the Wyman Street entrance to the current post office driveway is.

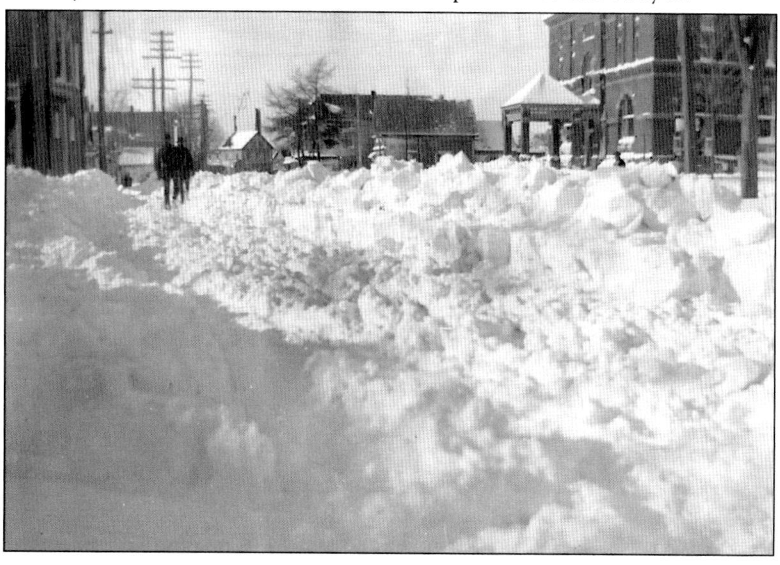

The view in this pre-1910 photograph looks west down Porter Street, which is nearly impassable. The corner of the Monk's Block is on the left. At right is the Stoughton Town Hall. Its portico was later removed.

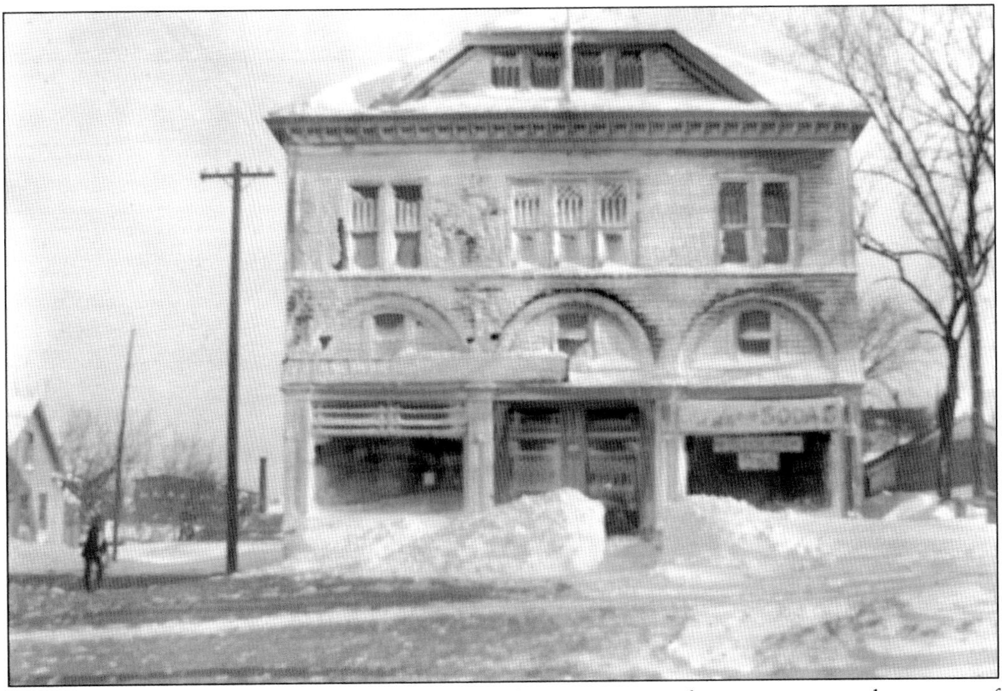

The snow-blasted front of the Henry E. Holbrook Store appears frozen in time at the corner of Washington and Freeman Streets. The Stretton Factory and smokestack can be seen on Porter Street in the distance at left.

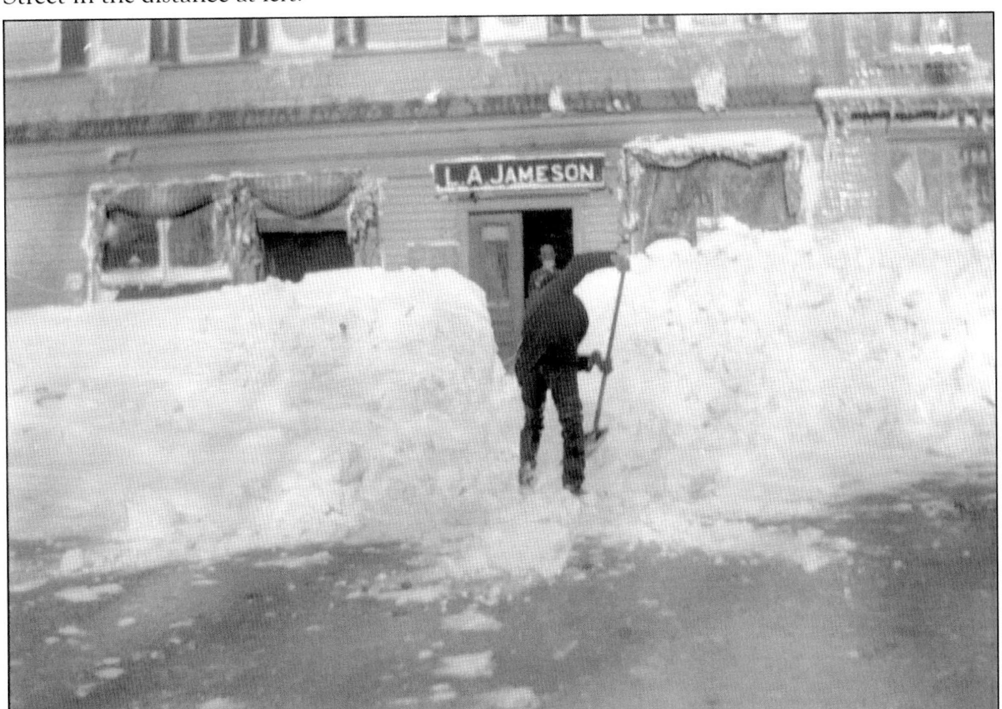

This man is digging a path to work, from Freeman Street to L.A. Jameson's storefront. Banks of snow are piled against the Freeman Street side of the Swan's Block sometime before 1919.

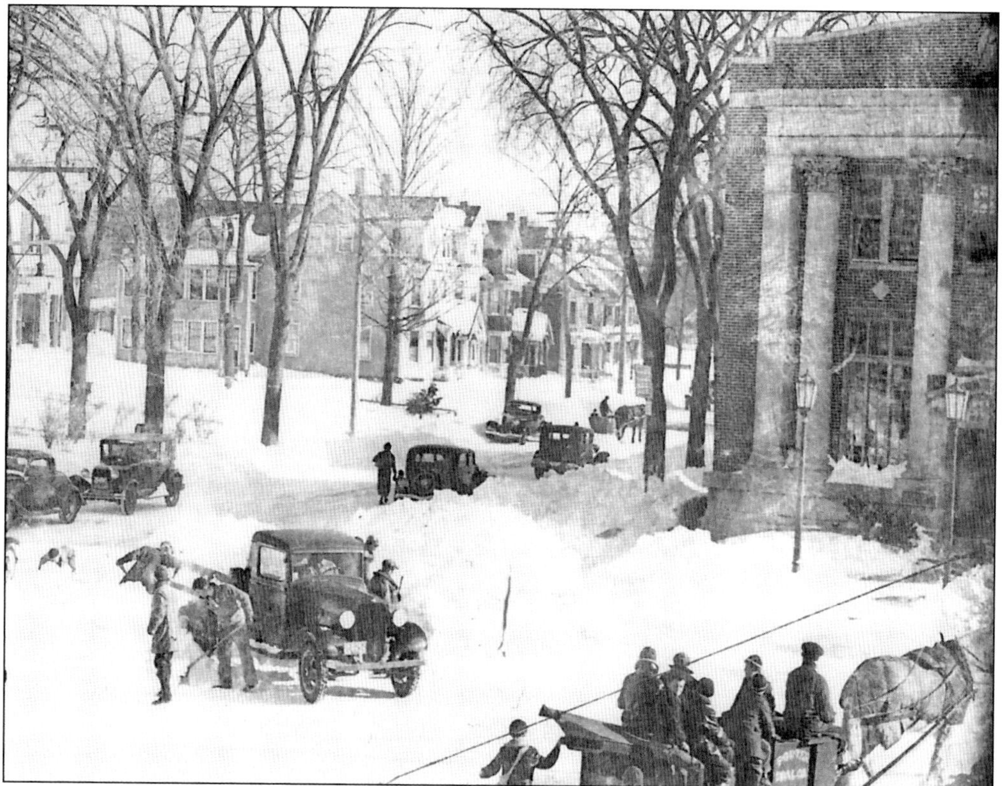

This photograph was taken from the John C. Stiles Fotakraft Studio in the Stoughton Building. Residents travel through the town's snow-buried streets. The Stoughton Public Library can be seen on the left, and the Stoughton Trust Co. is on the right.

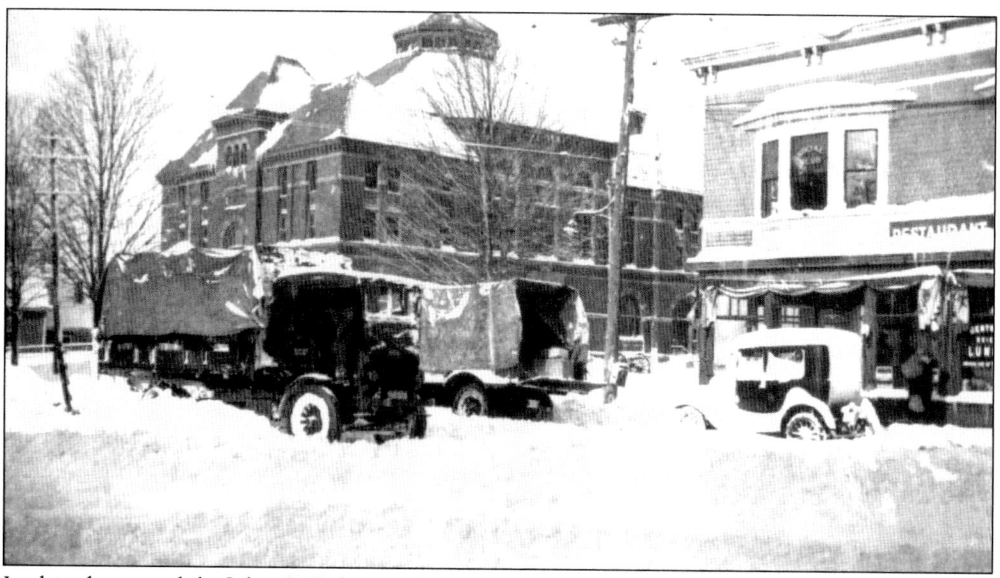

In this photograph by John C. Stiles, trucks appear to be operating in the snowbound intersection across from Stoughton Town Hall. Britton's Block (right) appears to be open for business and ready for restaurant customers.

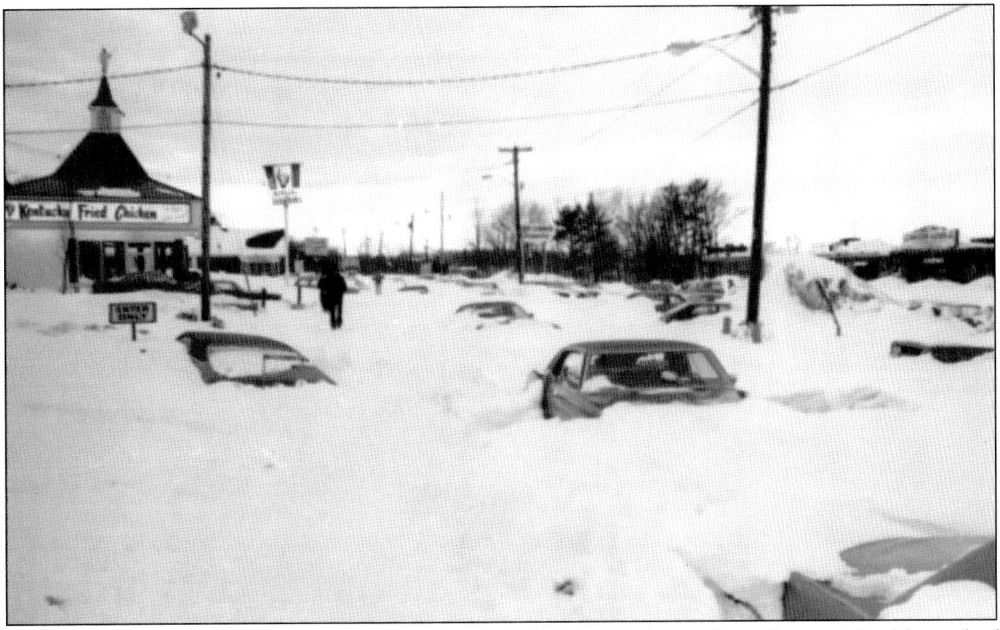

This photograph of Cobb's Corner, taken by Frank Maioli, shows the effects of the blizzard of 1978, which trapped many motorists in their cars. A person is walking on snow higher than the roofs of buried cars. Some Cobb's Corner dining favorites can be seen, including Kentucky Fried Chicken and Friendly's on the left, and Papa Gino's and Canton House Chinese restaurant on the right.

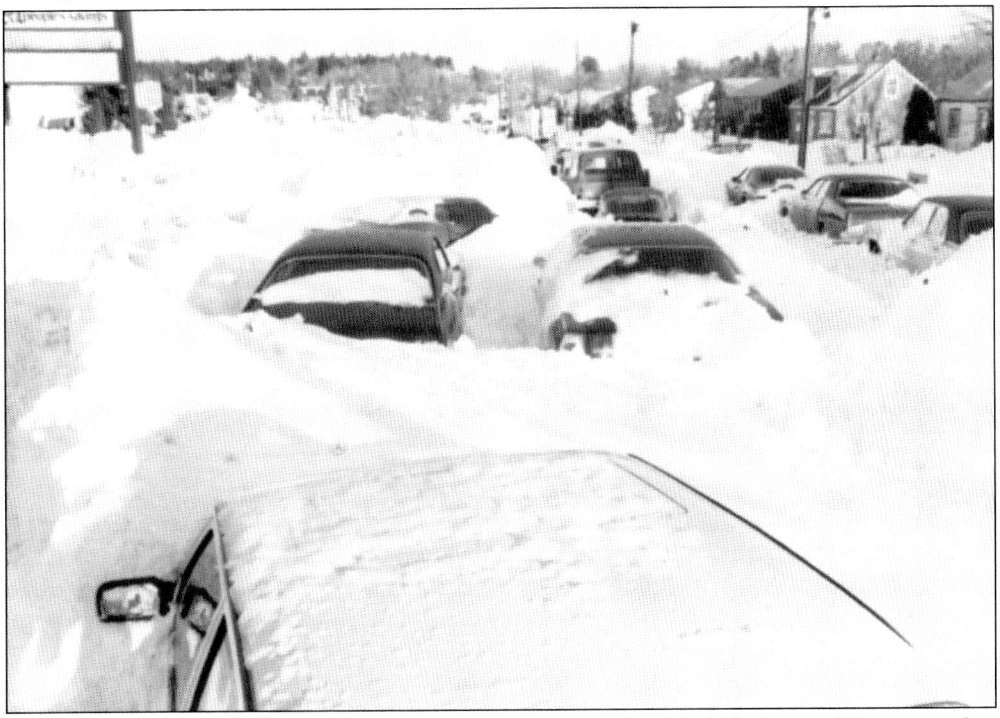

Cars are buried in their tracks on Central Street, just outside of Cobb's Corner. This is another photograph by Frank Maioli, taken during the great blizzard of 1978.

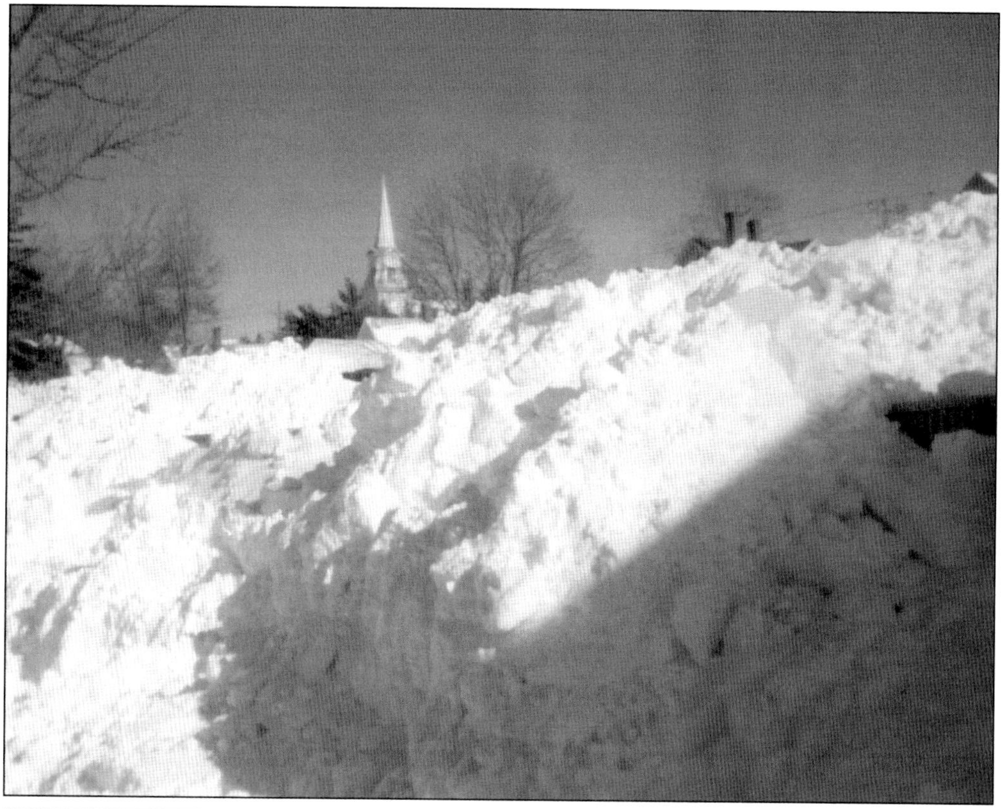

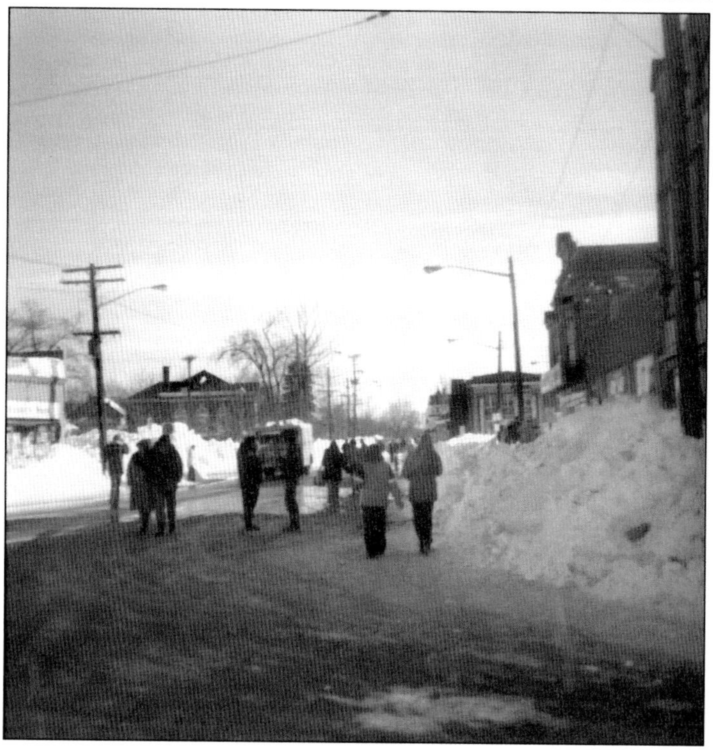

Only the steeple of the Methodist church and a couple of chimneys can be seen on Pleasant Street from Stoughton Square after the blizzard of 1978. This photograph was taken by Carol-Ann Lea after a walk to the square following the storm.

Stoughton Square in the wake of the blizzard of 1978 looks similar to how it must have been in the early 1900s, dominated by pedestrian traffic. This photograph by Carol-Ann Lea, with a view looking down Washington Street from Pearl Street, shows more people than cars in the square.

Five

STOUGHTON PARADES

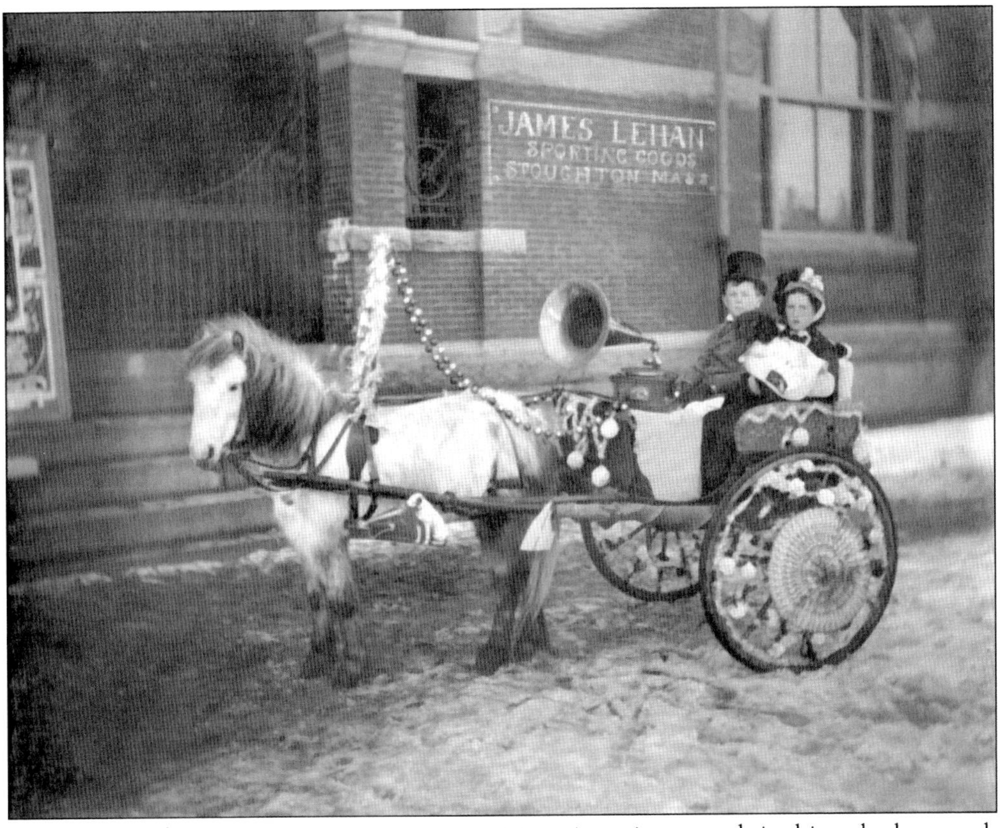

A pony cart and young passengers prepare to participate in a winter parade in this early photograph taken in front of Stoughton Town Hall. The stencil for James Lehan's Sporting Goods above the children was applied to the photographic negative. Lehan would later operate one of the longest-running Ford dealerships in the nation.

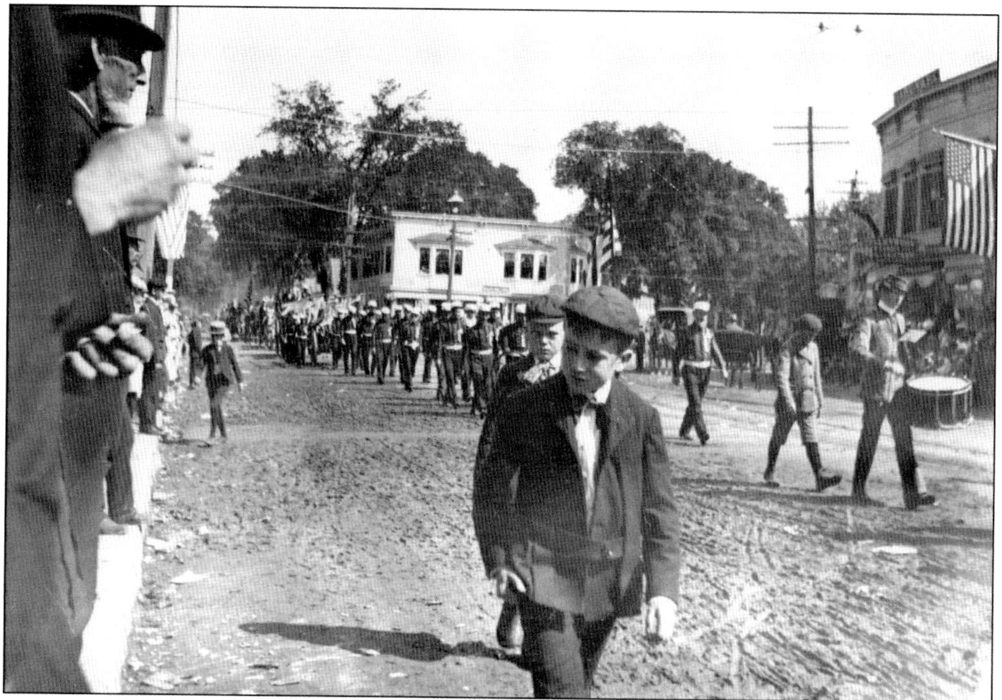

The dirt streets of Stoughton did not stop the fanfare of this early parade. This may be a Fourth of July parade or a Memorial Day parade. Britton's Block can be seen in the distance, at the intersection of Pearl and Washington Streets.

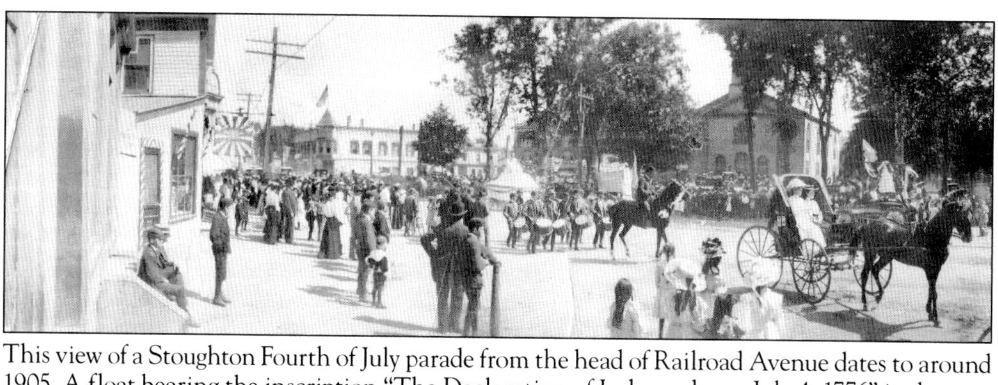

This view of a Stoughton Fourth of July parade from the head of Railroad Avenue dates to around 1905. A float bearing the inscription "The Declaration of Independence July 4, 1776" is about to pass the First Parish Universalist Church (right of center).

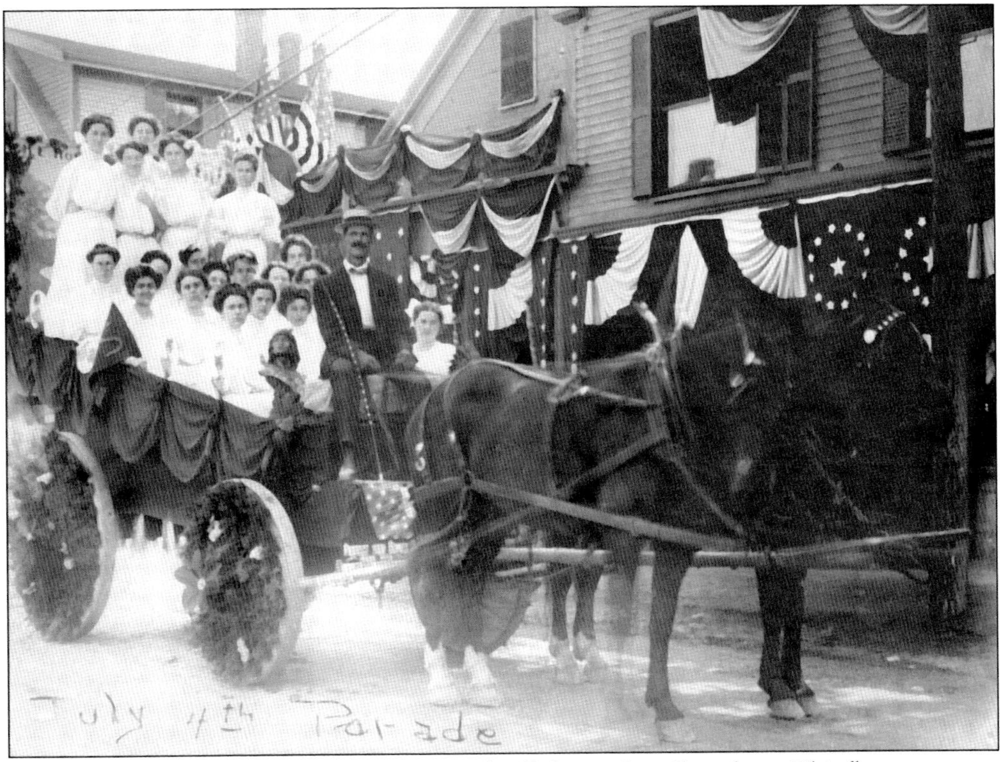

Ladies are driven in a two-horse float at a Fourth of July parade in Stoughton. This float appears to be sponsored by H.E. Holbrook, one of the leading real estate dealers in Stoughton at one time.

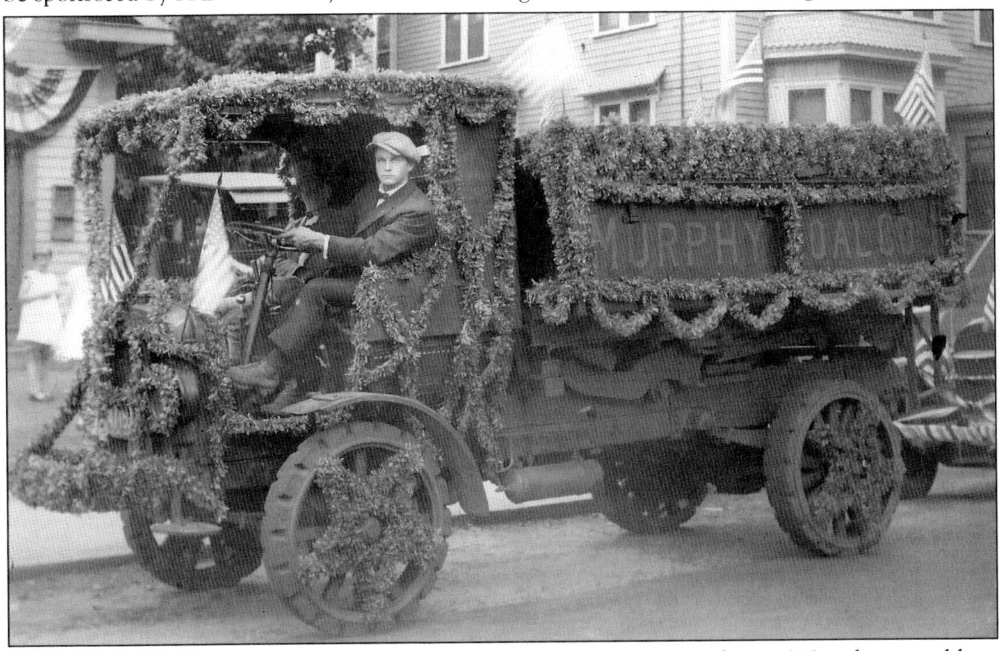

The Murphy Coal Co. truck is decorated in floral garland for a parade in 1919 to honor soldiers returning from World War I. The Murphy Coal Co. was started in 1886 by Irish immigrant Cornelius Murphy (1848–1929), and it is still operated by his descendants.

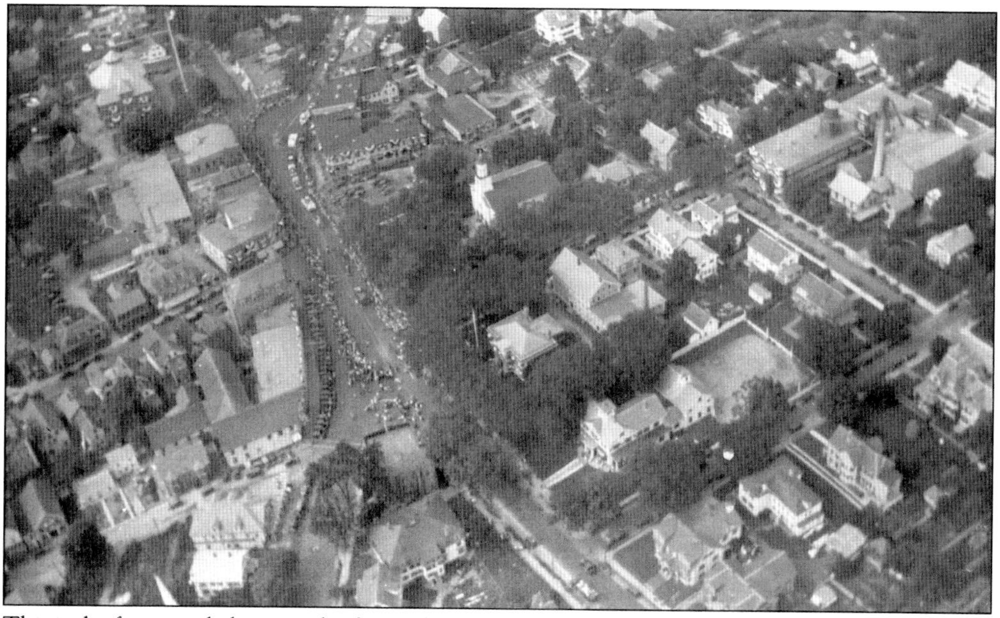

This is the first aerial photograph of Stoughton Square, taken by local photographer John C. Stiles. In this photograph, a parade honoring Stoughton's 200th anniversary heads down Washington Street in August 1926.

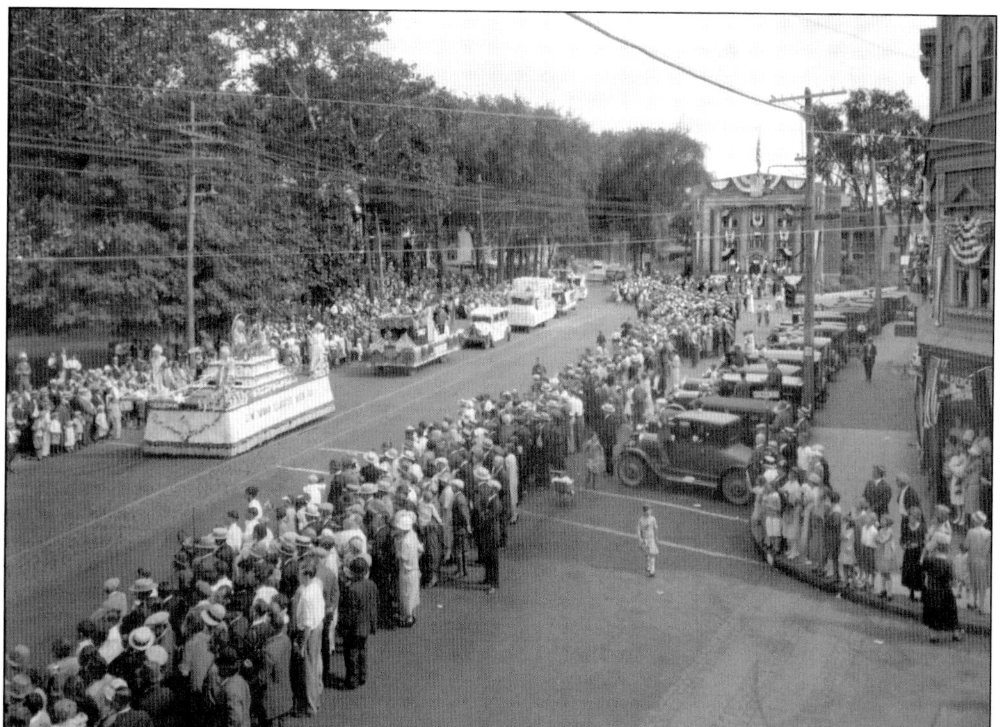

The town's 200th-anniversary parade heads through Stoughton Square. The float for the J.W. Wood Elastic Web Co. leads this portion of the procession. This photograph was taken by George A. Gerard from a second-story window of Swan's Building at Washington and Wyman Streets.

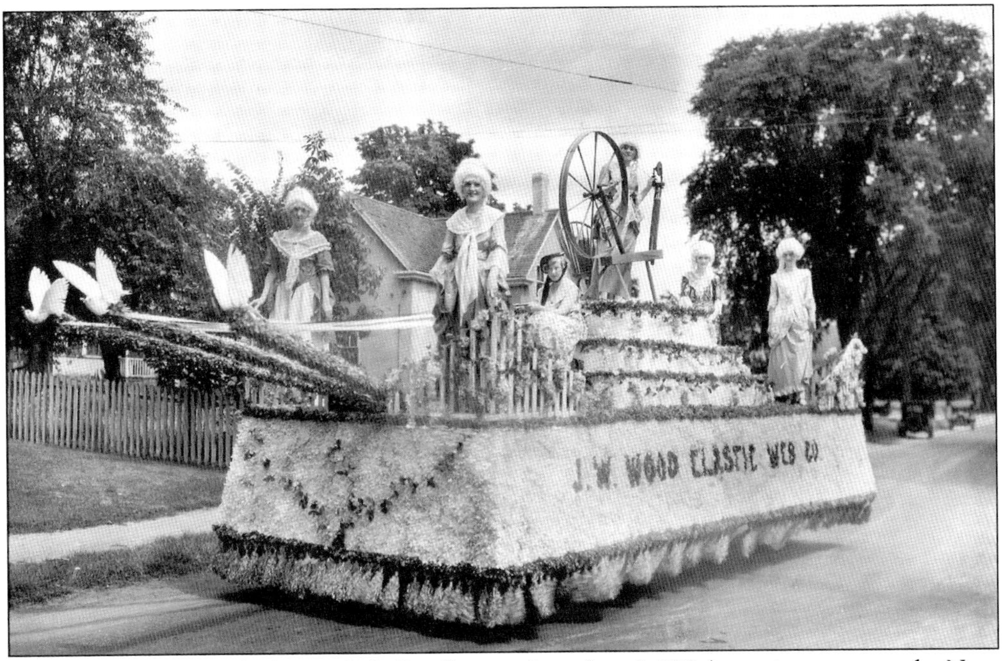

This is the J.W. Wood Elastic Web Co. float at Stoughton's 200th-anniversary parade. Note the ladies in Colonial dress and the spinning wheel on the top of this entry to honor the town's bicentennial.

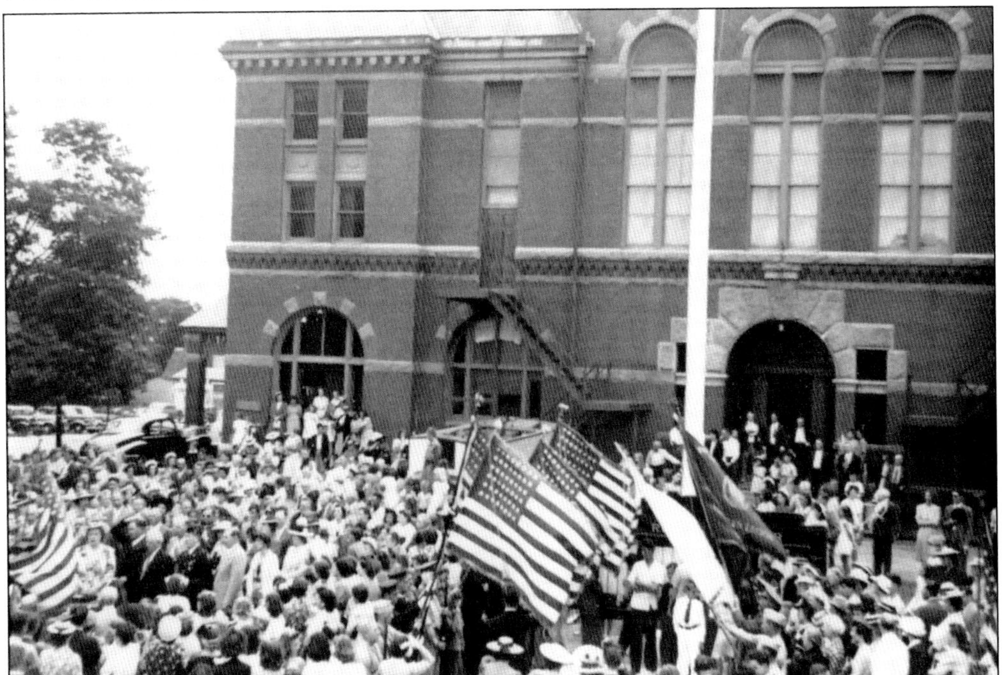

This photograph from the World War II years shows a scene familiar to most Stoughton residents over the years. The procession of this parade has stopped in front of Stoughton Town Hall for the reading of the names of the fallen veterans from the town's muster rolls. In recent years, this honor was given to beloved World War II veteran Charles Frederick "Charlie" Large (1924–2013).

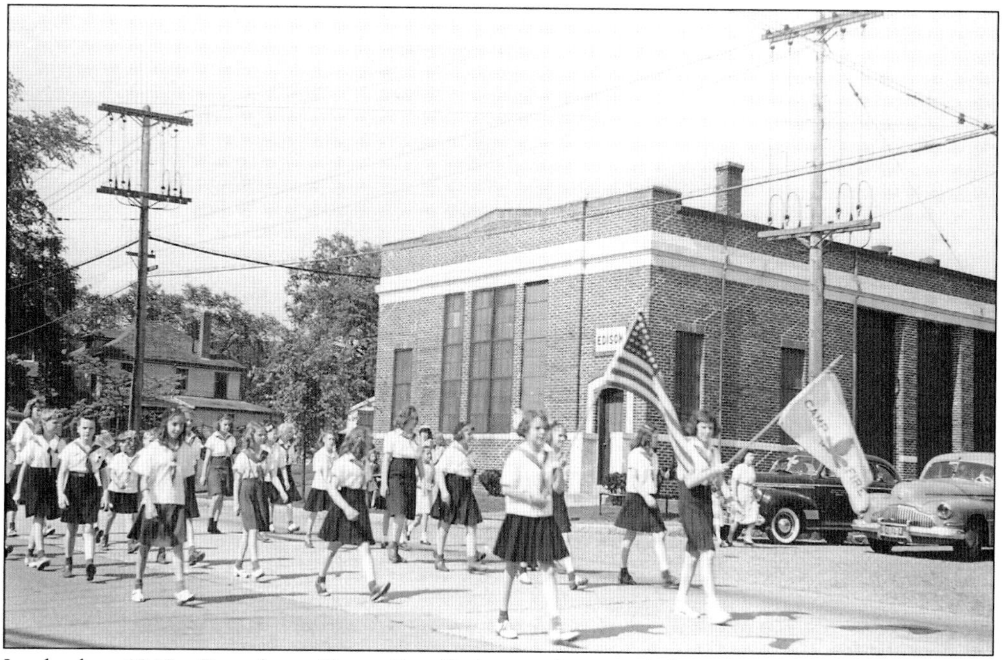

In the late 1940s, Stoughton Camp Fire Girls march toward the Evergreen Cemetery at the intersection where Brock and Kinsley Streets enter Washington Street. The old Edison Building is at center. The house on the left, at 918 Washington Street, is owned by the McGinley family.

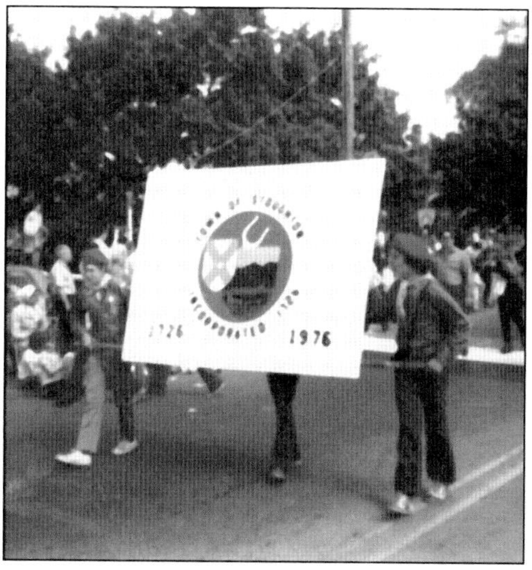

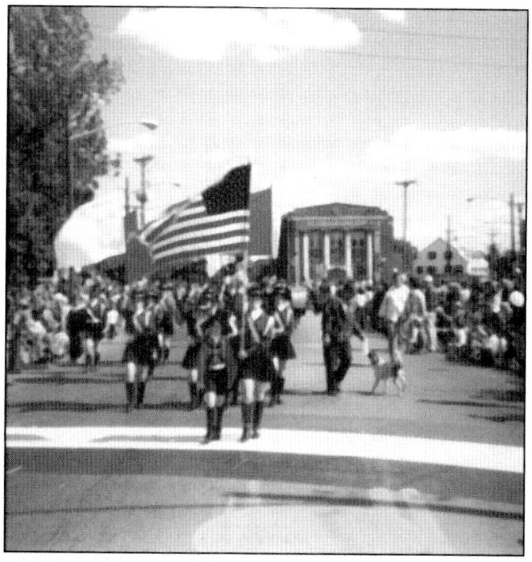

In 1976, when the nation celebrated its bicentennial, Stoughton celebrated the 250th anniversary of its incorporation. Stoughton Boy Scouts of Troop 57 carry the banner (left) as parade marchers pass the thousands of onlookers that lined the parade route in Stoughton (right). These photographs were taken by late Stoughton resident Robert Parsons, who was involved in coordinating many of the parades in Stoughton.

Six

Flying around Town

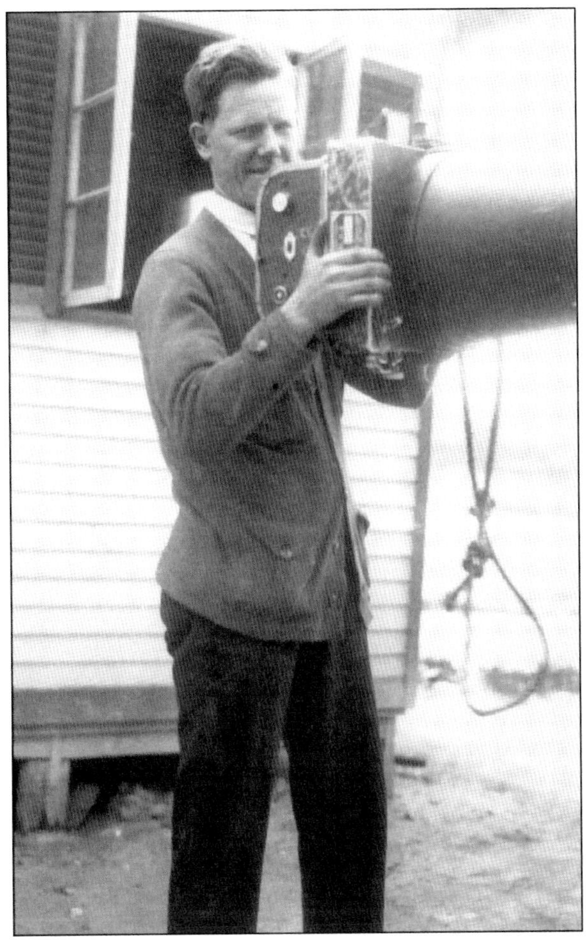

John C. "Johnny" Stiles (1906–2000) was an early Stoughton aviator and commercial photographer. Johnny took the first aerial photographs of Stoughton, in 1926. He operated a studio in Stoughton, known as Fotakraft, for many years. Stiles, a World War II veteran, was a postal carrier in Stoughton. He was the curator for the Stoughton Historical Society for many years and a mentor to current Stoughton historian (and the book's coauthor) David Allen Lambert.

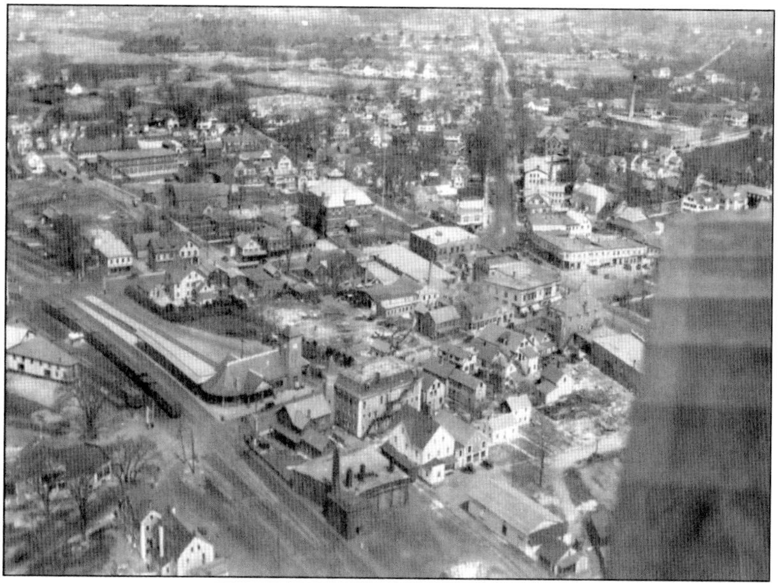

This photograph by Johnny Stiles shows Stoughton Square in the late 1920s. Clearly visible are the Stoughton train station and Stoughton Town Hall in the center. This view looks up Washington Street toward Central Street.

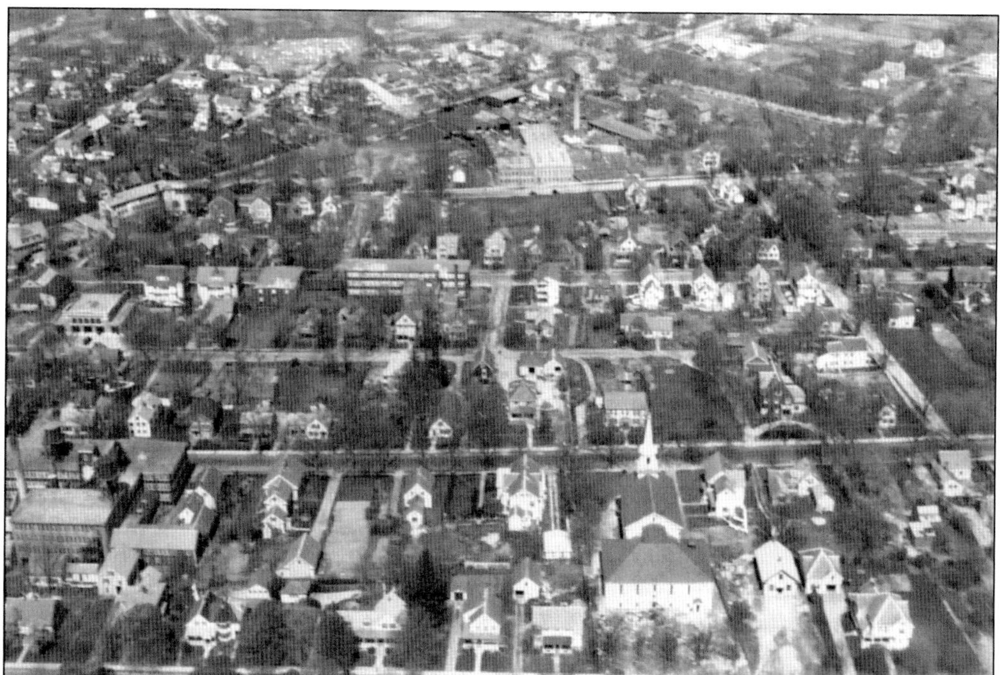

This is another photograph of Stoughton by Johnny Stiles, taken after 1927. The Panther Panco Rubber Co. on Monk Street can be seen at the top of the photograph. On the next street down, Porter Street, the Stretton Factory is in the center. On the far left of Freeman Street is the new Stoughton Fire Department station, built in 1927. The next street down is Pleasant Street, where the George E. Belcher Last Co. can be seen, as well as the steeple of the Methodist church. The street on the bottom is Seaver Street.

This aerial photograph was taken in 1929 by a commercial firm from Boston. The steeple of the First Congregational Church can be seen in the lower left, on Washington Street. The white steeple of the Universalist church is in the center of the photograph. All of Stoughton Square is visible. Canton, Pearl, and Washington Streets fade off into the distance. (Authors' collection.)

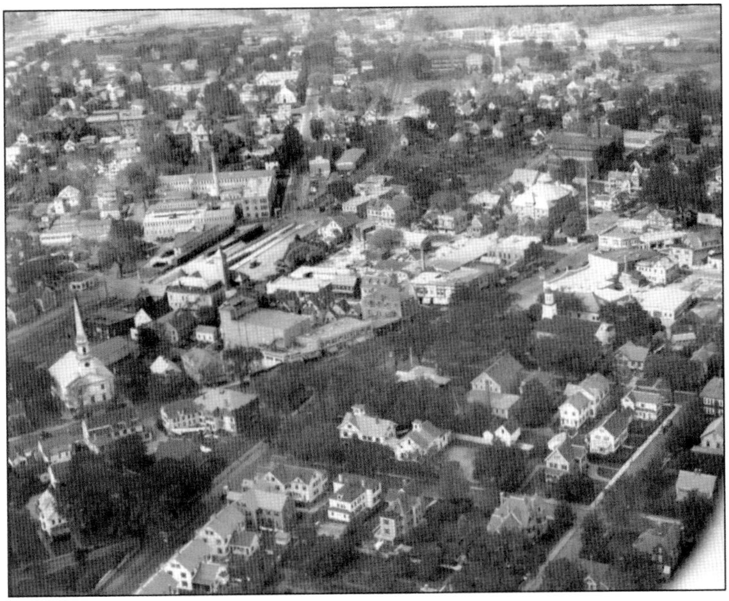

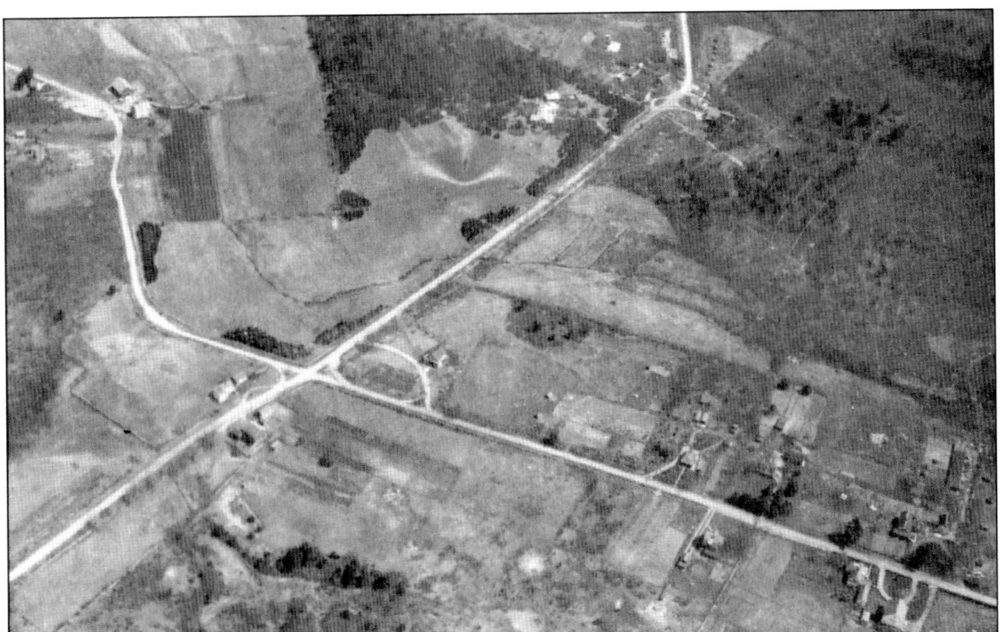

The countryside of the Dry Pond neighborhood was photographed by Johnny Stiles in the late 1920s. This view shows the intersection of Plain and West Streets, where the Dry Pond School stands with its circular driveway.

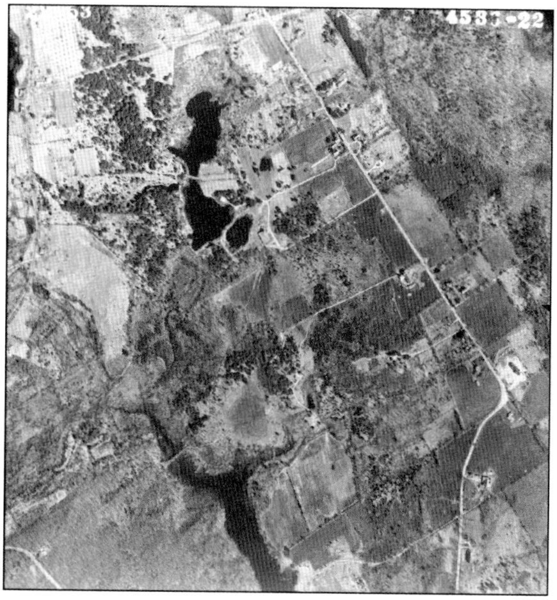

This aerial photograph of Stoughton is part of a series of images taken in 1953. This view of the Dry Pond neighborhood shows the southern end of West Street, including the top of Ames Pond. A section of Plain Street is seen here that begins near Dry Pond Cemetery and intersects with West Street at the top of the image.

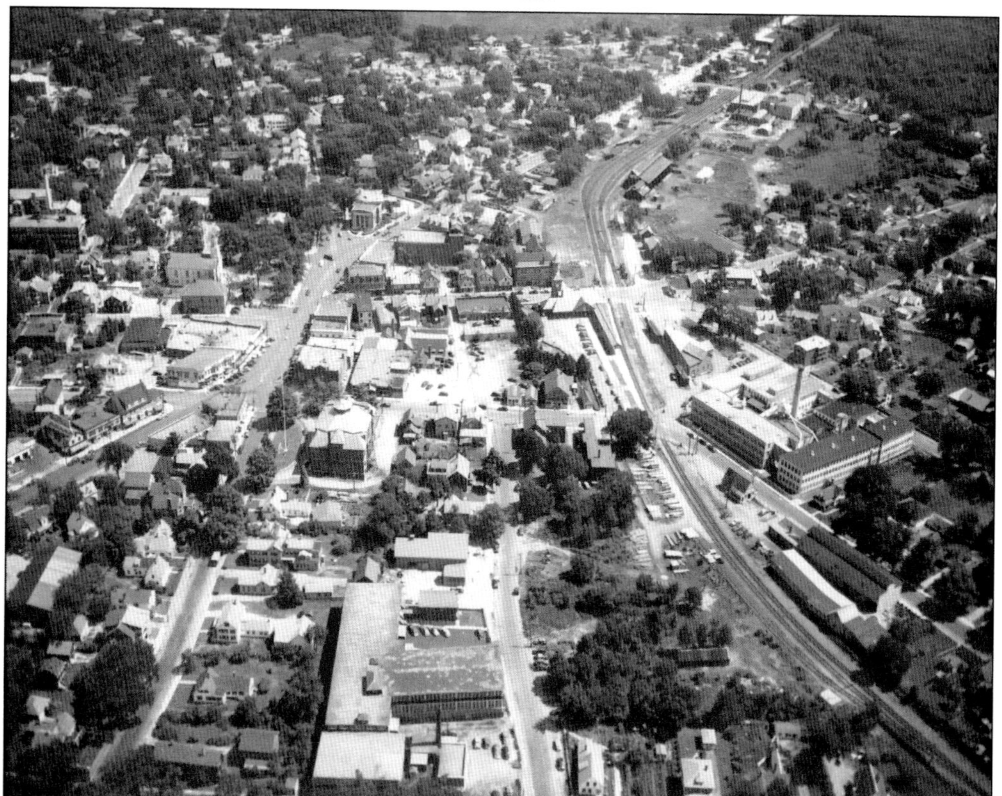

This photograph appears as the cover of the *Annual Report of the Town of Stoughton* in 1951. This view of Stoughton Square shows the J.W. Wood Elastic Web Co. on Rose and School Streets in the lower portion of the photograph. The Norfolk Country Trust Co. can be seen at the intersection of Park and Washington Streets in the far end of the square. This photograph can be dated to before 1951, as Darling's Block at Wyman and Washington Streets is still standing.

Seven

The Photography of George A. Gerard

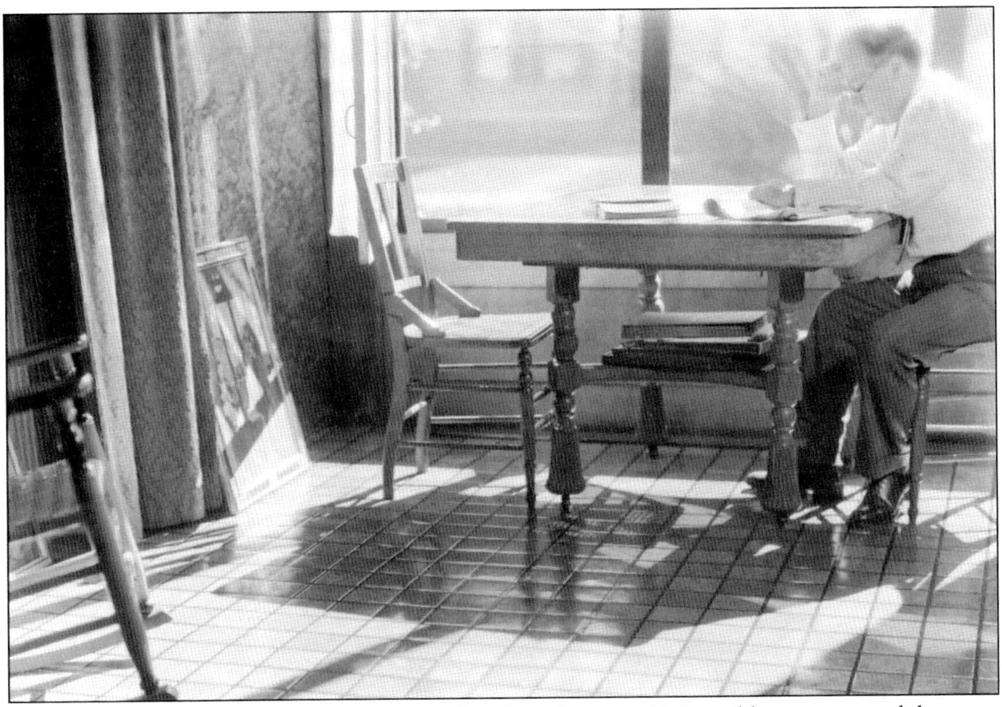

George Adolph Gerard (1872–1952) arrived in Stoughton in 1907 and became one of the most sought-after local photographers. He was born in Paris, France, and came to the United States as a child in 1881. He is seen here hard at work in his studio at 14 Capen Street. He also worked as a shoe last shaper in the Belcher Last Factory located just behind his home. Gerard would serve as a juryman in the infamous Sacco and Vanzetti trial with another Stoughton resident, J. Frank MacNamara.

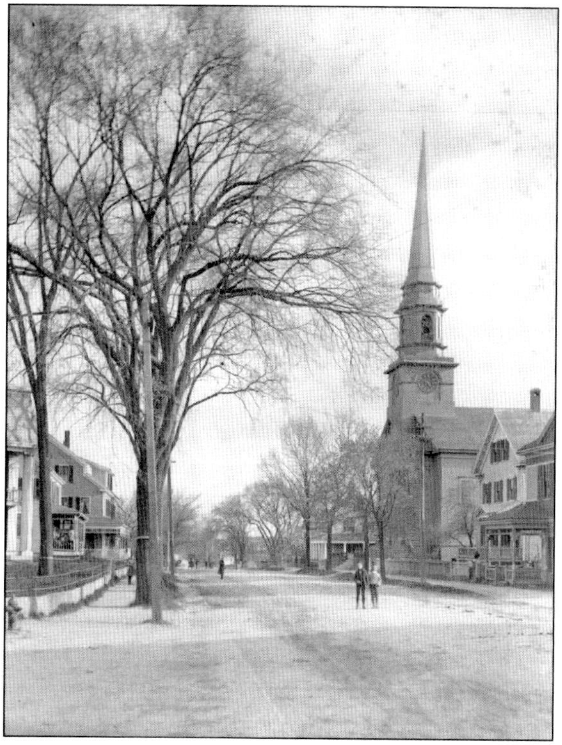

This 1908 photograph shows the First Congregational Church in the distance. On the far left are the columns of the former home of town clerk Martin Wales. To the right of the church is the parsonage of Rev. Albert Perry, which still stands today.

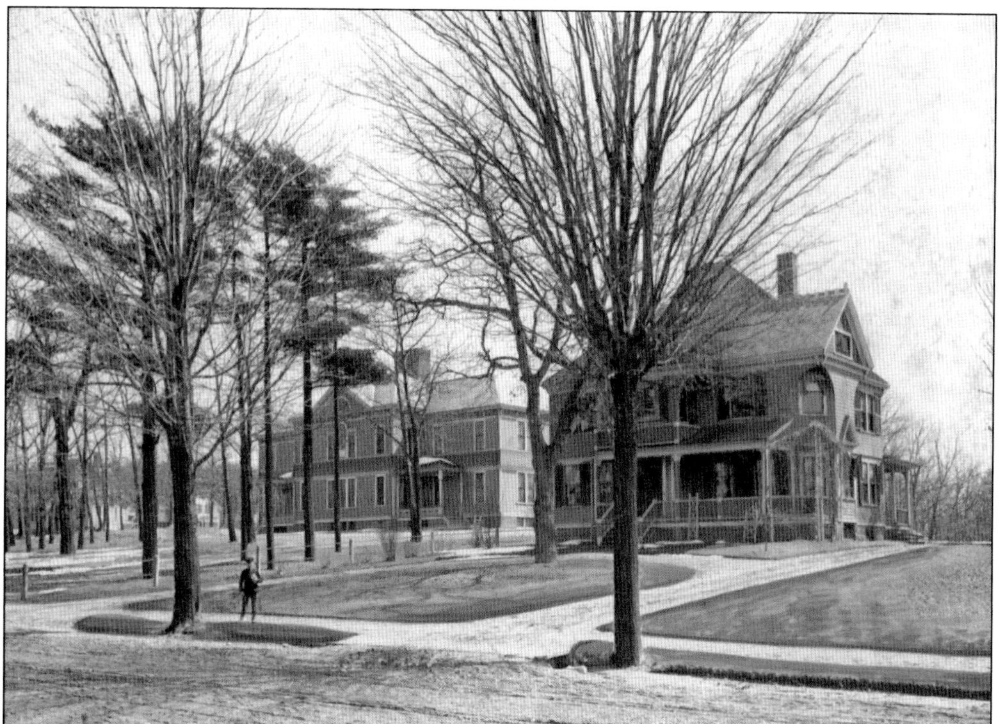

This view of Walnut Street shows the Clapp School (left) and the home of Ira Foss Burnham (1853–1929). Burnham was the president of the Stoughton Rubber Company on Canton Street.

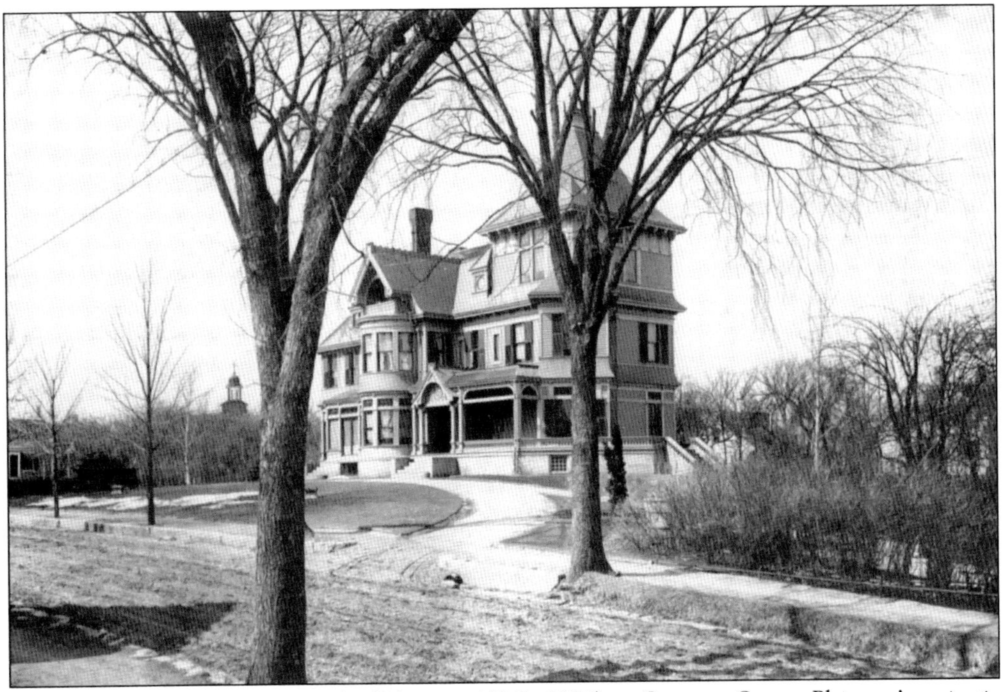

This is the home of John Greenleaf Phinney (1843–1888) on Summer Street. Phinney's majestic home still stands, now serving as a multifamily residence. Sections of his former Phinney Shoe Counter factory are still located diagonally across the street from this home.

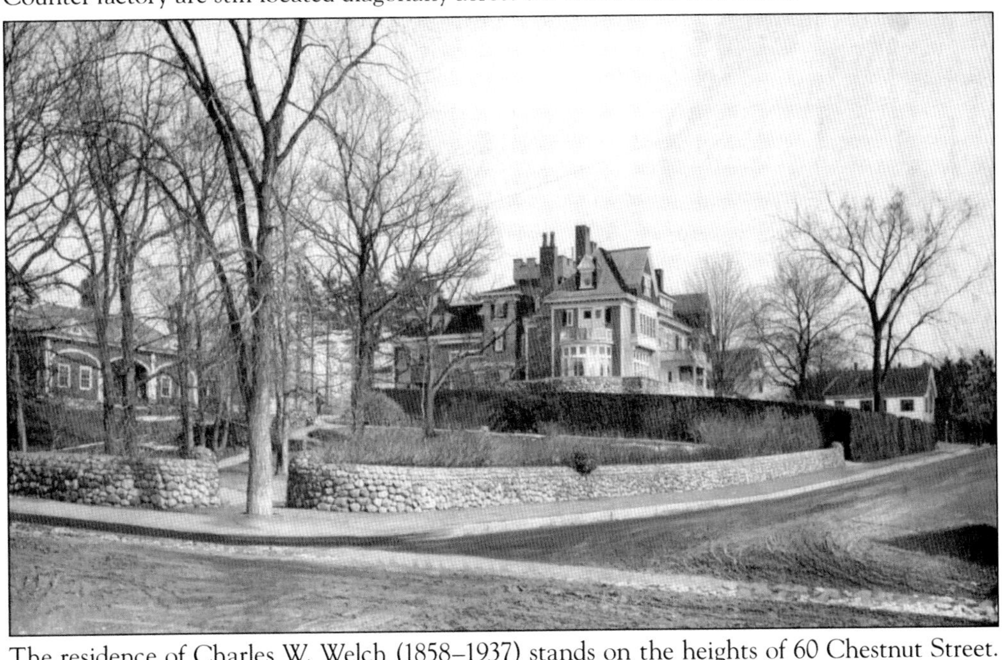

The residence of Charles W. Welch (1858–1937) stands on the heights of 60 Chestnut Street. This building was originally constructed in 1859 and greatly altered when purchased by Welch in 1883. Welch began working at the Phinney Shoe Counter factory and later became president of the company. Welch's land holdings off of Washington Street became the home of Stoughton Fish & Game in 1939.

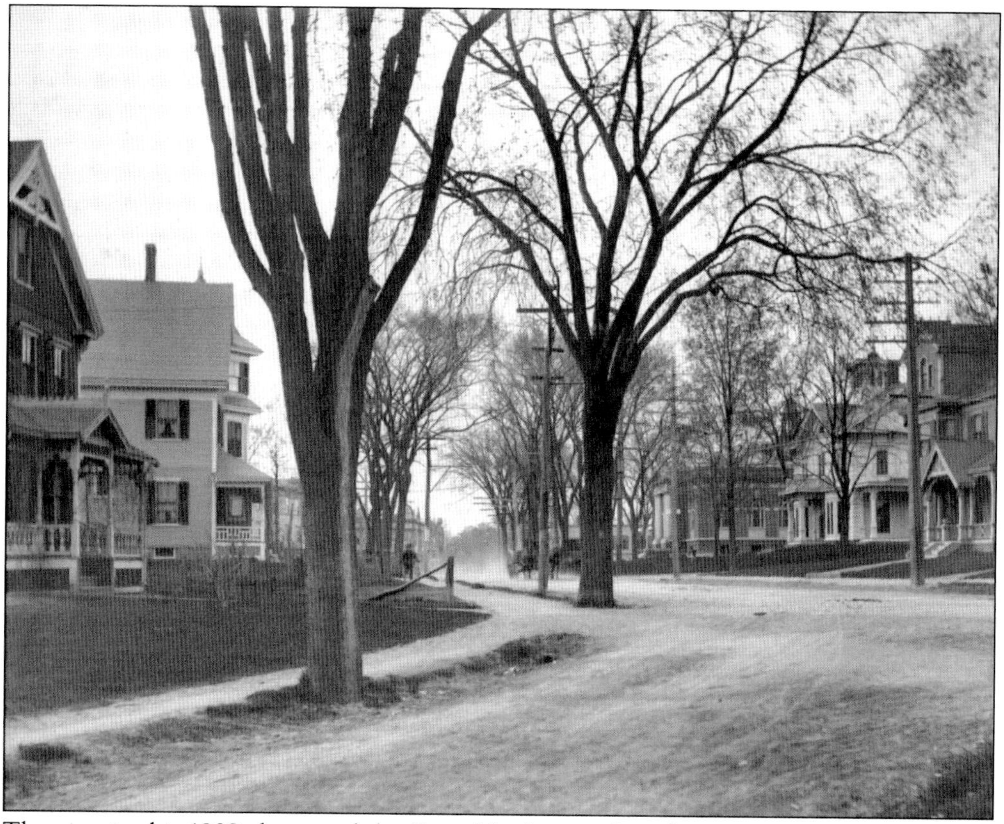

The view in this 1908 photograph by Gerard looks into Stoughton Center from Faxon Park. Here, Walnut Avenue heads to Park Street. The Stoughton Public Library and the Chicatabut Club are in the distance.

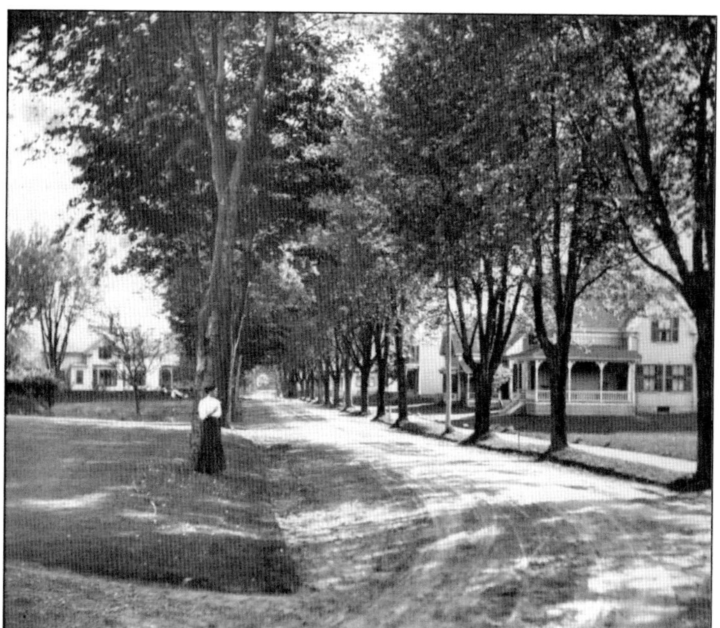

This Gerard photograph shows Monk Street from the eastern end, connecting with Grove Street. At left is the lawn of what is now Sheehan Funeral Home at 115 Monk Street, a business that has been in Stoughton since 1860.

The "Big Tree" is located off of Sumner Street at Sullivan's bog in Stoughton. This ancient landmark was at one time the oldest tree in Stoughton and was still growing in the 1930s.

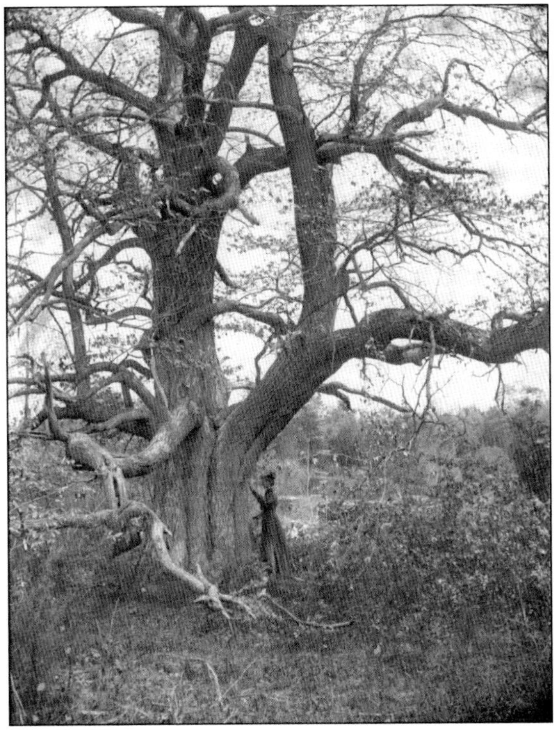

Seen here in 1908 is Murphy's Ice Pond in West Stoughton, off West Street. In the distance are homes at the intersection of West and Chemung Streets.

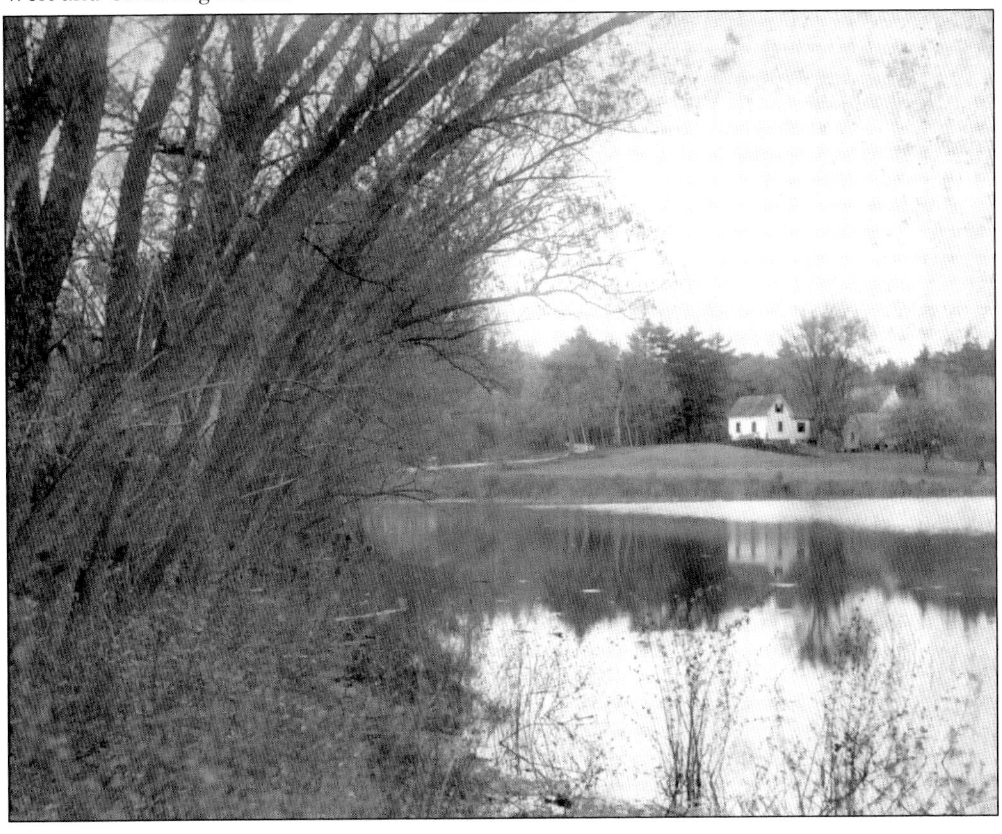

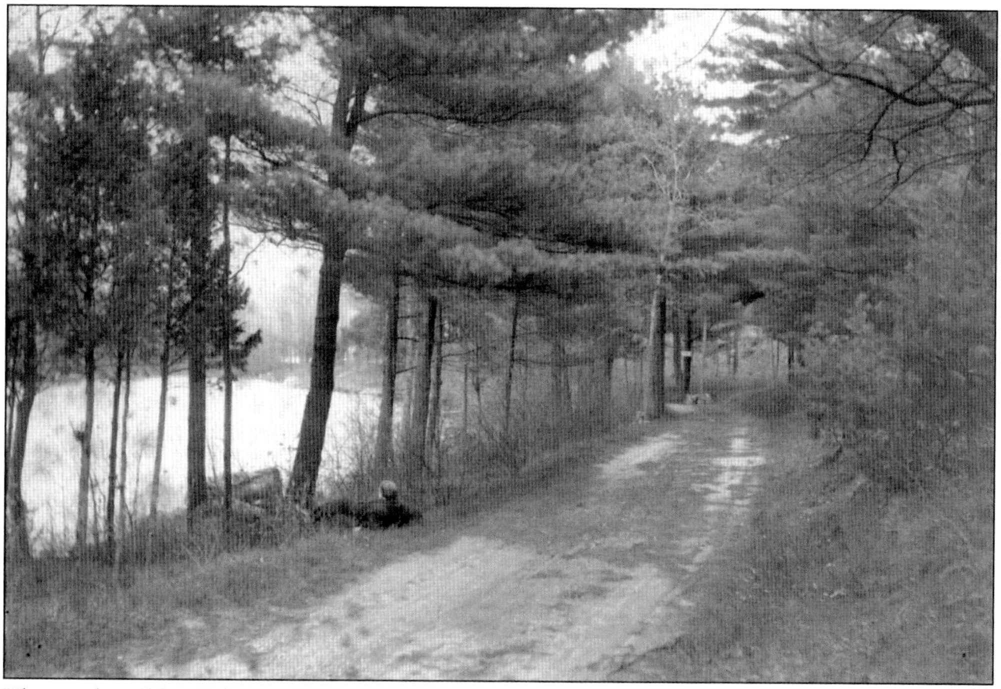

The road to Glen Echo Park in Stoughton is captured by Gerard in 1908. Glen Echo served the community for many years as a site for recreation. It was recently purchased by the Town of Stoughton to be returned to use by residents in the future.

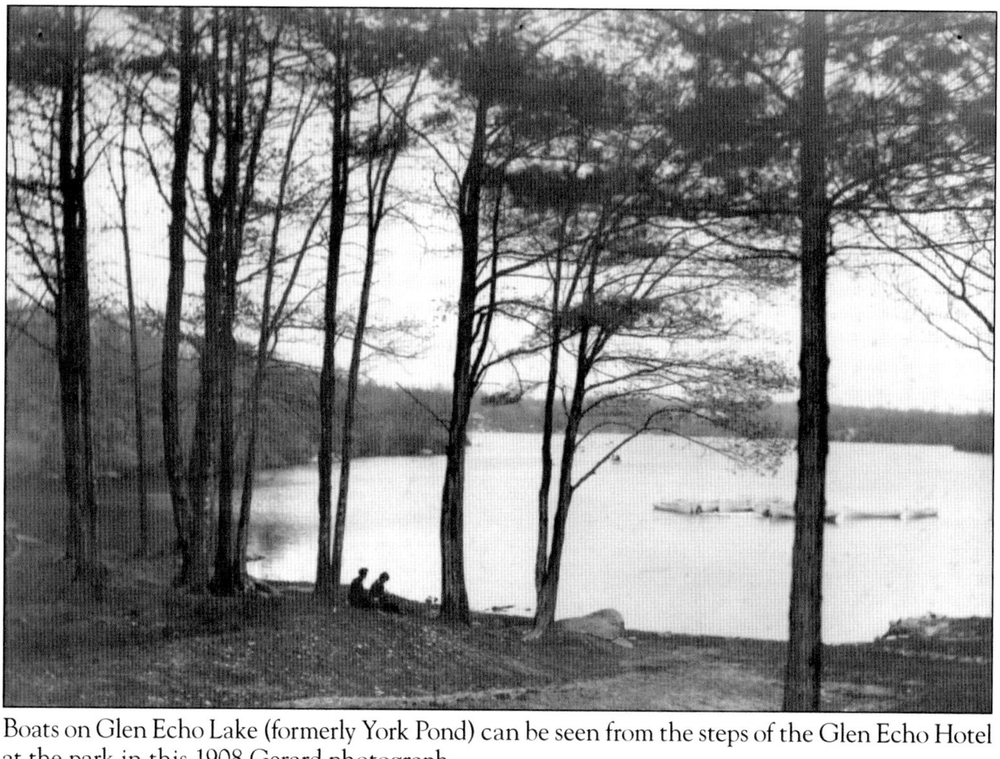

Boats on Glen Echo Lake (formerly York Pond) can be seen from the steps of the Glen Echo Hotel at the park in this 1908 Gerard photograph.

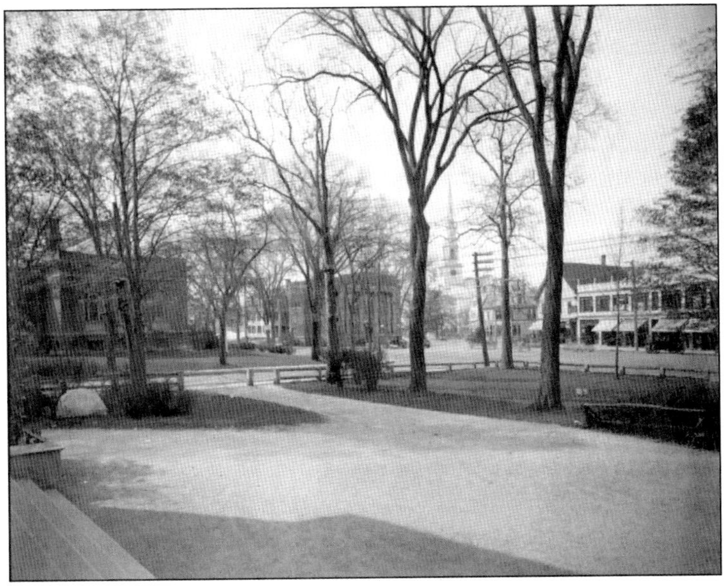

This photograph by Gerard was taken from the steps of the First Parish Universalist Church in 1925. The Stoughton Public Library is on the left, the Stoughton Trust Co. is at center, and the First Congregational Church is next to it, in the distance. The old Atwood's Market, which burned down in 1927, can be seen next to the Stoughton Building, which has stood in Stoughton Square since 1923.

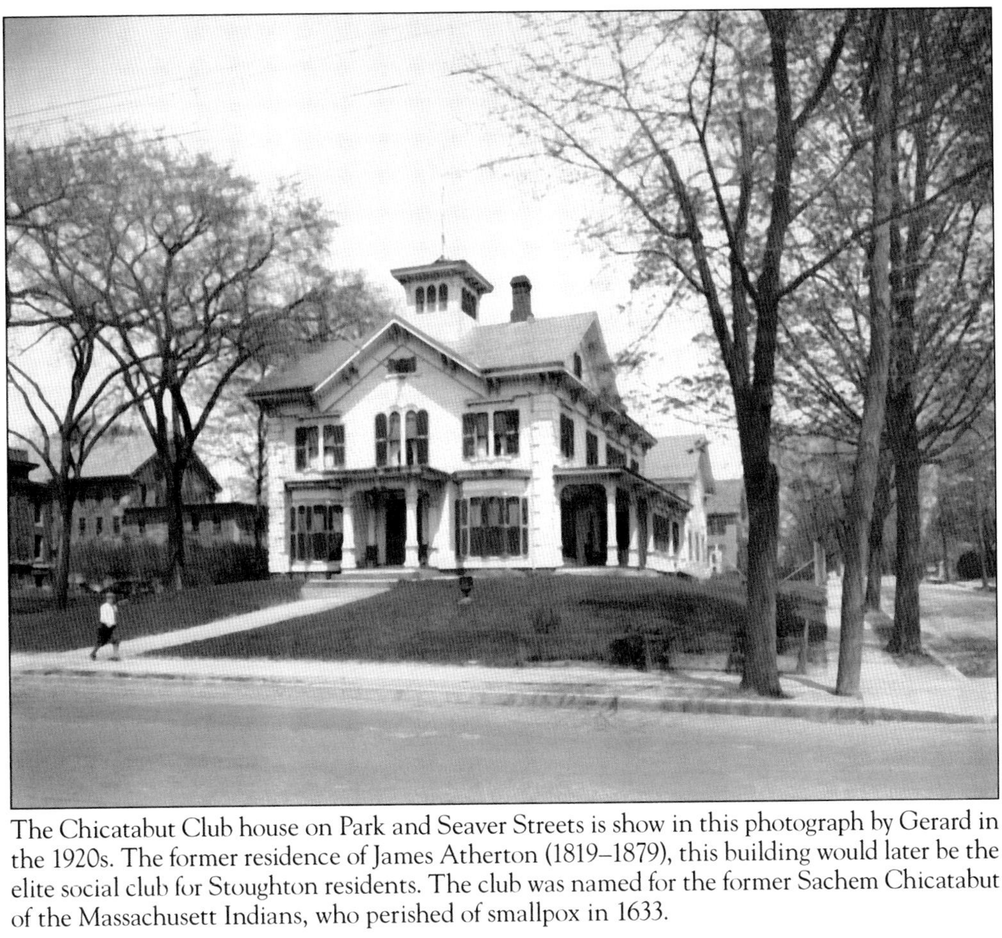

The Chicatabut Club house on Park and Seaver Streets is show in this photograph by Gerard in the 1920s. The former residence of James Atherton (1819–1879), this building would later be the elite social club for Stoughton residents. The club was named for the former Sachem Chicatabut of the Massachusett Indians, who perished of smallpox in 1633.

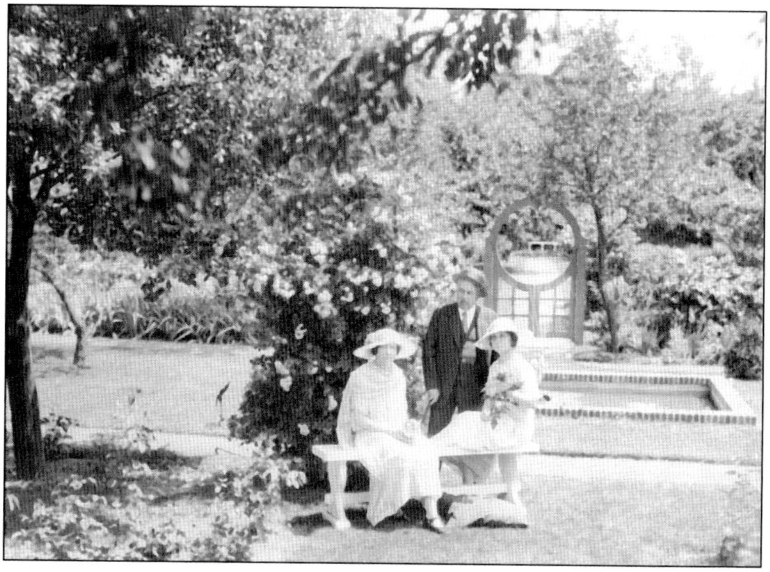

The George E. Belcher family poses in the back garden of Belcher's stately home at 33 Seaver Street in the early 1920s. Pictured are, from left to right, Gertrude Hervey Belcher; her father, George Edward Belcher; and her mother, Elva A. (Pope) Belcher. This photograph was taken by George Gerard.

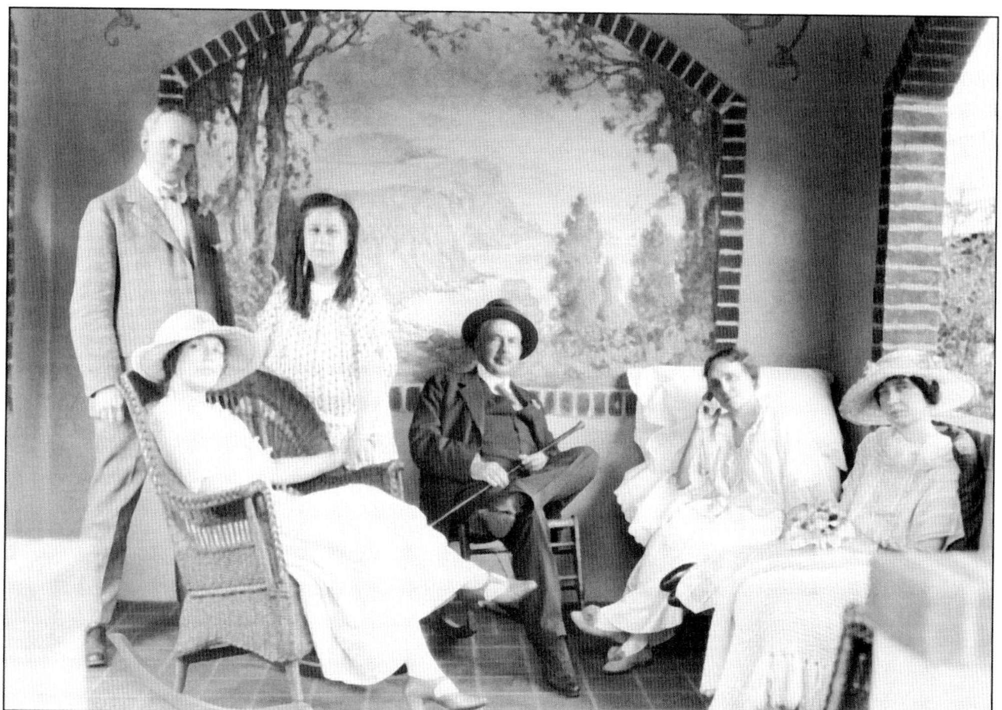

This George Gerard photograph shows the Belchers with the family of Ernest Southworth. They are posing at the teahouse on the Belcher property on Seaver Street. The mural in the background was painted by Stoughton artist F. Mortimer Lamb. This building and mural still exist on the old Belcher estate. Pictured, from left to right, are Mr. and Mrs. Ernest B. Southworth, unidentified, George E. Belcher, his wife, Elva A. (Pope) Belcher, and their daughter Gertrude Hervey Belcher. Southworth was the president of Belcher's Last Company, at Pleasant and Capen Streets.

Eight

Police and Fire Departments

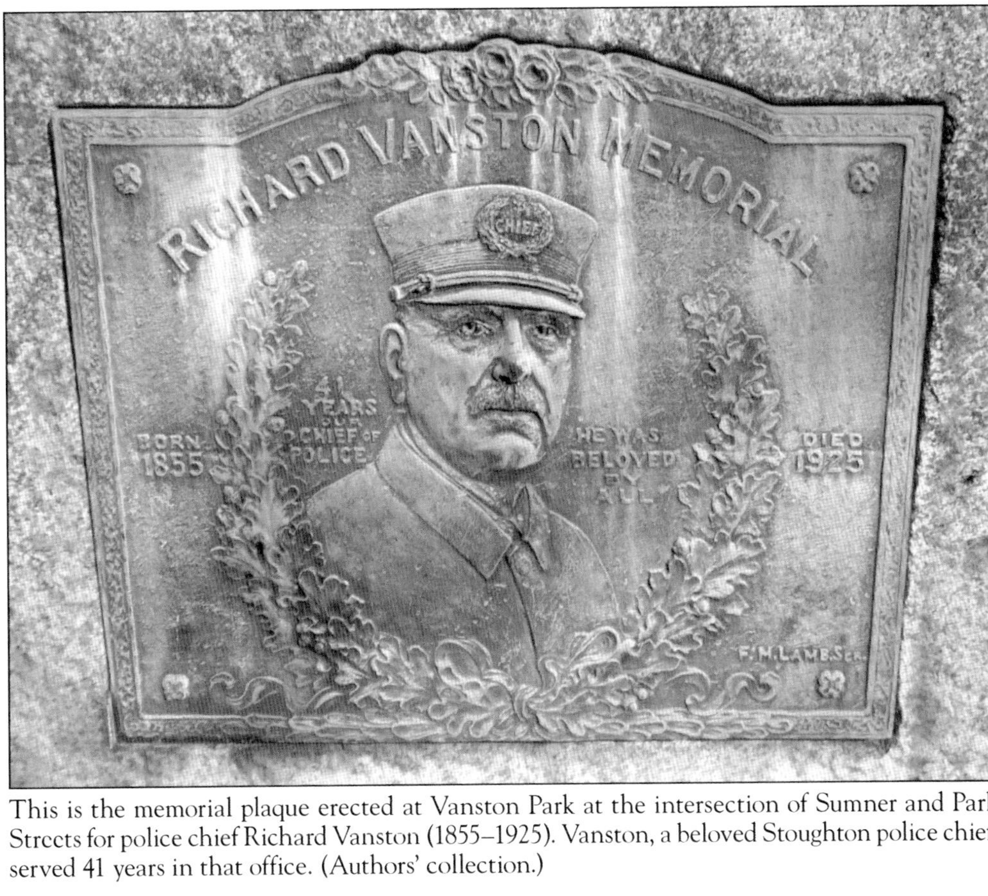

This is the memorial plaque erected at Vanston Park at the intersection of Sumner and Park Streets for police chief Richard Vanston (1855–1925). Vanston, a beloved Stoughton police chief, served 41 years in that office. (Authors' collection.)

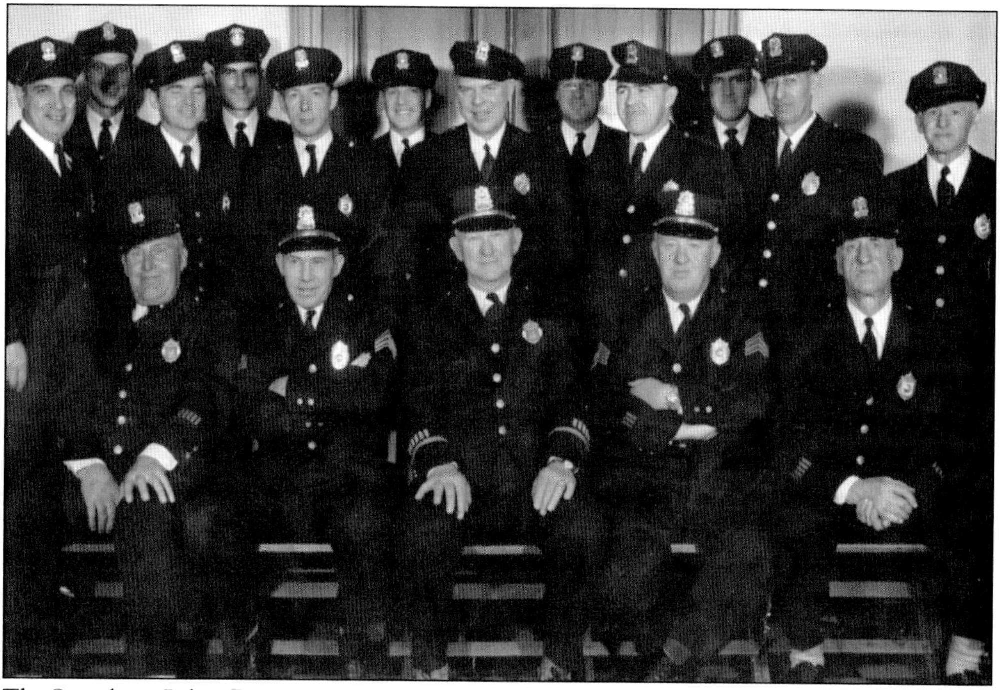

The Stoughton Police Department is seen here in the early 1950s. The men are, from left to right, (first row) Tim Roach, Jerome Flynn, Chief Peter McGarvey, Thomas Mara, and unidentified; (back row) Officer Silva, two unidentified men, J. Kelly, Pete Lucas, Officer Silva, Ellie Smith, John Sousa, "Bulldog" Kelly, John Donahue, William B. Hodges, and unidentified.

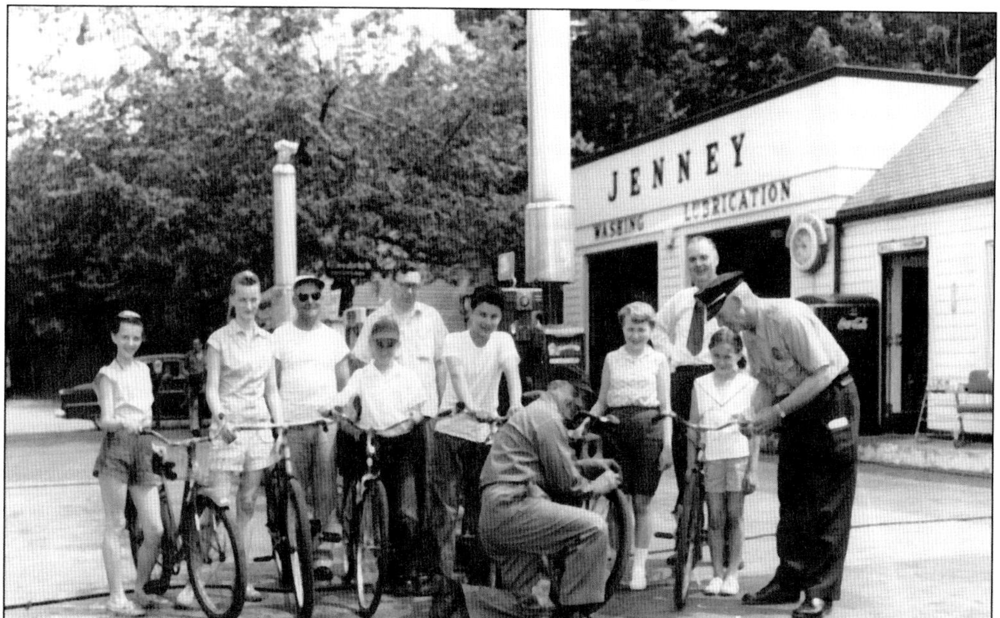

The Town of Stoughton would issue license plates for bicycles, and bikes could be inspected. Here, Chief Peter McGarvey conducts a crack inspection with kids at the Jenney Station in Stoughton in the early 1950s.

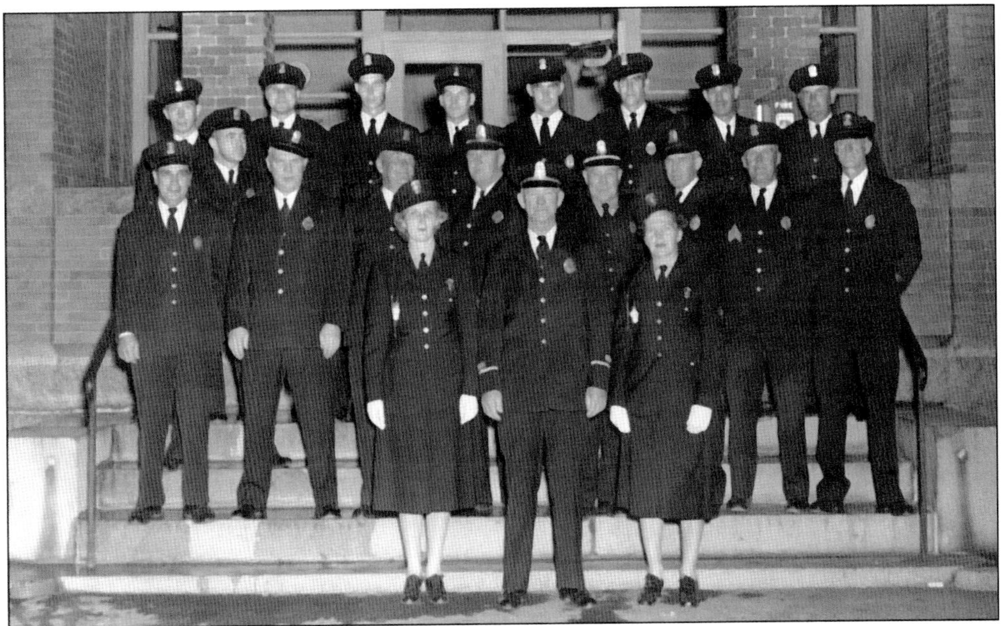

The Stoughton Police Department poses in 1955. Shown here are, from left to right, (first row) unidentified, Chief Peter McGarvey, and Susan Walsh; (second row) John Donahue, Ellis Smith, Louis Swanson, Tom Mara, Sid Morey, Jerry Flynn, Tim Roach, and Duncan Fleming; (third row) Peter Lucas, unidentified, John Sousa, Dick Conrad, unidentified, Jim Kelly, two unidentified persons, and Tom Smith.

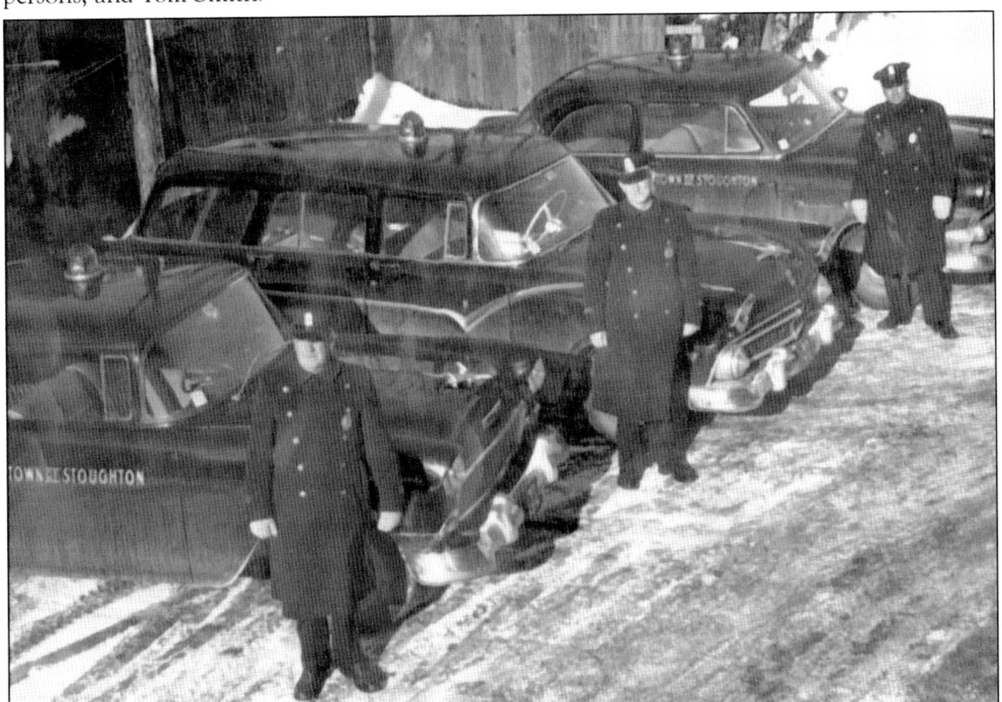

Some of the Stoughton Police Department's fleet of vehicles are seen here. Chief Peter McGarvey (center) poses with two unidentified officers in this winter photograph taken in the 1950s.

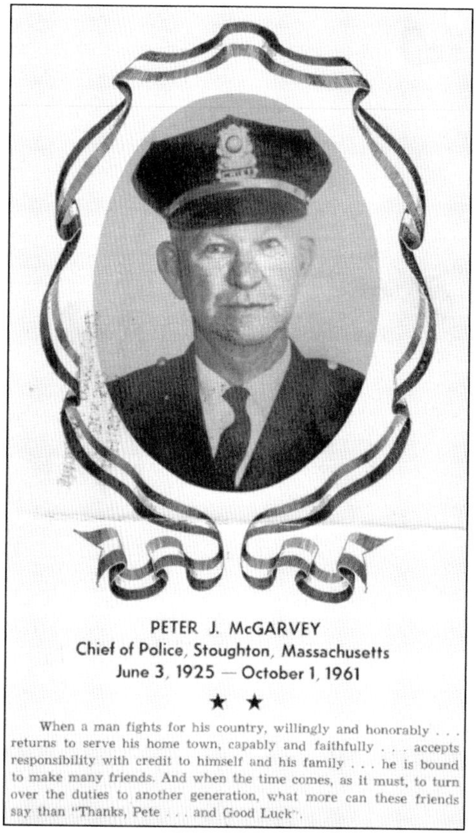
PETER J. McGARVEY
Chief of Police, Stoughton, Massachusetts
June 3, 1925 — October 1, 1961

★ ★

When a man fights for his country, willingly and honorably . . . returns to serve his home town, capably and faithfully . . . accepts responsibility with credit to himself and his family . . . he is bound to make many friends. And when the time comes, as it must, to turn over the duties to another generation, what more can these friends say than "Thanks, Pete . . . and Good Luck".

Peter Joseph McGarvey (1896–1976) served as the chief of police in Stoughton from June 3, 1925, until his retirement on October 1, 1961. A park across from Swan's Tavern at the intersection of Central and Turnpike Streets was dedicated in his honor.

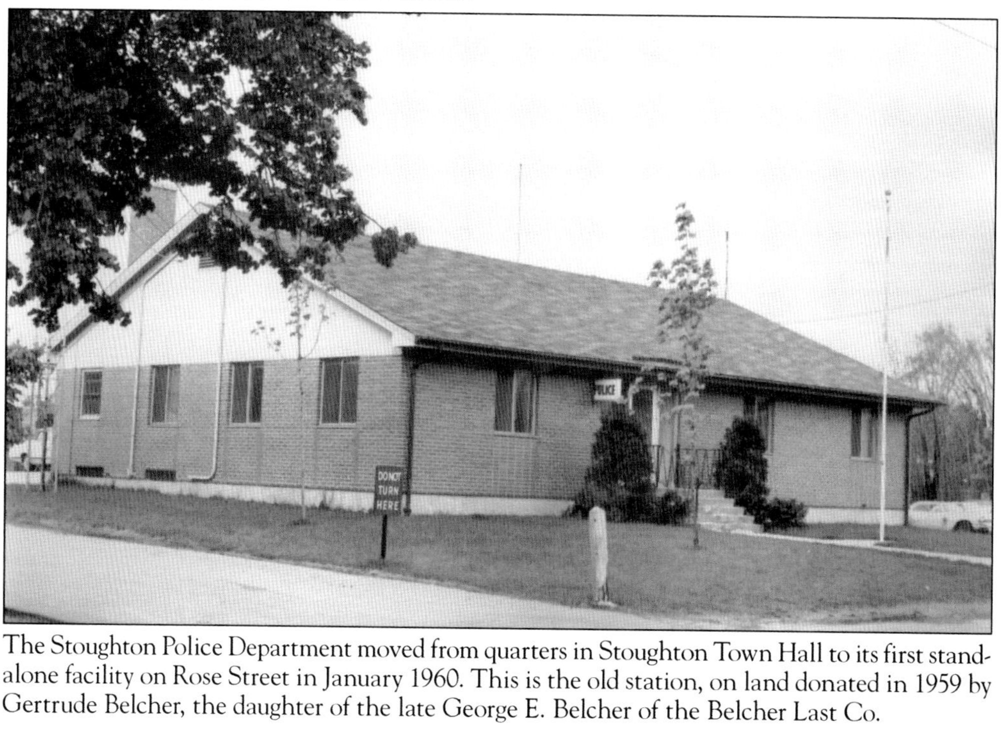

The Stoughton Police Department moved from quarters in Stoughton Town Hall to its first stand-alone facility on Rose Street in January 1960. This is the old station, on land donated in 1959 by Gertrude Belcher, the daughter of the late George E. Belcher of the Belcher Last Co.

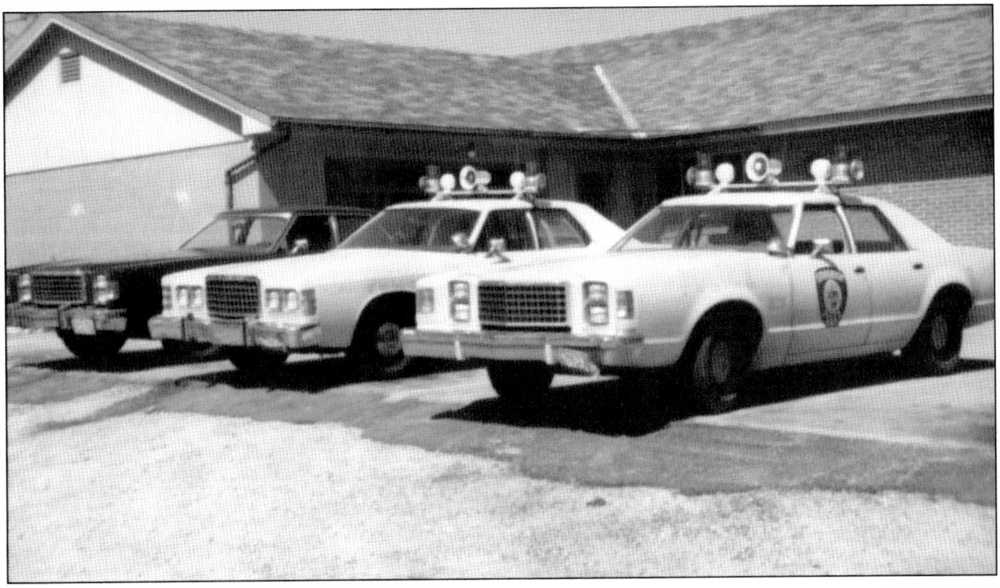

This photograph shows the yellow police cars that were a common sight in Stoughton in the mid-1970s. These cars, parked behind the old station on Rose Street, were photographed by the late Robert Parsons of Stoughton.

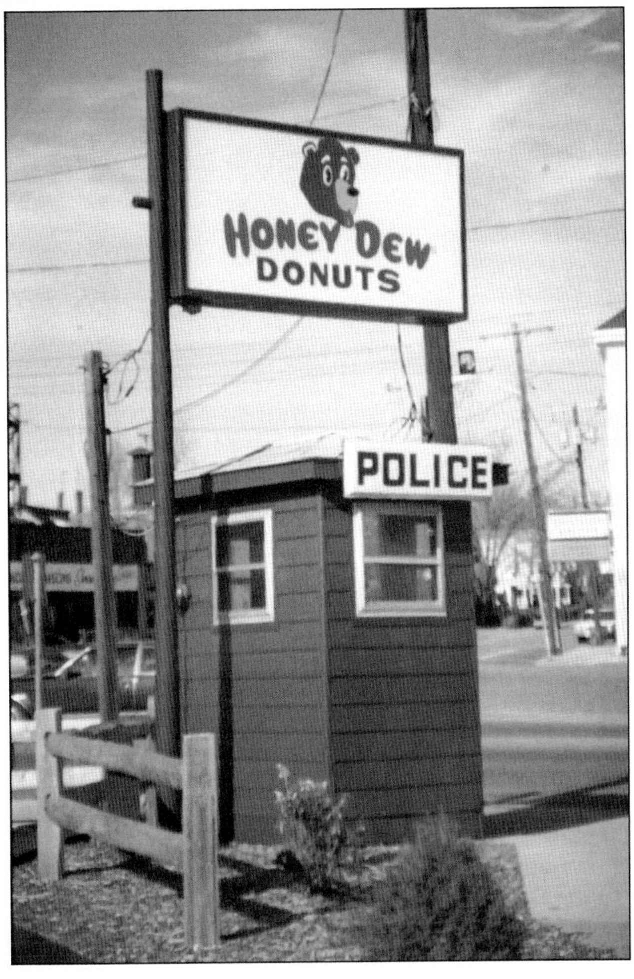

This photograph, taken in the early 1980s, shows the old police box at the crossing in Stoughton Square at Washington and Rose Streets. This box sheltered the member of the police force who assisted in crossing citizens at this busy intersection. Honey Dew Donuts, located at this location until 2014, was the only business to replace the former Swan's Building, which burned down in 1969.

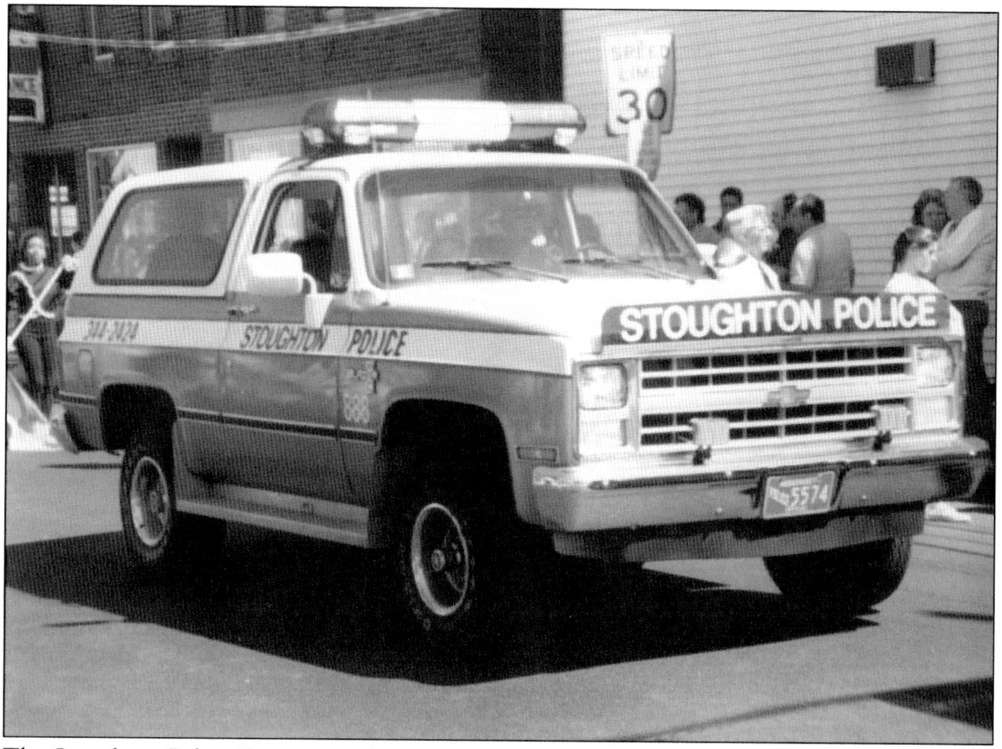

The Stoughton Police Department had a four-wheel-drive vehicle in the 1980s. This blue-and-white Chevy Blazer, part of the department's fleet, was numbered 888.

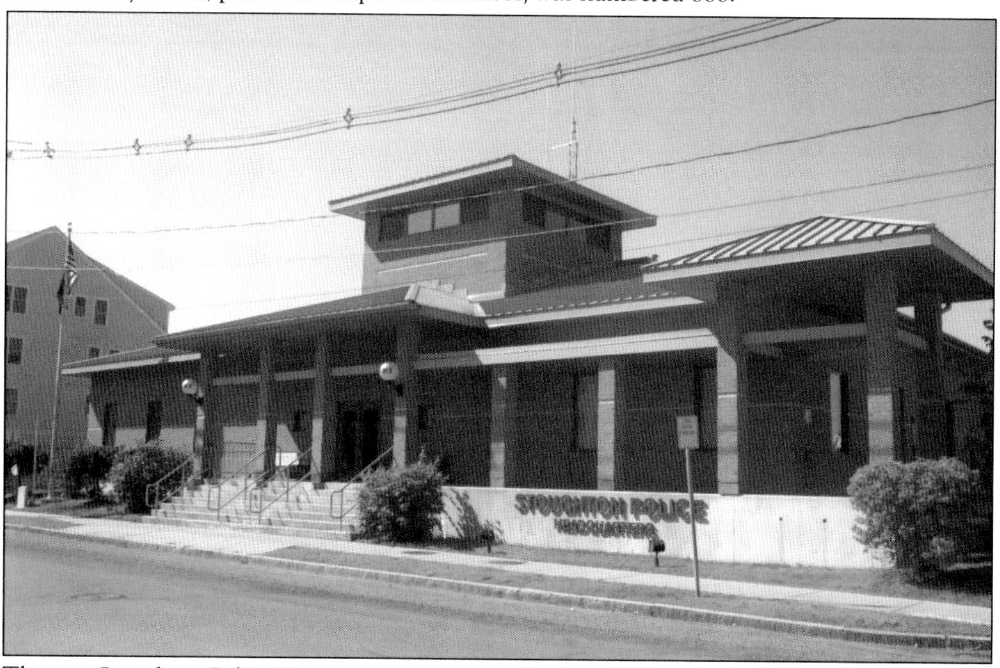

The new Stoughton Police Department station was built in 1998 at the location of the old station on Rose Street. Included in this expanded station is a community room, which serves the town of Stoughton as additional meeting space. (Authors' collection.)

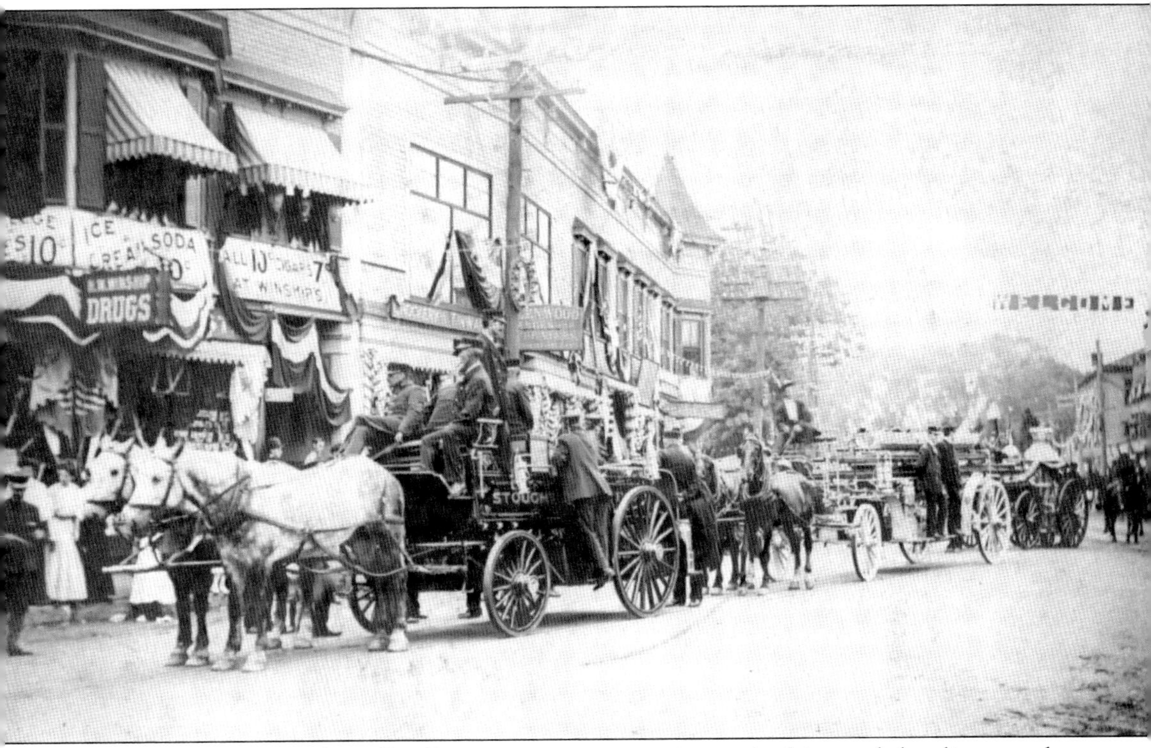

The horse-drawn Stoughton Fire Department equipment is seen in this parade heading past the Swan's Building on Washington Street before 1912. The second apparatus is a ladder wagon, purchased in 1896. Behind it is the old Sibley Steamer from 1880.

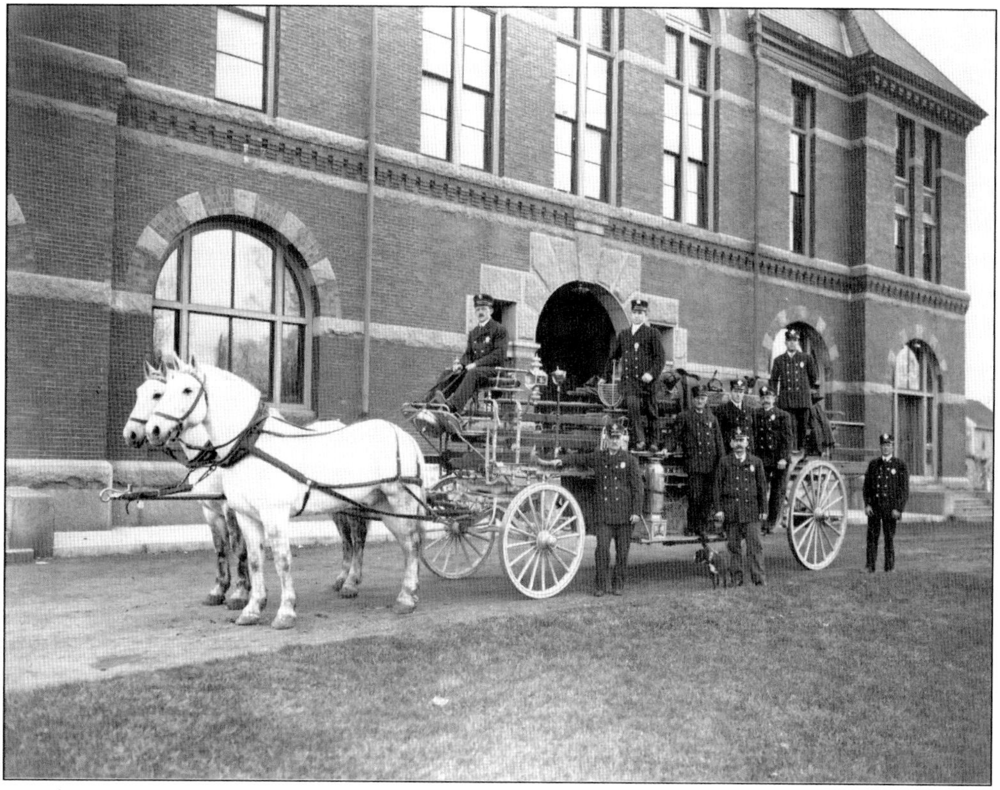

Members of the Stoughton Fire Department are seen in a photograph by George A. Gerard. They are posing in front of Stoughton Town Hall with the 1896 ladder wagon and team. This apparatus was called the "White Angel." Until 1927, the Stoughton Fire Department housed its equipment under the town hall.

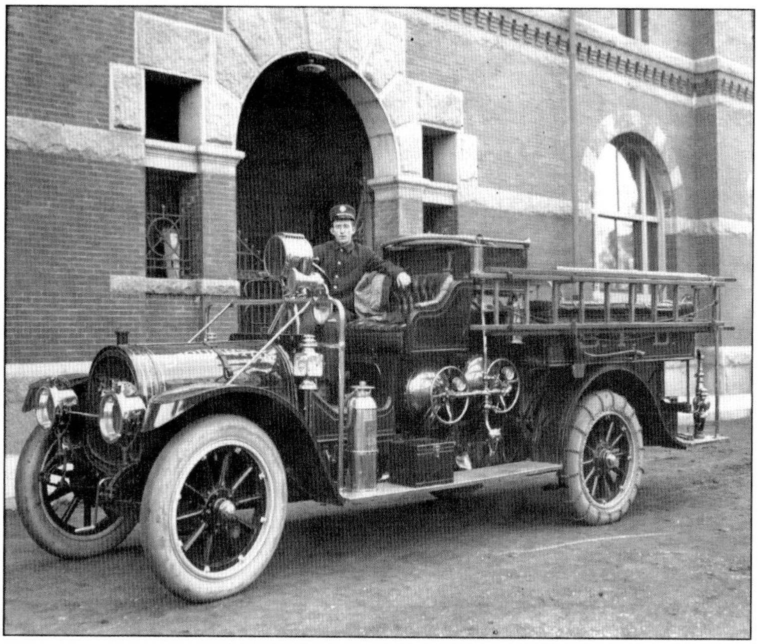

This photograph by George A. Gerard shows future fire chief Frederick H. Pye (1891–1971) at the wheel of the 1912 Pope Hartford fire engine. This was the first motorized fire engine purchased by the Town of Stoughton. Pye joined the Stoughton Fire Department on April 12, 1910. He became chief on May 23, 1933, and retired on January 31, 1962.

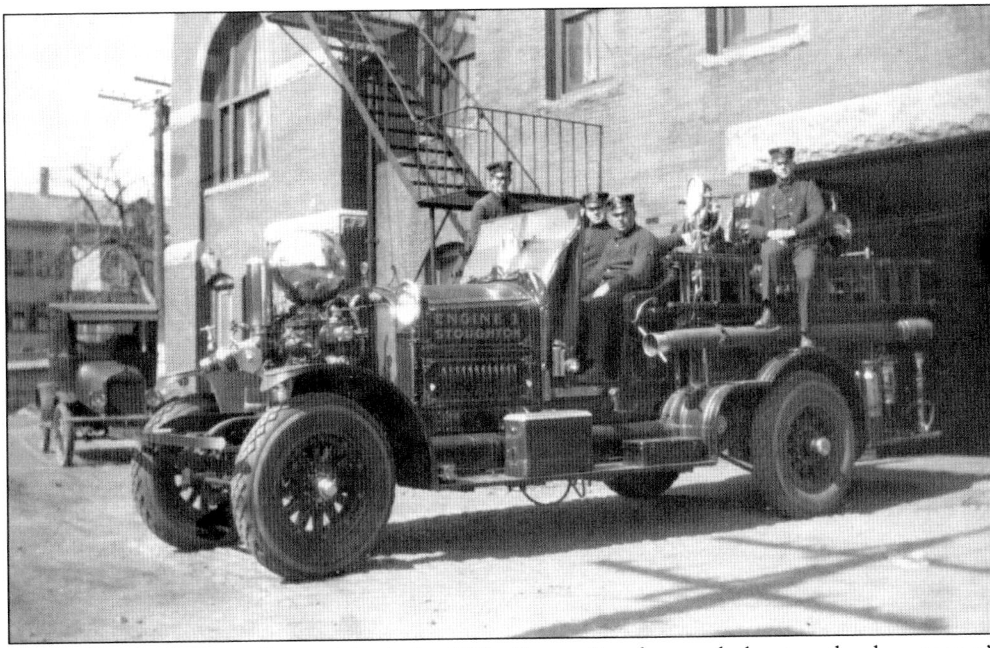

This photograph shows Engine No. 1, the 1921 Ahrens-Fox fire truck, leaving the department's location at Stoughton Town Hall in the 1920s. Future chief Fred Pye, on the far left, stands on the vehicle.

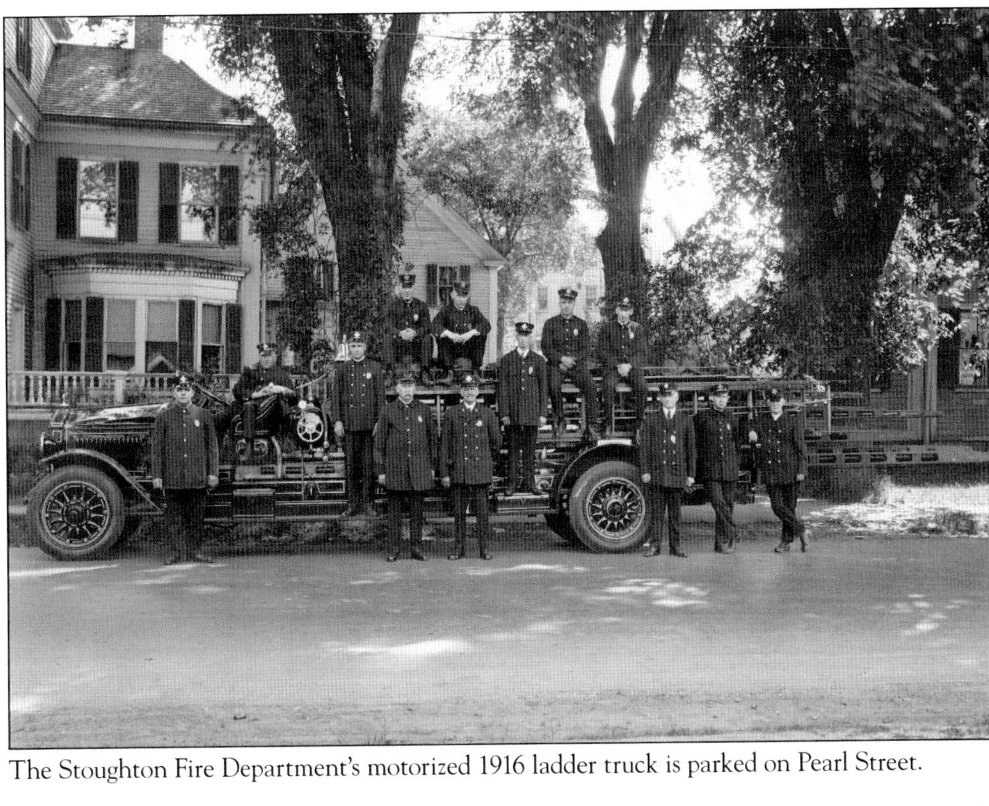

The Stoughton Fire Department's motorized 1916 ladder truck is parked on Pearl Street.

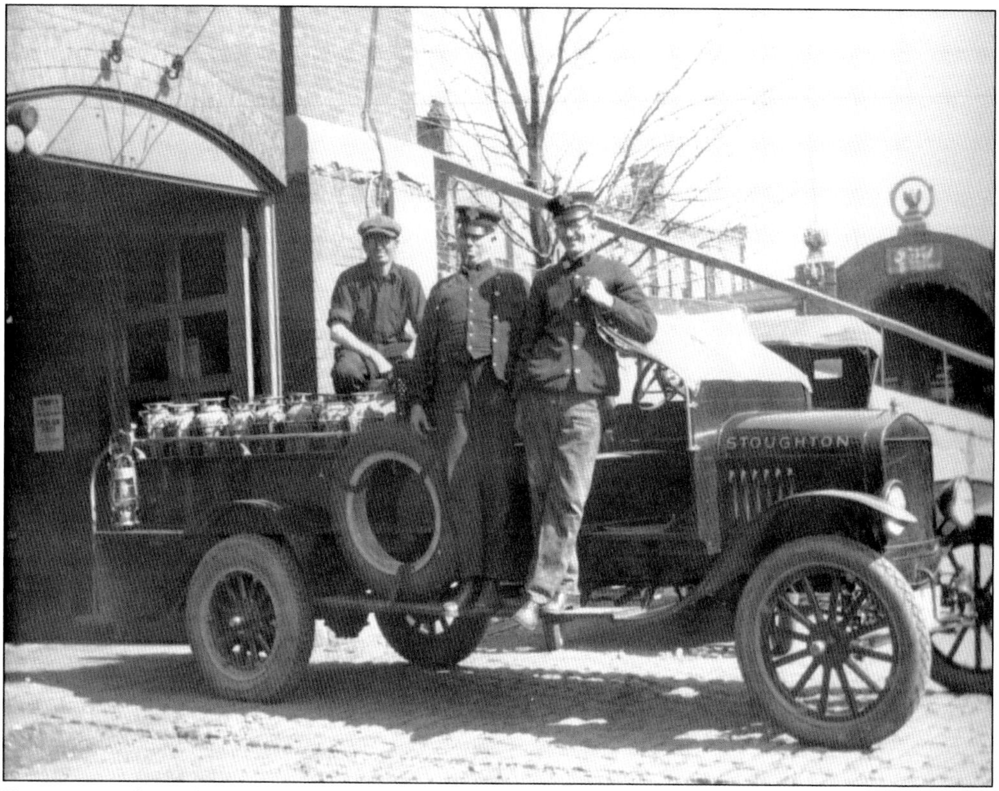

Fireman Fred Pye (far right) poses with the small fire extinguisher vehicle used in the 1920s by the Stoughton Fire Department. The former James Lehan Ford dealership can be seen in the background on Porter Street. The other men are unidentified.

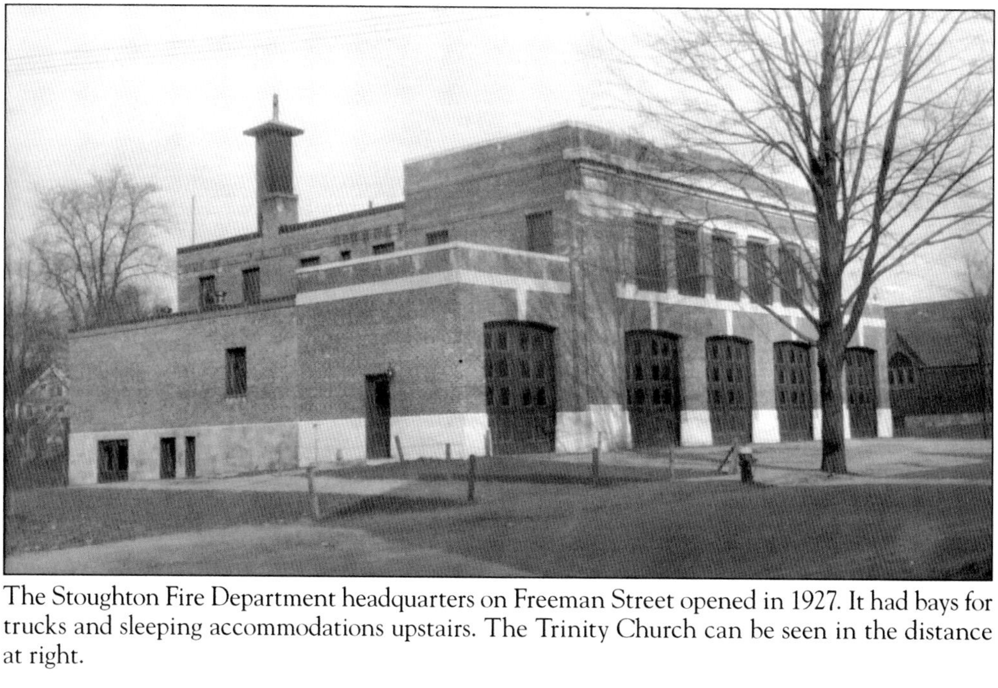

The Stoughton Fire Department headquarters on Freeman Street opened in 1927. It had bays for trucks and sleeping accommodations upstairs. The Trinity Church can be seen in the distance at right.

Fire chief Fred Pye (left) and an unidentified man pose with an exploded fire extinguisher.

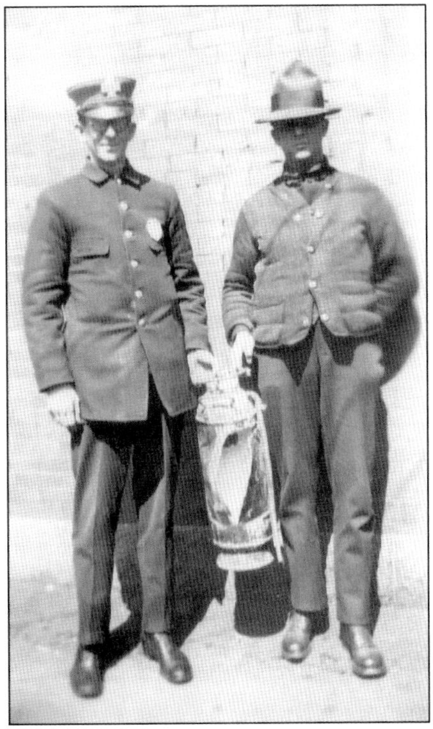

Members of the Stoughton Fire Department pose in the headquarters on Freeman Street in 1955. They are, from left to right, (first row) Lt. John E. Noonan, Lt. Arthur N. Corbett, Assistant Chief Chester C. Smith, and Chief Frederick H. Pye; (back row) Pvt. Leo F. Roche, Pvt. Clyde R. Holmes, Pvt. Paul J. Roach, Pvt. Joseph F. Kelley, Pvt. Wallace S. Billings, and Pvt. James M. Haron.

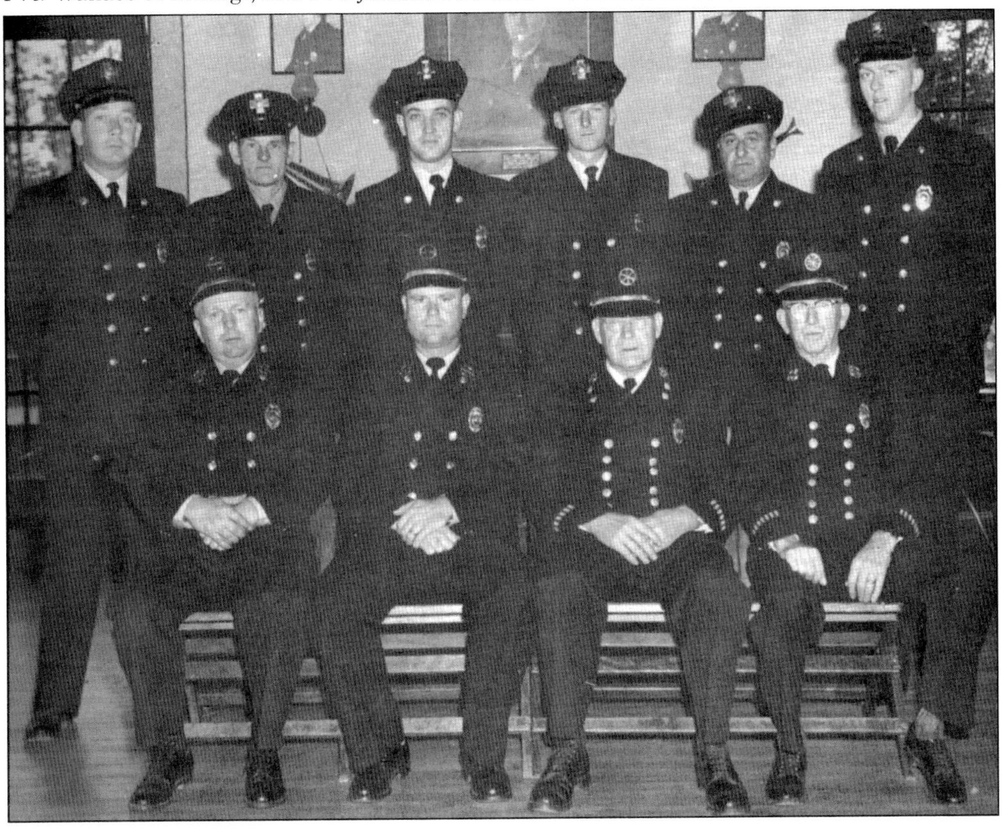

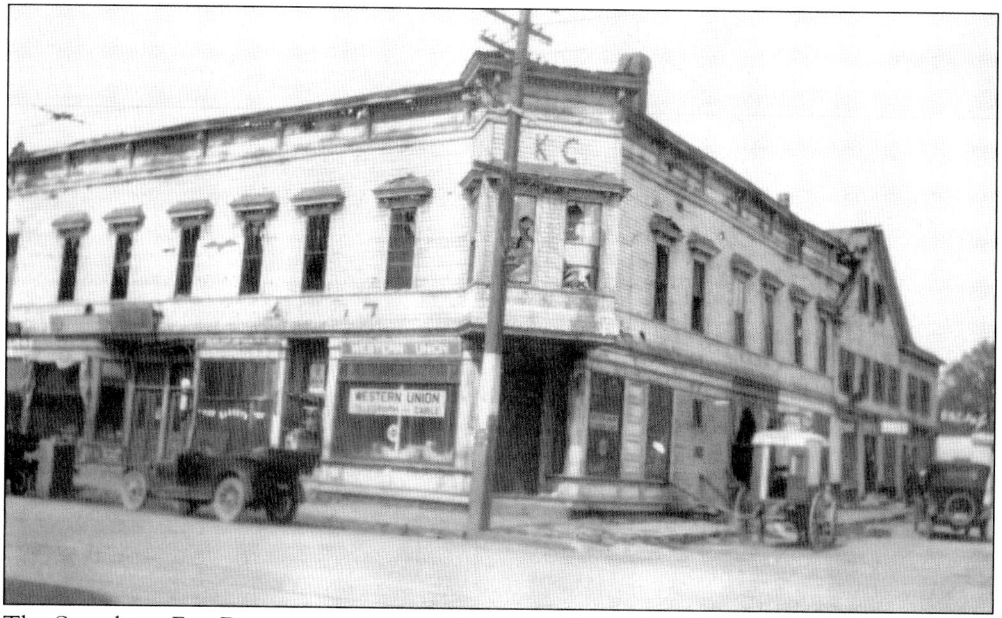

The Stoughton Fire Department came to the scene of countless fires and rescues in the 20th century. This fire at the southern end of the Swan's Block at Washington and Porter Street occurred in 1919. At this time, the Knights of Columbus was located in the upper floors of the structure, and Western Union had an office downstairs. In recent years, this location has been home to the Malcolm & Parsons insurance company.

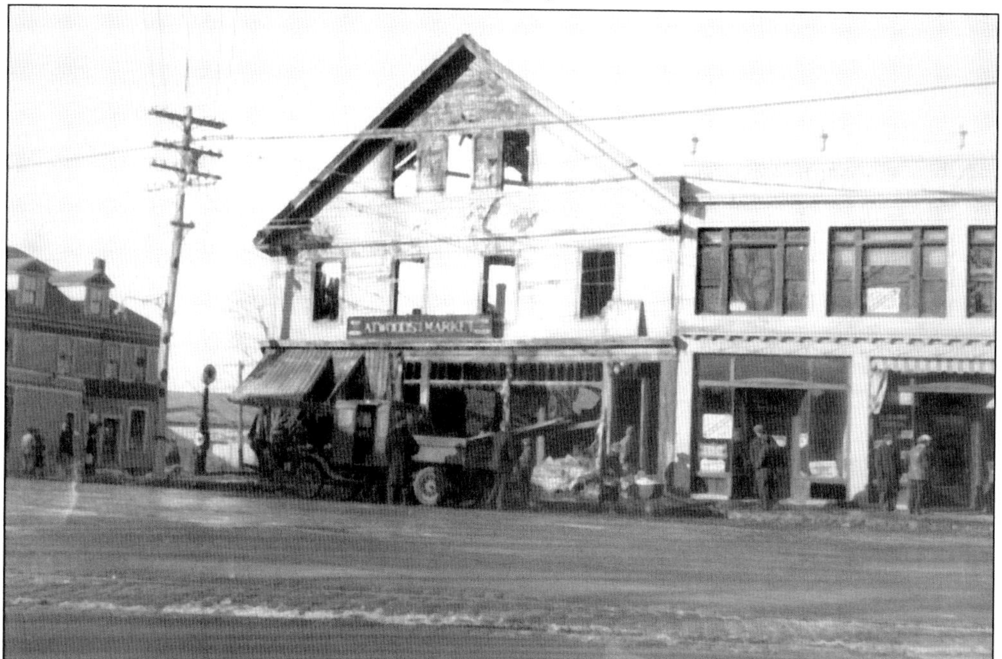

In 1927, Atwood's Market, at the corner of Washington Street and Railroad Avenue, was destroyed by fire. Ironically, this was the site of a fire that destroyed the entire block on February 27, 1880. In December 1927, this location opened its doors as the State Theatre. This building and a restaurant next door still stand today in Stoughton Square.

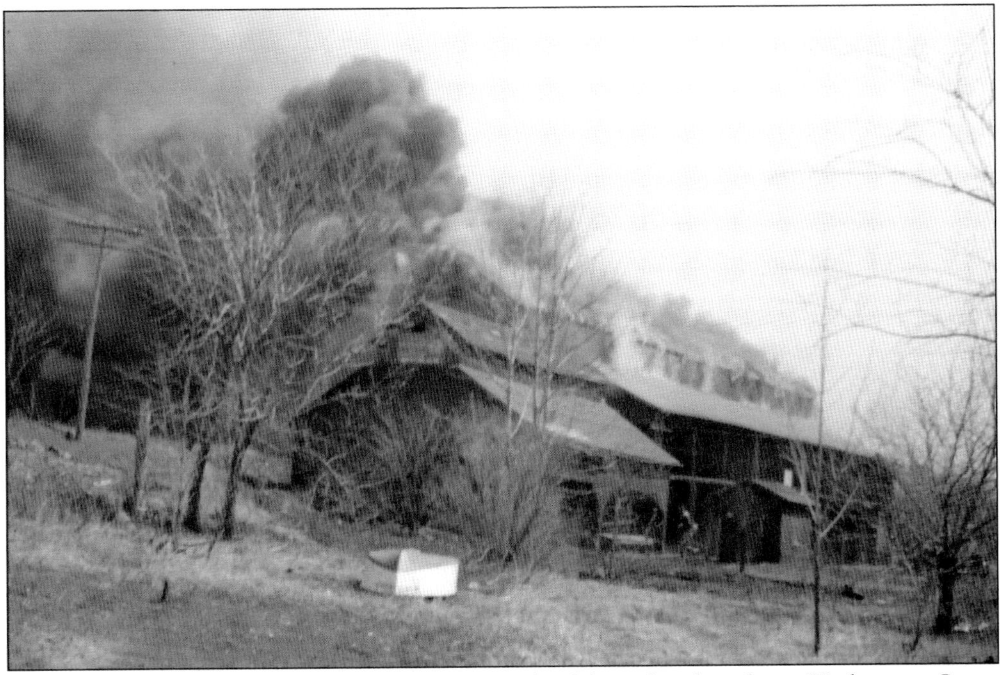

The Murphy Coal Co. sheds located on the west side of the railroad tracks on Washington Street were destroyed by fire on April 6, 1963. The Murphy family still maintains part of its business at this site in a rebuilt structure.

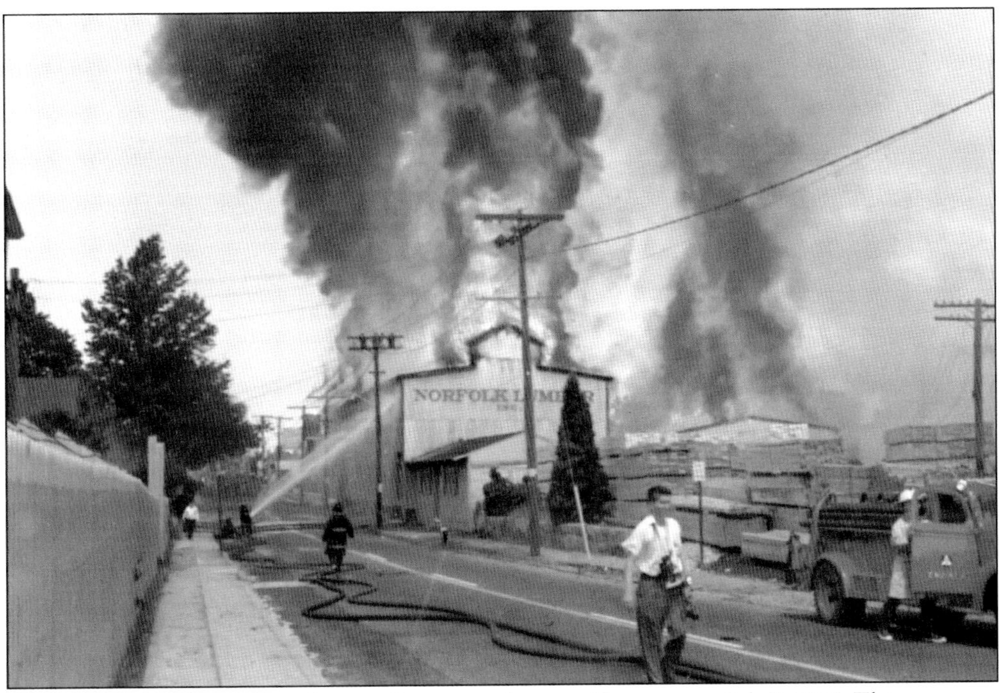

The Norfolk Lumber Co. on Canton Street was destroyed by arson on July 3, 1966. This company was owned at one time by Ellery P. Clapp, Charles Dodge, and Henry Lyons.

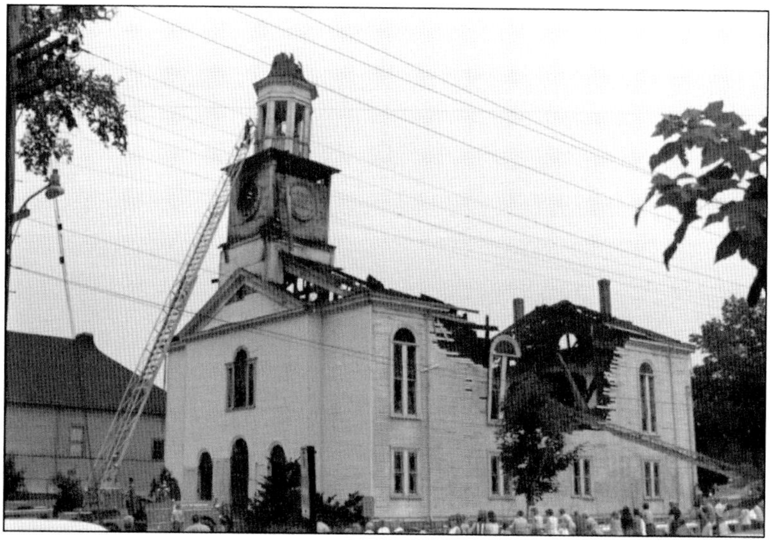

The Universalist church in Stoughton Square, built in 1808, was destroyed by fire on June 29, 1966. The loss of this historic landmark was very sad for both the parishioners and the people of Stoughton.

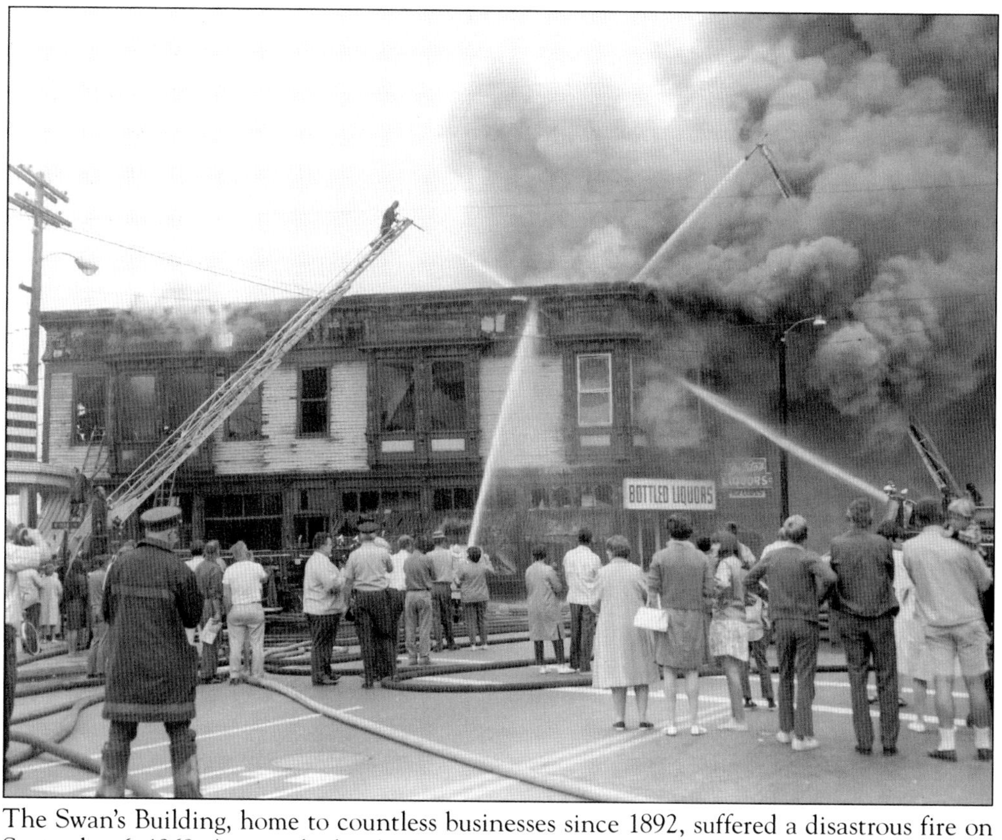

The Swan's Building, home to countless businesses since 1892, suffered a disastrous fire on September 6, 1969. Among the last businesses at this location was the DeVito Liquor Store on the street level.

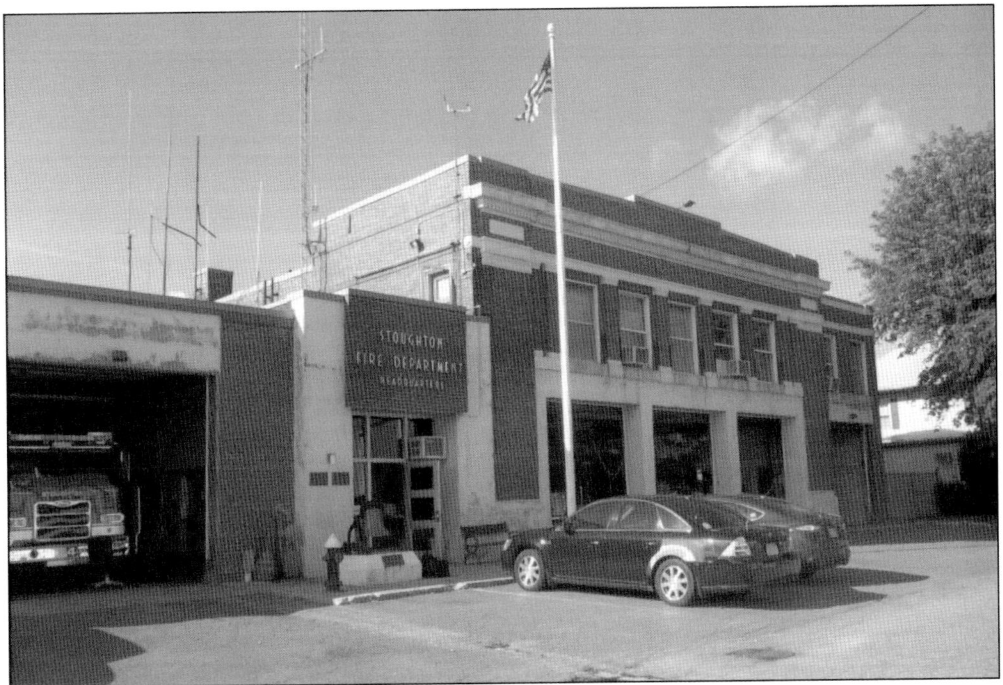

The Freeman Street Fire Station has continued to be used for nearly 90 years by the Stoughton Fire Department. It is hoped that a new facility at this location will be constructed in the near future. (Authors' collection.)

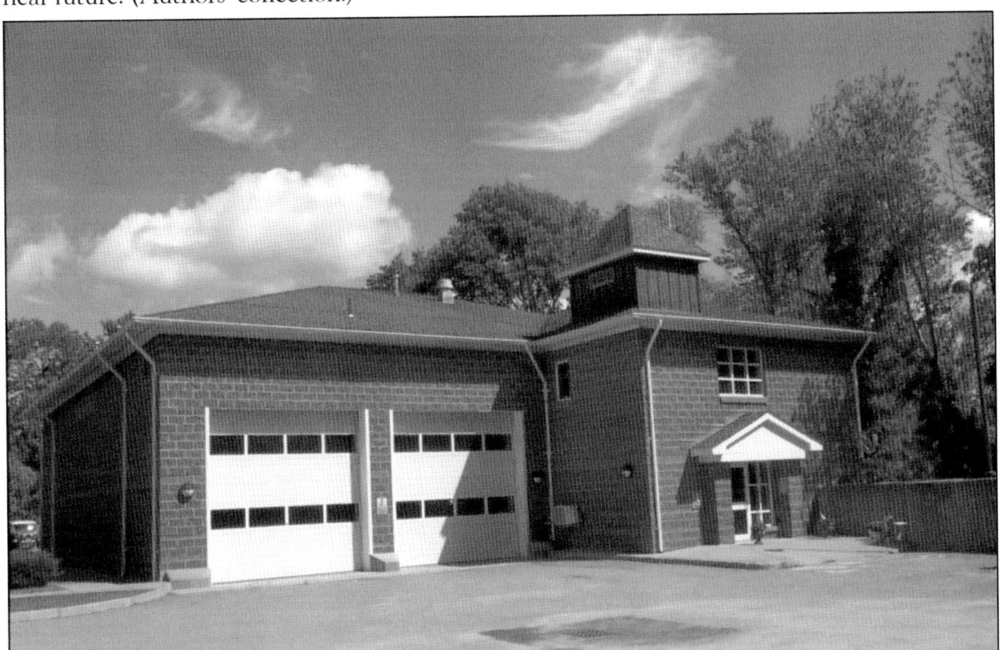

The Stoughton Fire Department headquarters is located on Central Street. This location provides Stoughton with fire protection on the other side of the railroad tracks. Not far from here, on Canton Street, was the site, at one time, of the barn housing the fire horses used in the 19th and early 20th centuries. (Authors' collection.)

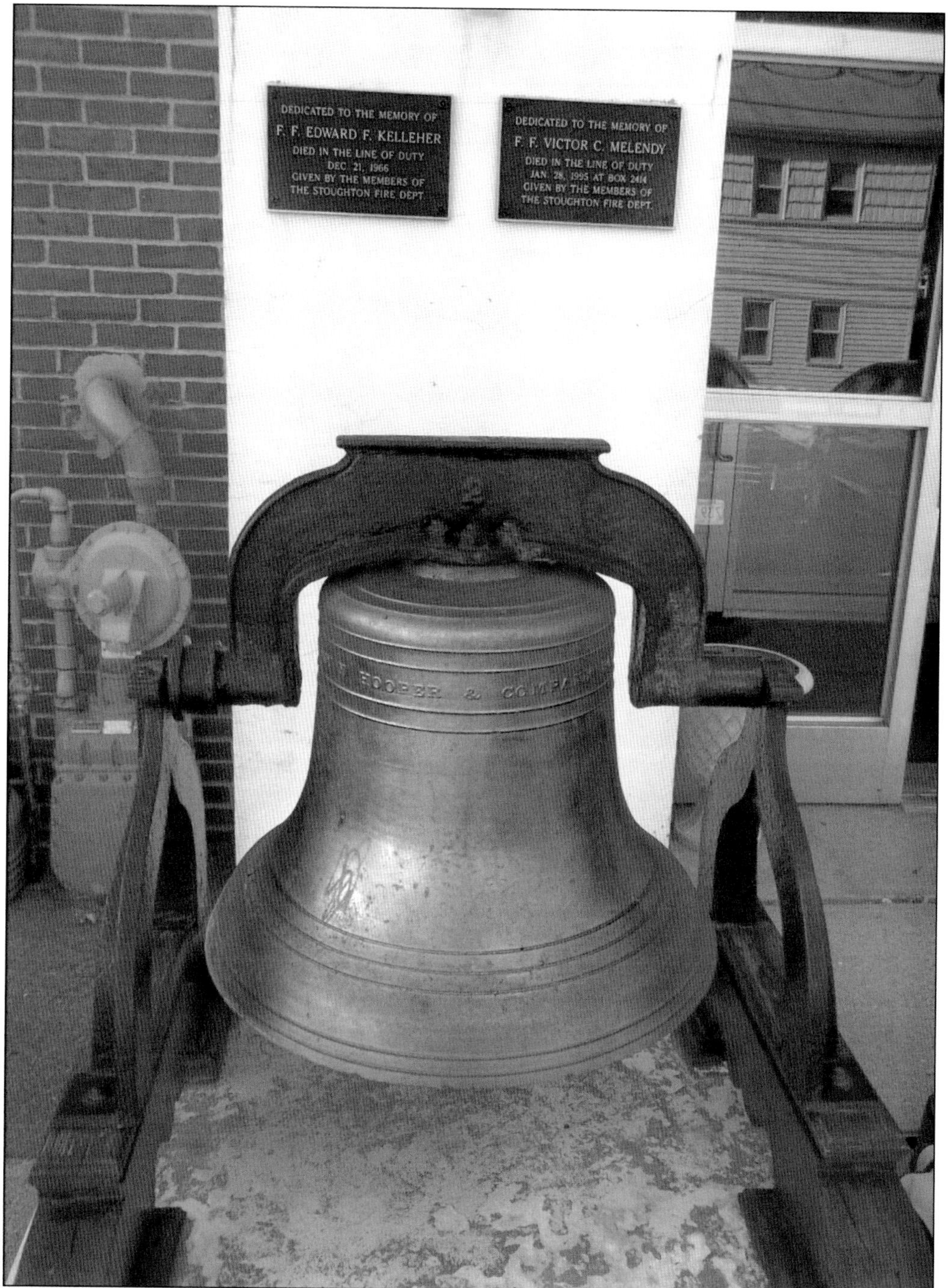

This 19th-century fire bell stands as a memorial, dedicated on November 11, 1957, to all Stoughton firefighters. The memorial was constructed from an old fire bell that once hung over town hall. The bell was cast in 1856. The plaques behind it are in memory of two Stoughton heroes of the fire department who lost their lives: On December 21, 1966, firefighter Edward F. Kelleher died in the line of duty. And tragedy struck again on January 28, 1995, when firefighter Victor C. Melendy died in a fire on Rose Street at Box 2414. (Authors' collection.)

Nine

Stoughton Business and Local Transportation

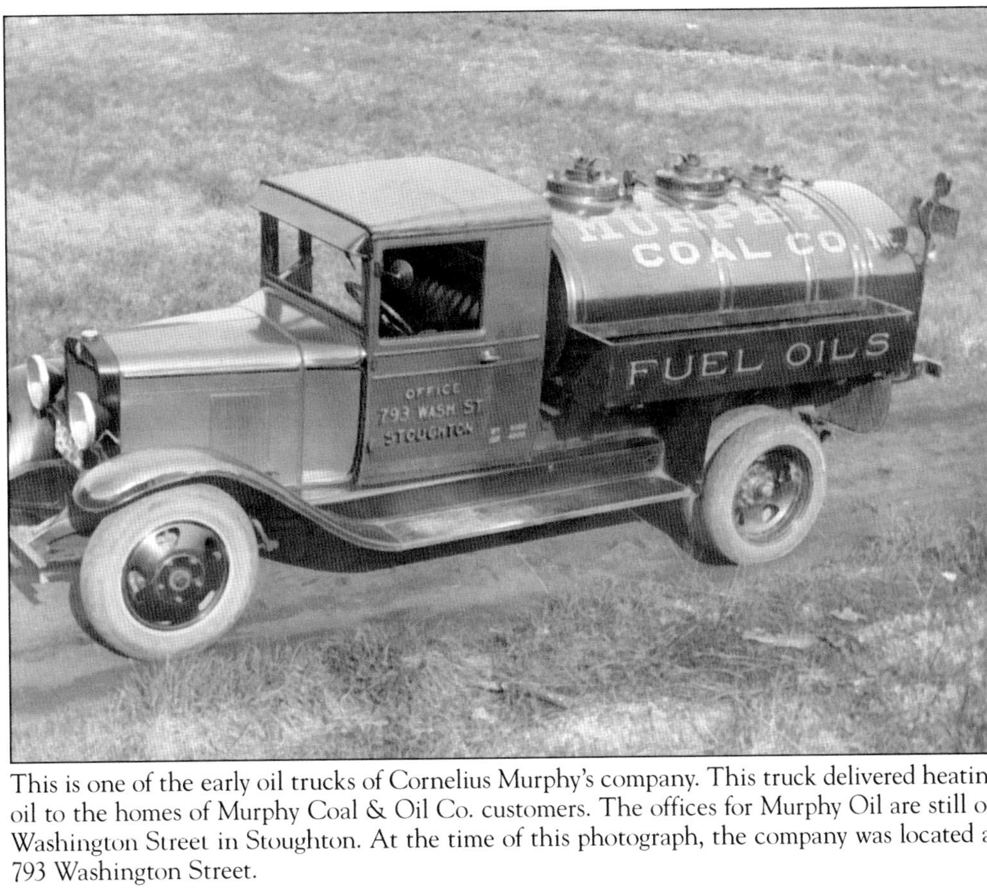

This is one of the early oil trucks of Cornelius Murphy's company. This truck delivered heating oil to the homes of Murphy Coal & Oil Co. customers. The offices for Murphy Oil are still on Washington Street in Stoughton. At the time of this photograph, the company was located at 793 Washington Street.

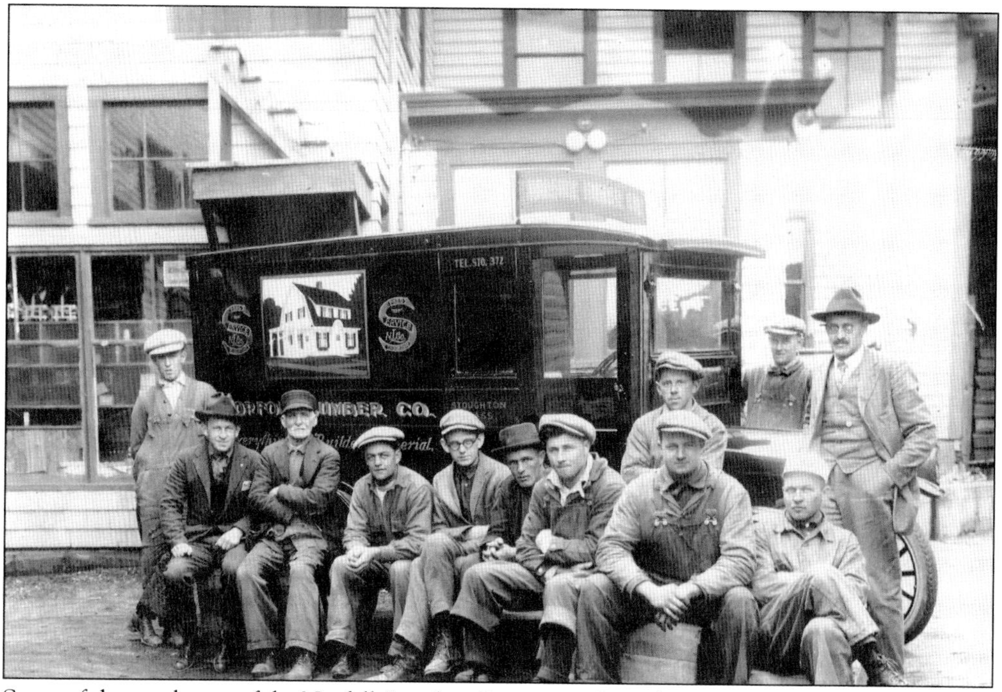

Some of the employees of the Norfolk Lumber Co. pose in Stoughton in the 1920s. The company, located on Canton Street in Stoughton, served as the lumberyard providing supplies for the construction of homes and other building projects throughout the town.

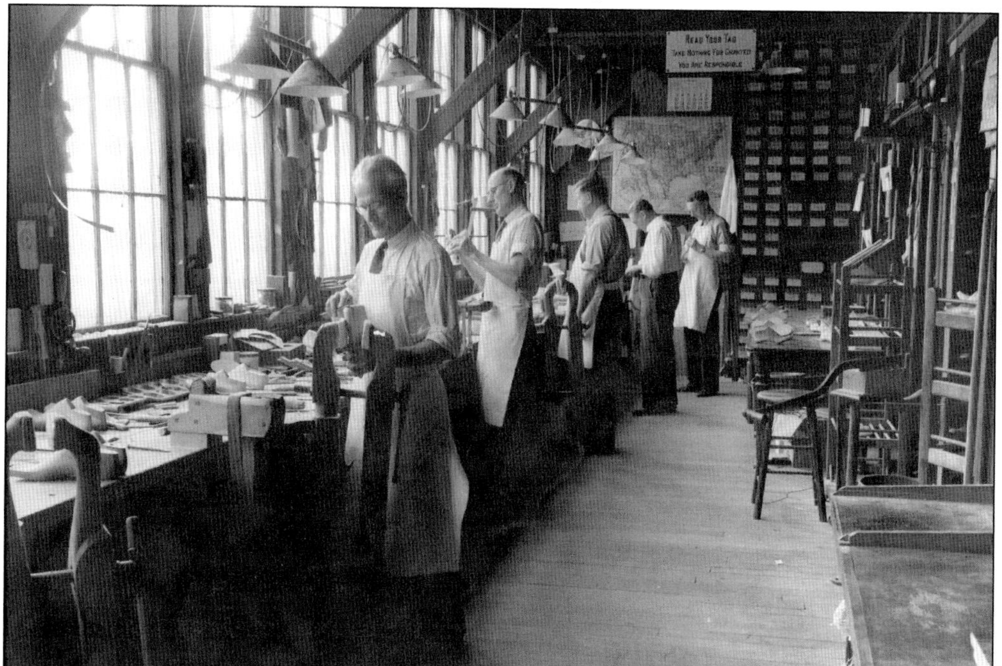

Workers are seen inside the George E. Belcher Last Co. factory on Pleasant and Capen Streets. The precision work to make a shoe last for a customer was done completely by hand by these craftsmen.

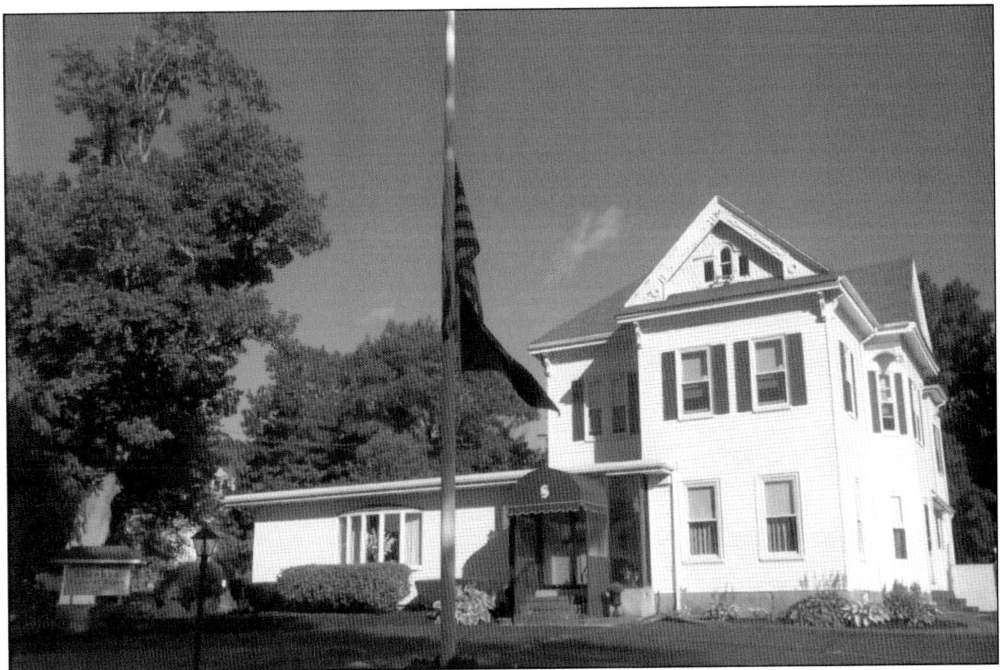

The Sheehan Funeral Home at 115 Monk Street is one of the oldest continuously operating Stoughton businesses. This location was used after the Lowe & Powers Funeral Home moved from its address at Porter and Rose Streets in 1928. The business, started by Phineas M. Withington in 1860, later became Withington & Lowe, and served as both furniture dealers and undertaker.

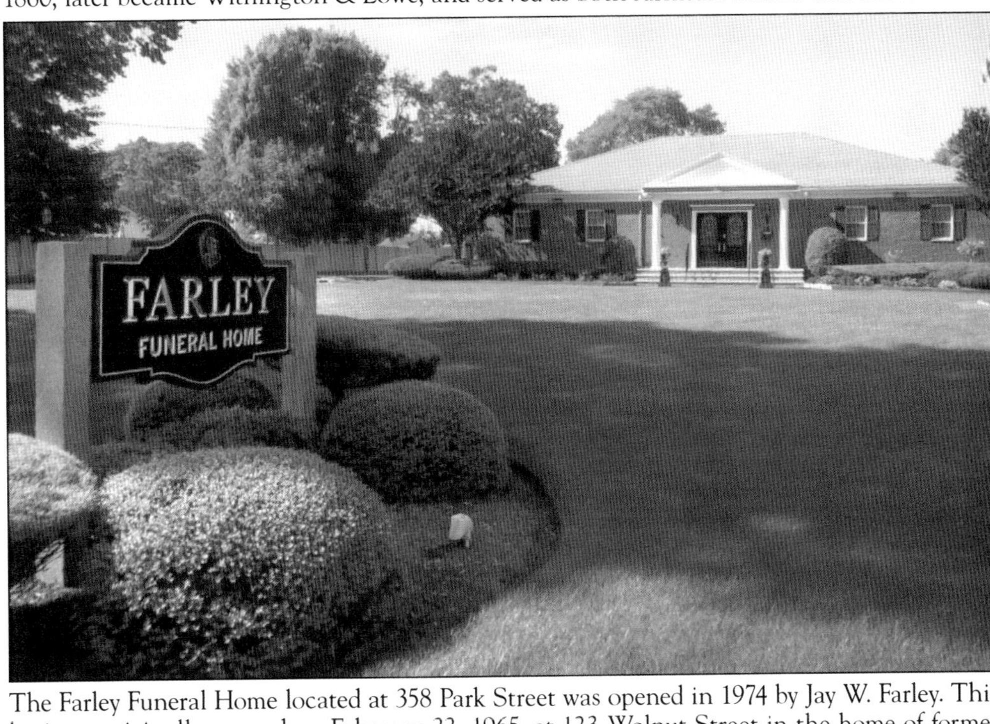

The Farley Funeral Home located at 358 Park Street was opened in 1974 by Jay W. Farley. This business originally opened on February 22, 1965, at 123 Walnut Street in the home of former attorney Francis X. Greeley.

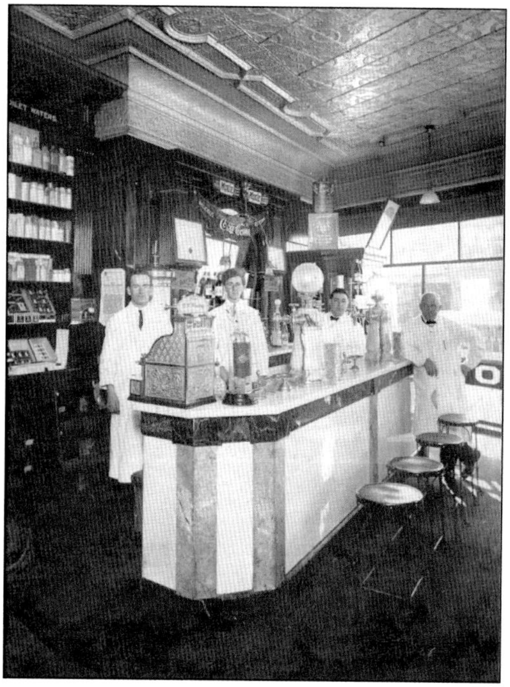

This is the drugstore and soda fountain at the Henry W. Winship Pharmacy. The pharmacy was located in the Swan's Block when this photograph was taken in 1909. Shown here are, from left to right, Timothy Murphy, Edwin Pollycutt, H. Ward Winship, and Charles Winship.

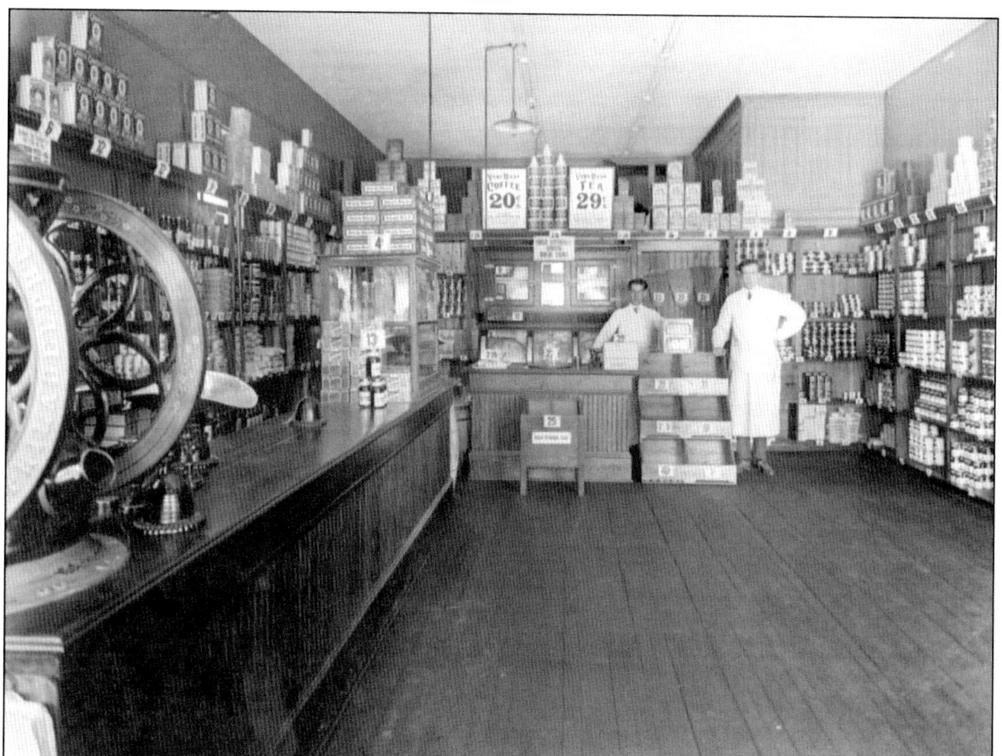

The interior of Malcolm's store at 330 Morton Street at the intersection with Plain Street is seen here in the early 1900s. Still in operation by the Bento family as a corner store, the establishment has for decades been known as Andy's Food Market.

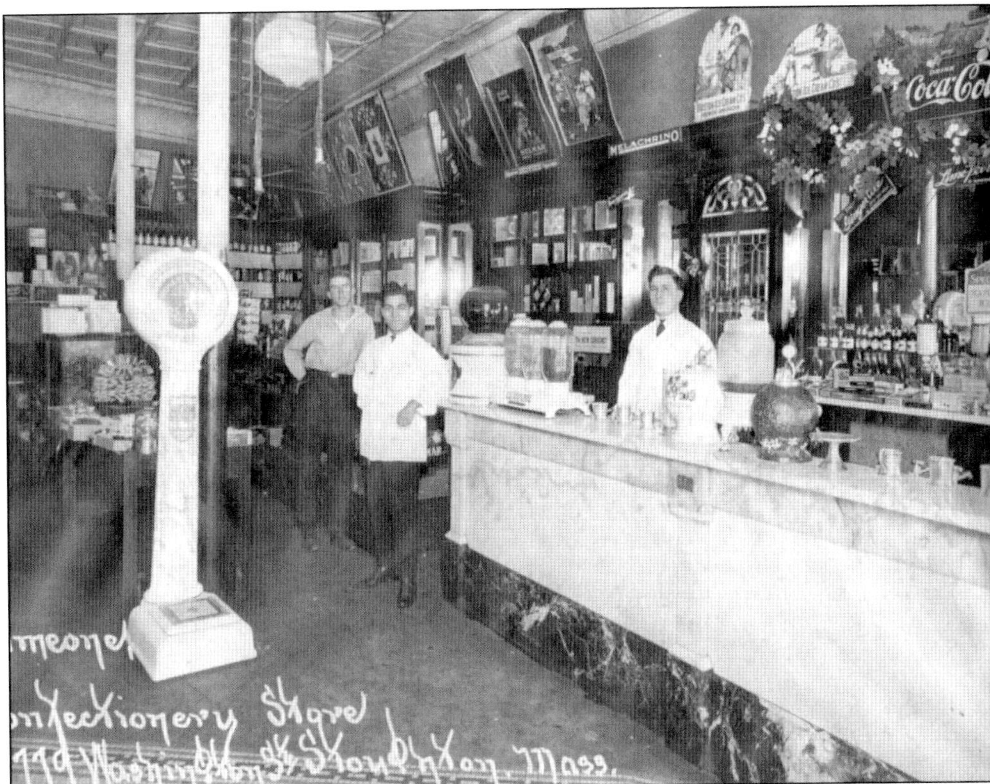

The Simeone and DeVito Confectionery Store was located at 779 Washington Street in the Swan's Building. The scale in this photograph was donated by the DeVito family to the Stoughton Historical Society.

The DeVito Liquor Store would later occupy the location of the confectionery store at 779 Washington Street. The proprietor, Joseph DeVito (1897–1979), is seen here with his daughter Evelyn (DeVito) Callanan. This store and the old Swan's Building were destroyed by fire on September 6, 1969.

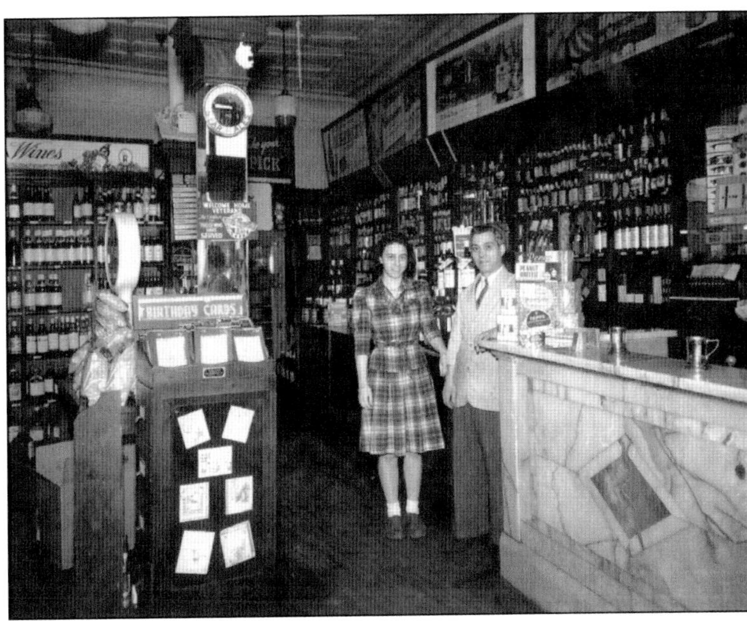

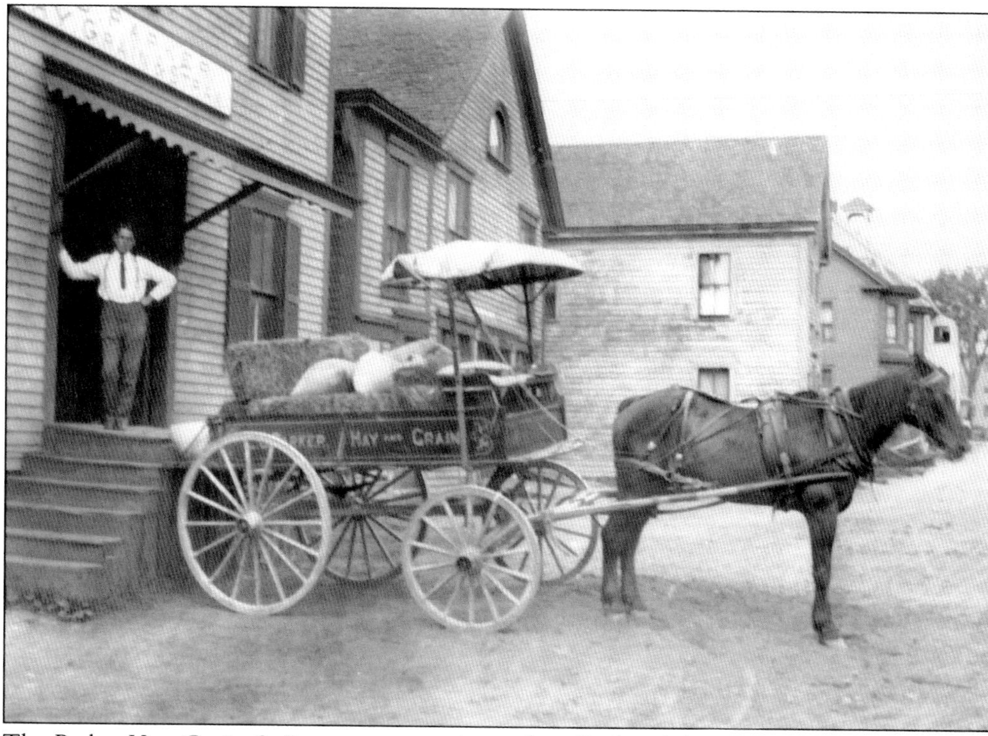

The Parker Hay, Grain & Straw store was located on Railroad Avenue near the train tracks. This business offered delivery to customers' homes, specializing in goods that suited the twilight years of farming in Stoughton. This store was located where the back of the Portuguese National Club stands today.

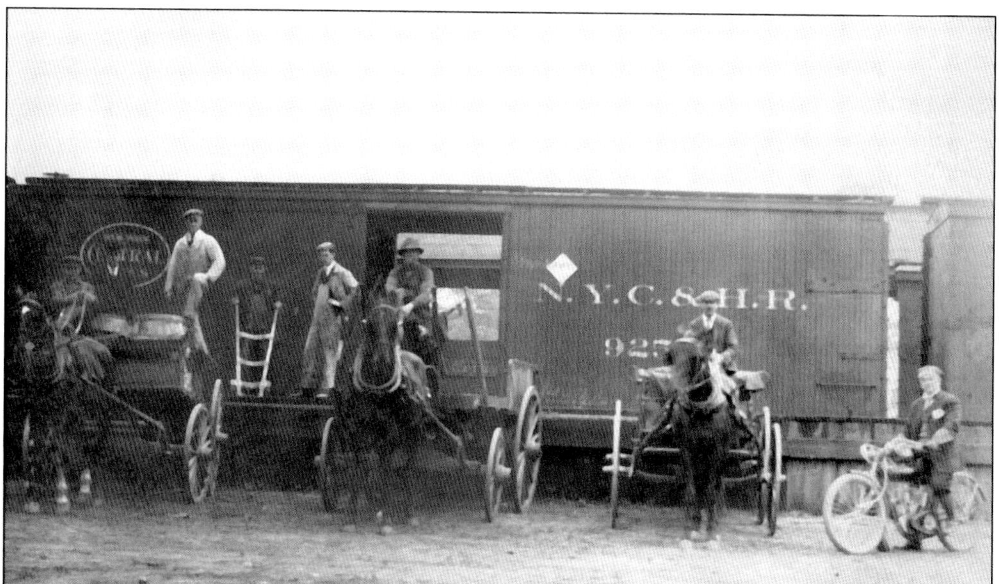

This New York Central & Hartford Railroad freight car unloads at the Stoughton freight yard outside Stoughton Square. This freight yard was located south of the Stoughton Rubber Company factory off Porter Street.

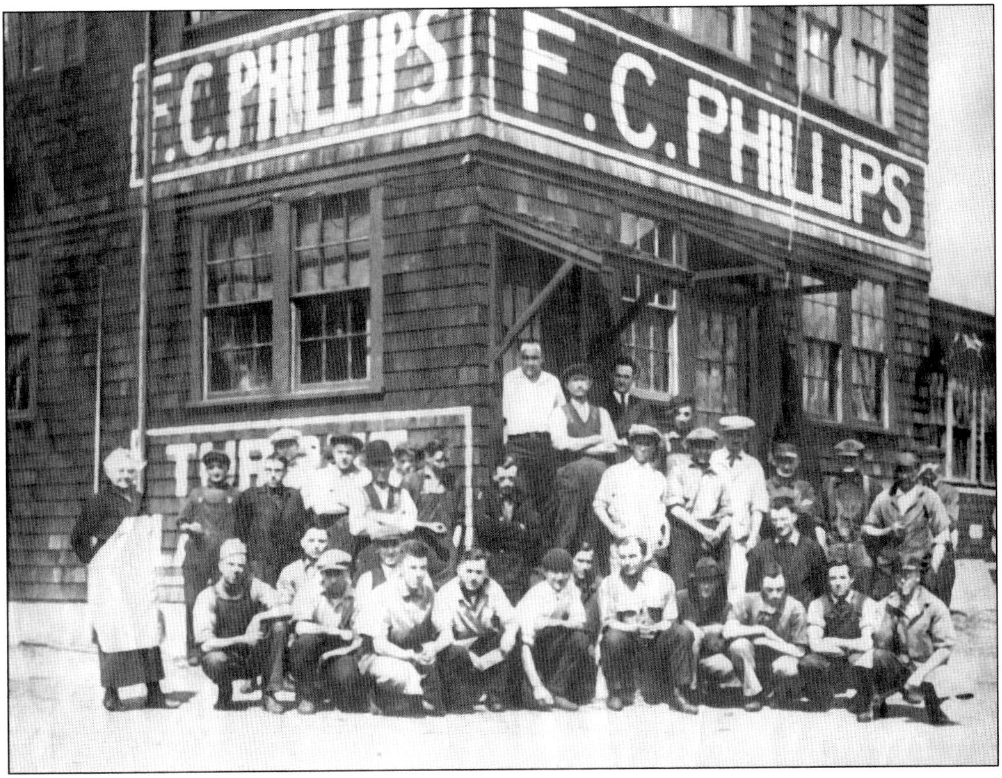

The F.C. Phillips Company came to Stoughton in 1911 and is still in business more than a century later. This view of the factory, built in 1916 at 473 Washington Street, shows employees in the 1920s. This company was well known years ago for the production of detachable golf spikes.

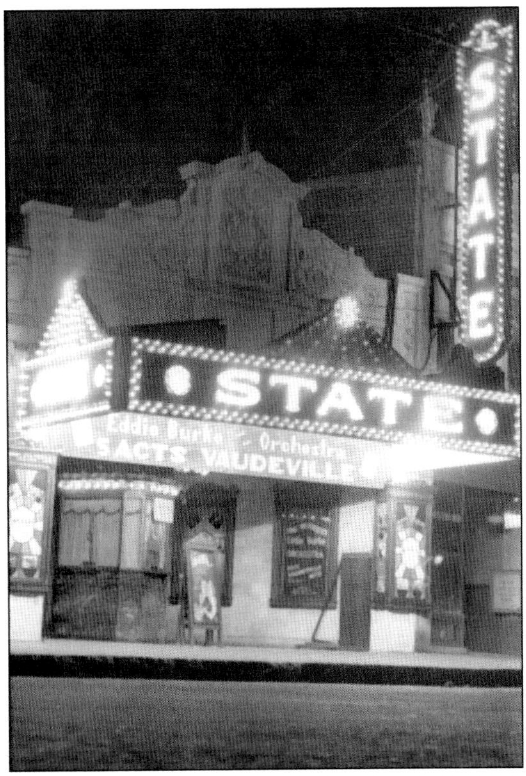

The State Theatre in Stoughton on Washington Street opened its doors to the public in 1927. This vaudeville stage and movie theater entertained many generations of Stoughton families until it closed recently. This view at night shows the marquee lit up, advertising a performance by Eddie Burke and His Orchestra and five vaudeville acts.

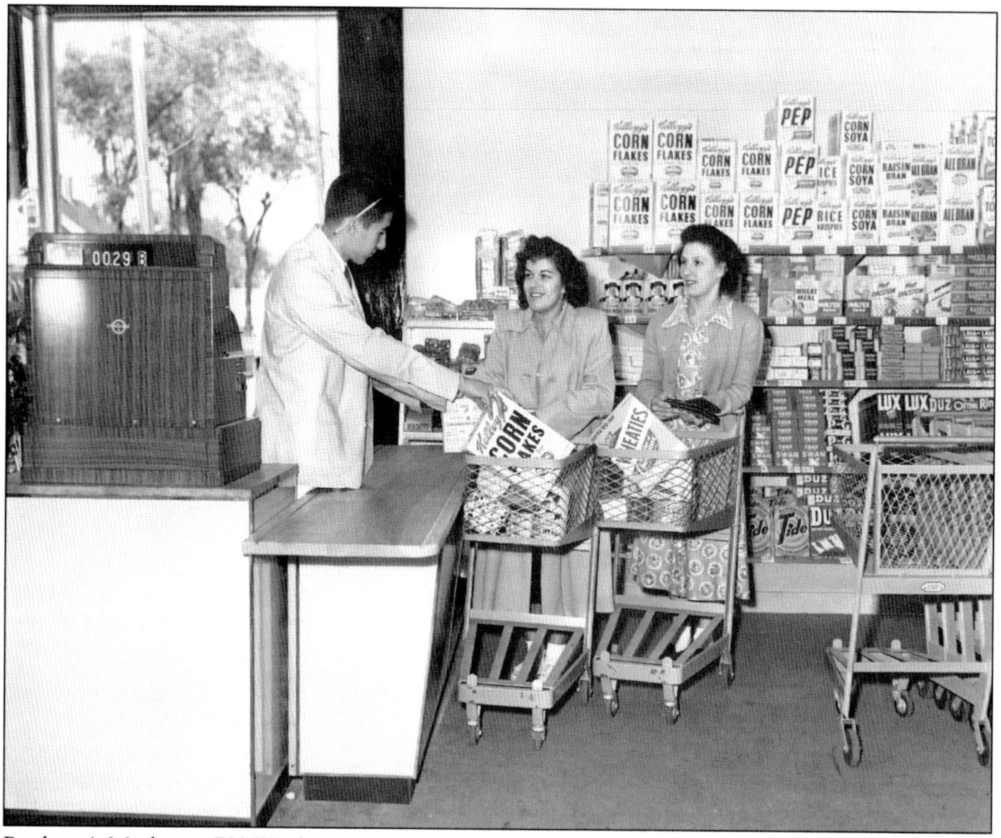

Perdigao's Market at 732 Washington Street in Stoughton offered convenient downtown grocery shopping. Here, ladies stock up on groceries, including Kellogg's Corn Flakes and General Mills' Wheaties, in the 1950s.

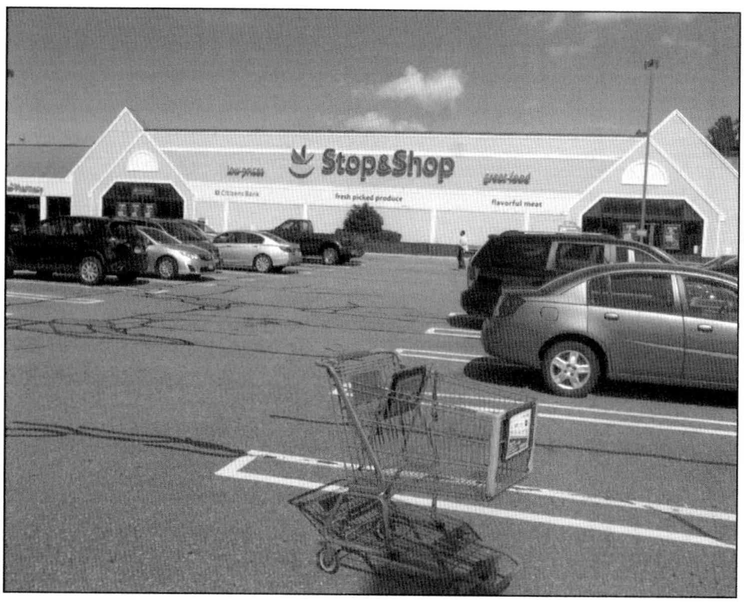

In 1988, a Stop & Shop opened at 278 Washington Street. In 2014, it remains the only full-scale local grocery store still open. In the 1970s and 1980s, Stoughton consumers also shopped at places on Washington Street such as Roxies, BPM, and, finally, Shaw's Supermarket, which closed in 2013. (Authors' collection.)

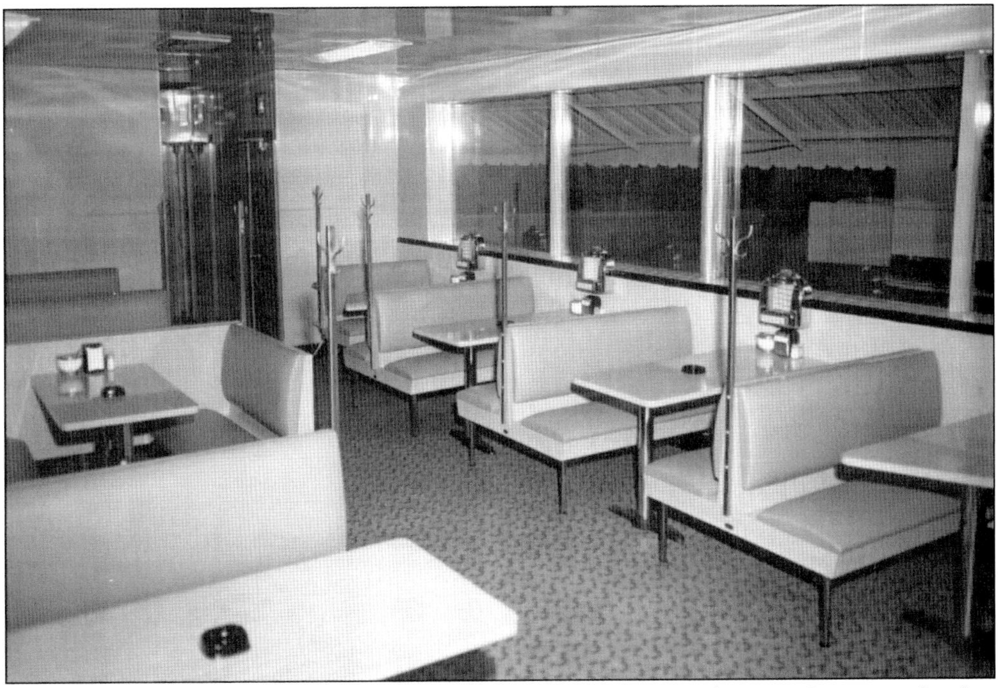

The spotless, stainless-steel interior of Stoughton Diner at 657 Washington Street is a familiar sight for many residents. The Stoughton Diner closed in the 1980s, but this location has housed a variety of restaurants ever since. Currently, the Cheng Du restaurant offers both food and entertainment to its customers. This location has also been home to Ebenezers, the Ground Round, and Phatt Boys since the diner closed.

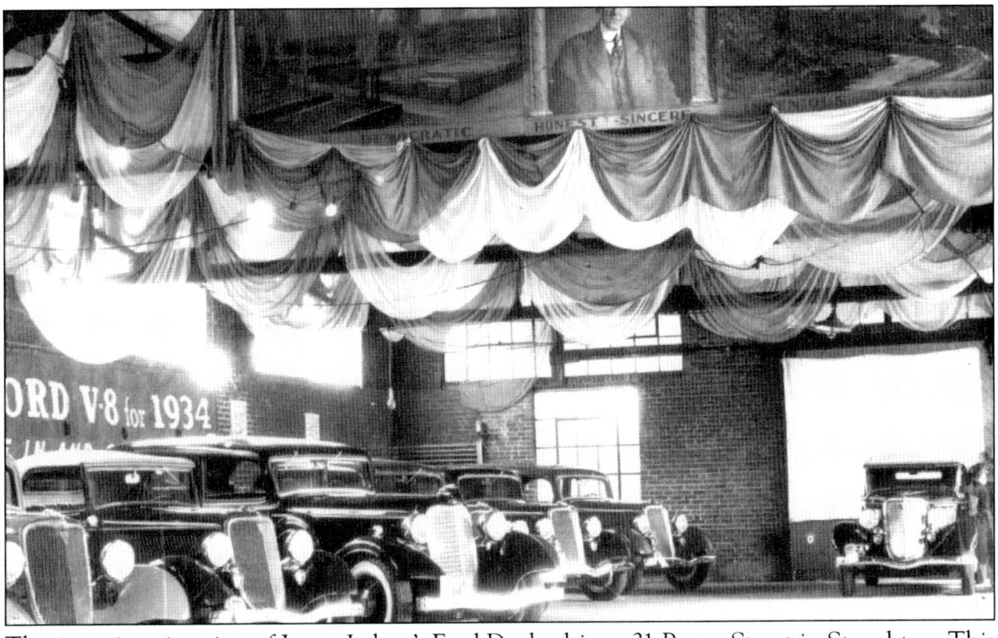

This is an interior view of James Lehan's Ford Dealership at 31 Porter Street in Stoughton. This location was built in 1916 and remained until the 1970s. The Stoughton Post Office now stands where residents could purchase a Ford V-8 in 1934.

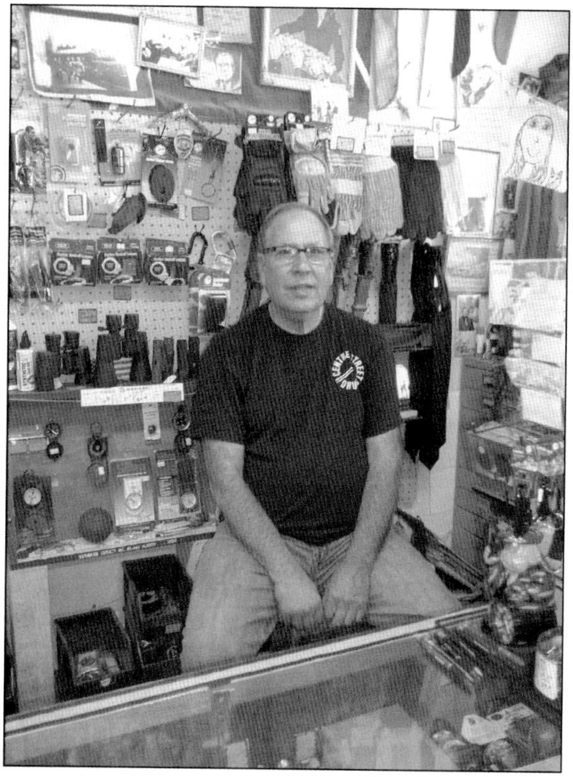

Stoughton Army Navy Store has been in Stoughton Square since 1977. Shown here is proprietor Rob Kushner. His parents, Milton and Anita Kushner, started the business. Many former Stoughton students remember getting their jackets from this location, or perhaps having dog tags produced on its original 1941 Graphotype machine. A cigar store Indian stands guard at this store at 763 Washington Street in the old Lehan Block.

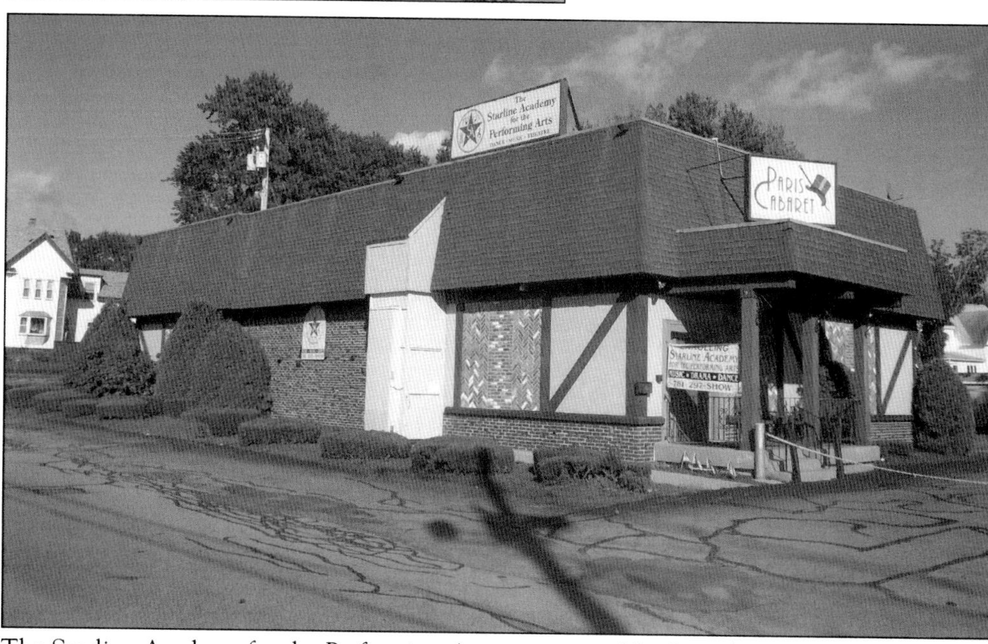

The Starline Academy for the Performing Arts was opened by Stoughton music teacher Paris Kampanelas in 2005. Residents may remember that this originally was Sherwood's Restaurant, where lobster dinners were a specialty. The Starline Room and Dinner Theatre was started by Kampanelas in 1981. Many talented performers are educated and perform at this facility at 49 Monk Street.

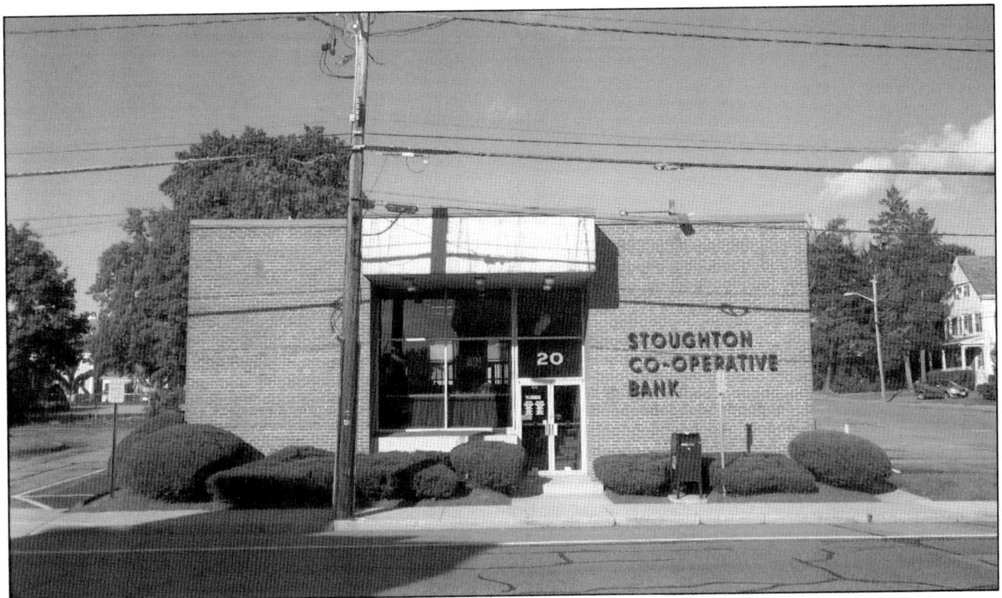

The Stoughton Co-operative Bank was started in 1886, and it has had a location at 20 Park Street since 1952. The Chicatabut Club and former home of James Atherton (1819–1879) stood on this site until it was razed to make way for this structure.

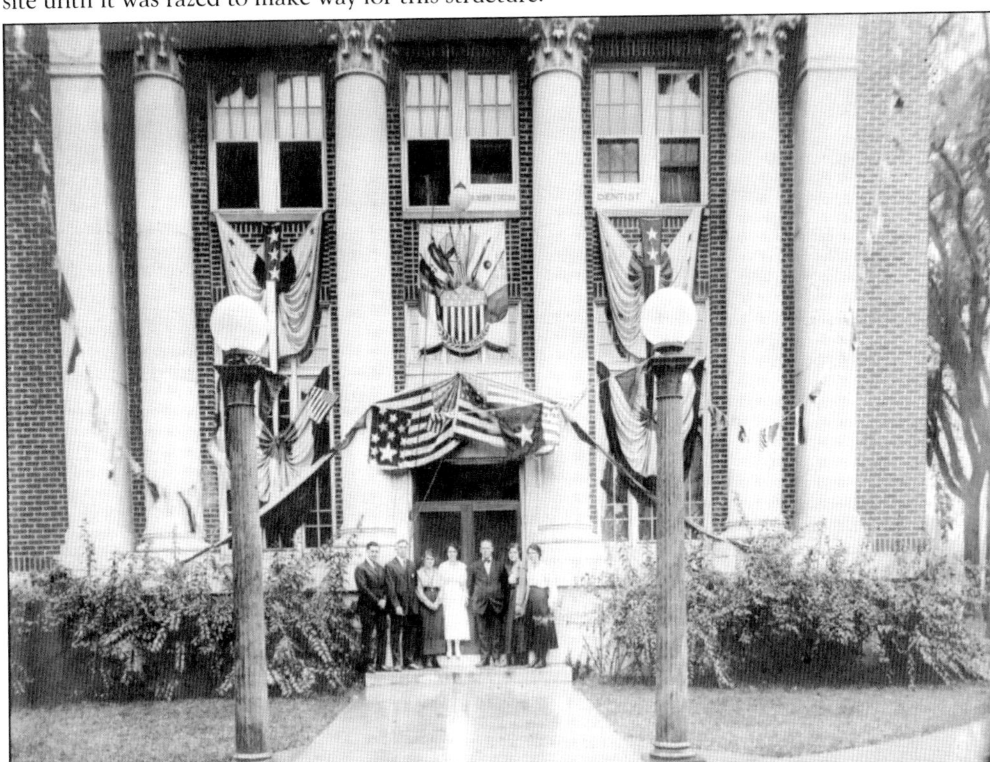

The Stoughton Trust Company, at the intersection of Park and Washington Streets, opened its doors in 1916. This 1919 photograph shows the company honoring returning World War I soldiers. Employees pose in front of this Stoughton landmark.

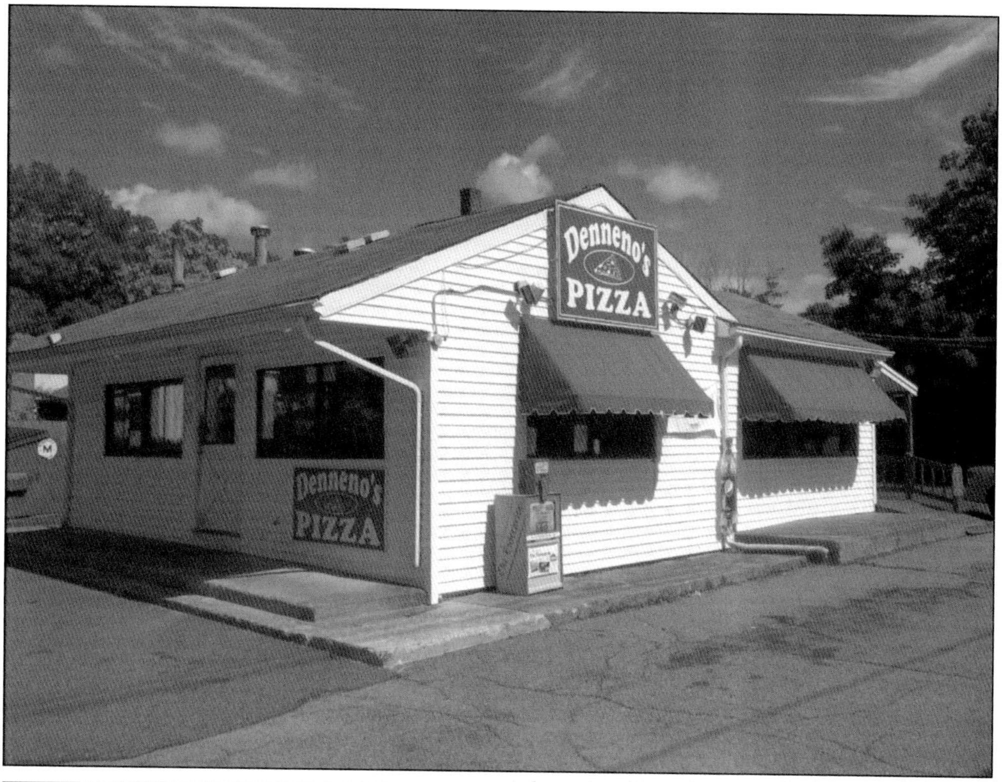

A longtime Stoughton tradition at 545 Pearl Street is Denneno's Pizza. It has been serving pizza to generations of Stoughton residents since 1955. (Authors' collection.)

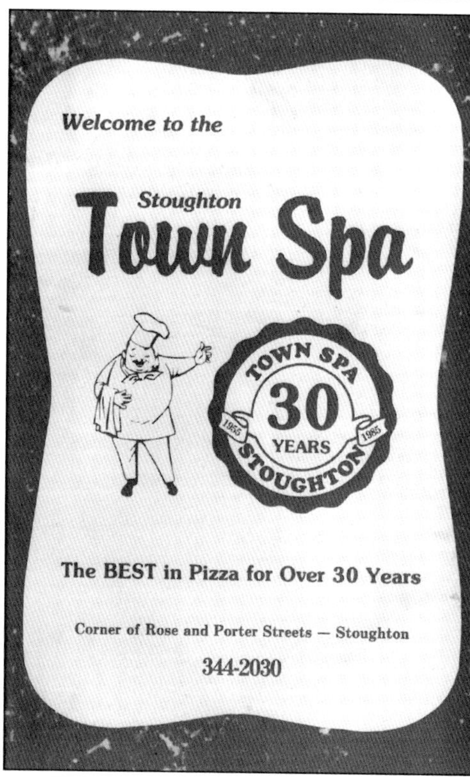

The Town Spa opened in 1955, when Henry and Rena Phillips started making pizzas at the old Porter Street location. On September 8, 1986, the business moved to a brand-new structure at 1119 Washington Street, where Cal's Ice Cream bar had stood for many years. The Town Spa has been a favorite of customers for nearly 60 years. (Authors' collection.)

Daniel Deacon opened Deacon Plumbing in 1886 on Pleasant Street. Over a century later, the business is still going, located across the street at 32 Pleasant Street. The company occupies a 19th-century former home of the Stoughton Post Office. (Authors' collection.)

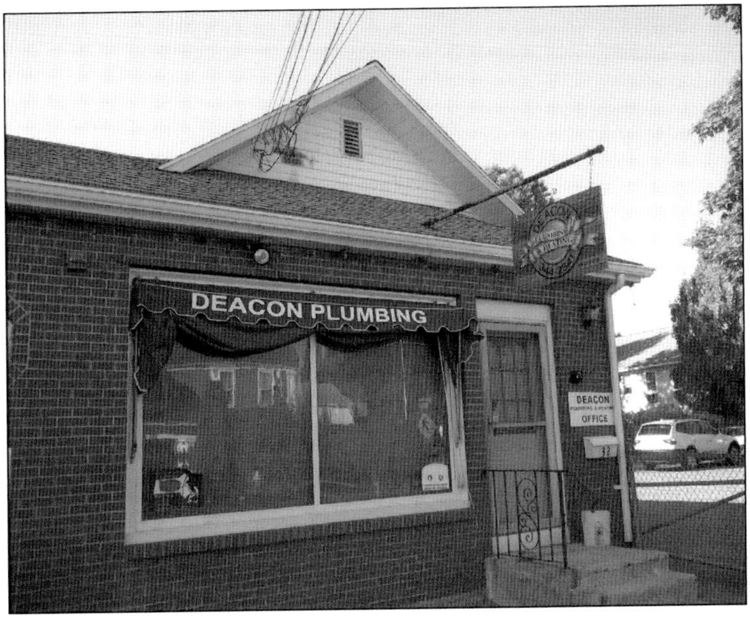

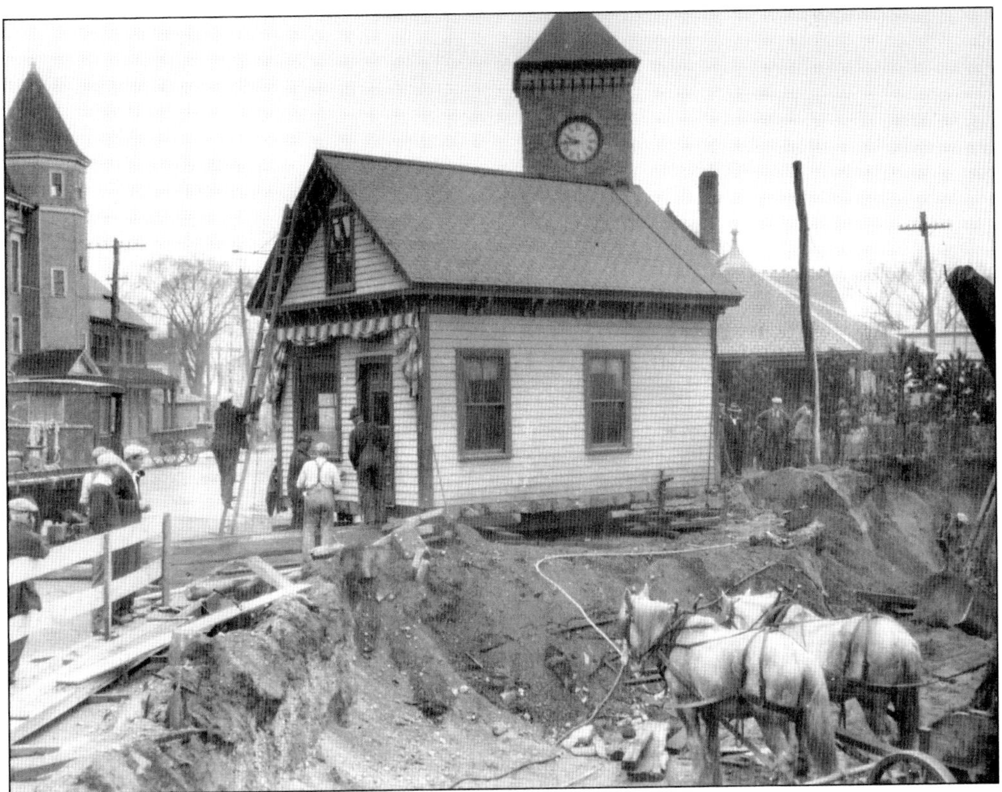

The Vanston Coal office was moved in 1927 to make way for the New Atwood's Market, and it was moved once before to open up the post office site on Wyman Street. Since December 1, 2009, this location has housed the popular Stoughton Bakery, serving train commuters and the community with coffee and some of the finest baked goods around.

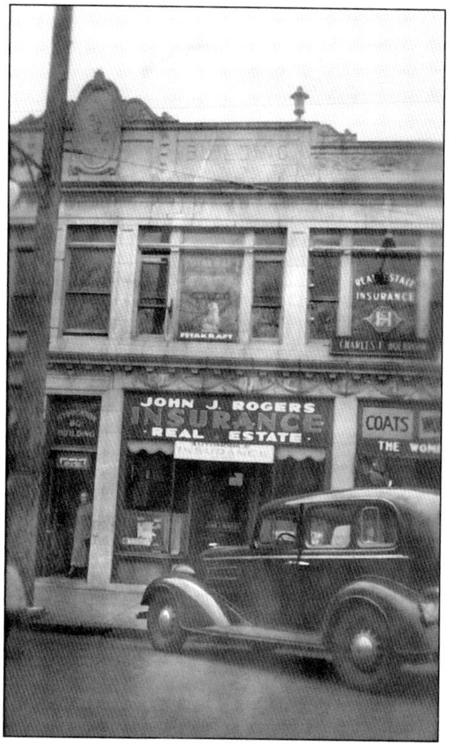

Seen here is the John J. Rogers Insurance Agency in the Stoughton Building in the 1930s. The John C. Stiles Fotakraft Studio can be seen above the Rogers Insurance office. A competitor to the Rogers firm, Charles F. Holbrook's Real Estate Insurance operated upstairs. John J. Rogers opened his company's first office in 1904, and, after 110 years, it is still a respected Stoughton business, now at 1 Cabot Place.

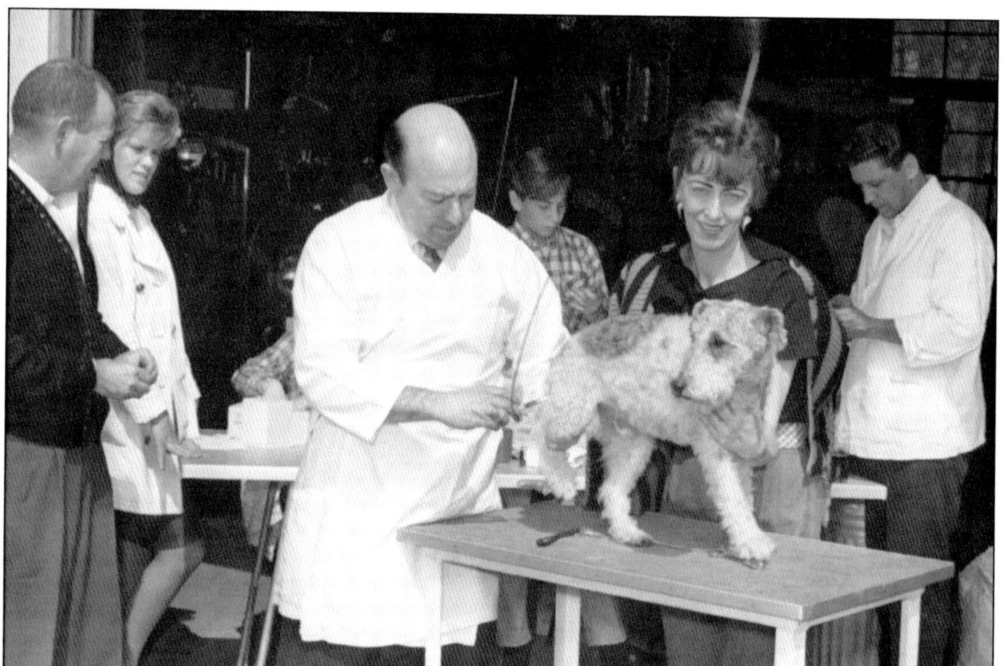

Dr. William Lloyd started an animal hospital in Stoughton in 1945. Here, Dr. Lloyd gives a vaccination at the annual rabies clinic at the Stoughton Department of Public Works Yard in the 1970s. Lloyd Animal Medical Center is still operating, in a facility built in 1995 at the old location at 1995 Washington Street.

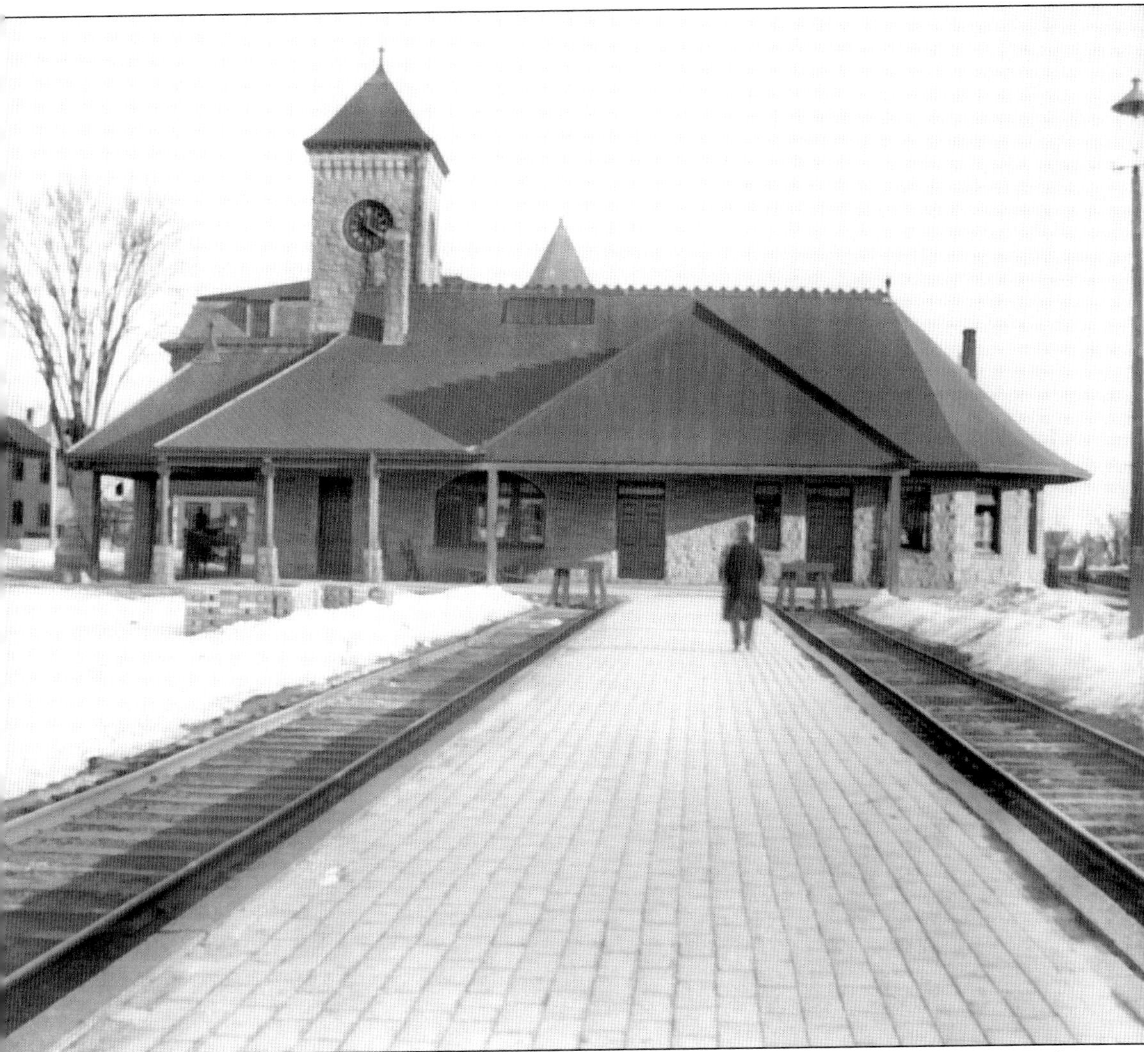

The Stoughton railroad station opened its doors in 1888 to serve commuters. This rare photograph, taken around 1905, shows a double set of tracks going up to the station. Today, the former tracks area is dedicated to commuter parking. Note the horse and carriage going through the portico on the left-hand side of the station.

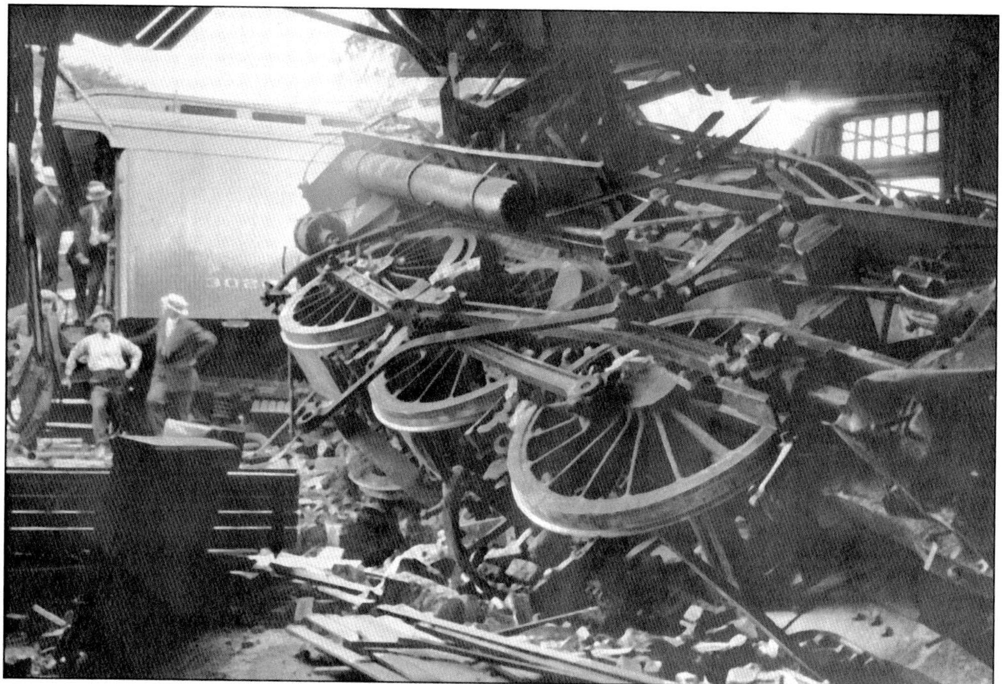

On August 4, 1924, a Newport train running express to Boston from Taunton derailed after children put railroad spikes on the tracks. This image shows the engine after it crashed through the granite walls of the ladies' waiting room at the Stoughton station on Wyman Street.

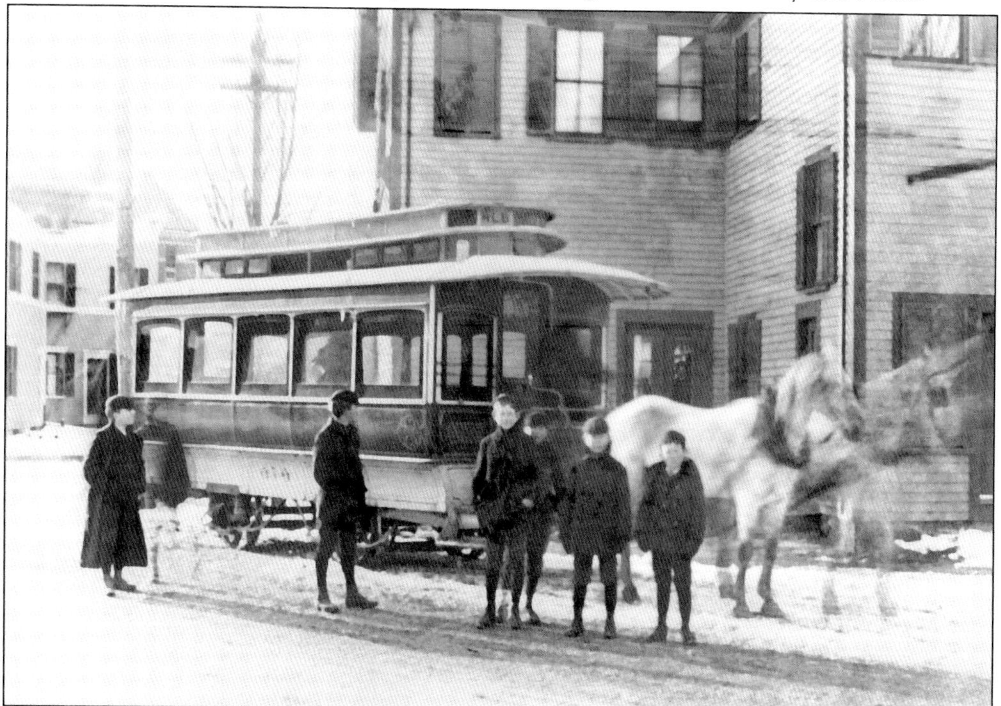

The horse-drawn trolley car makes its first trip on the Porter Street tracks in 1901. Stoughton Town Hall is visible at upper left.

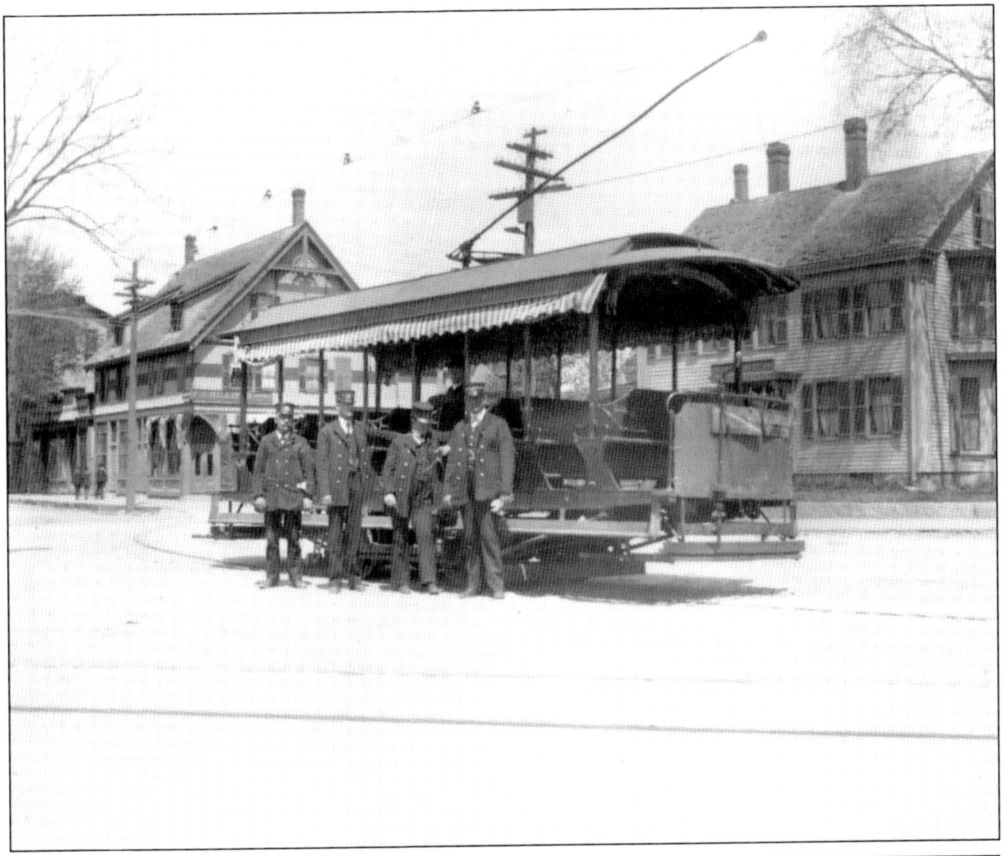

This view shows a trolley and conductors after the approach into Stoughton Square on the electric lines. The Washington Street Inn, seen directly behind the trolley car, would be moved north, farther up Washington Street, to make room for the Swan's Block.

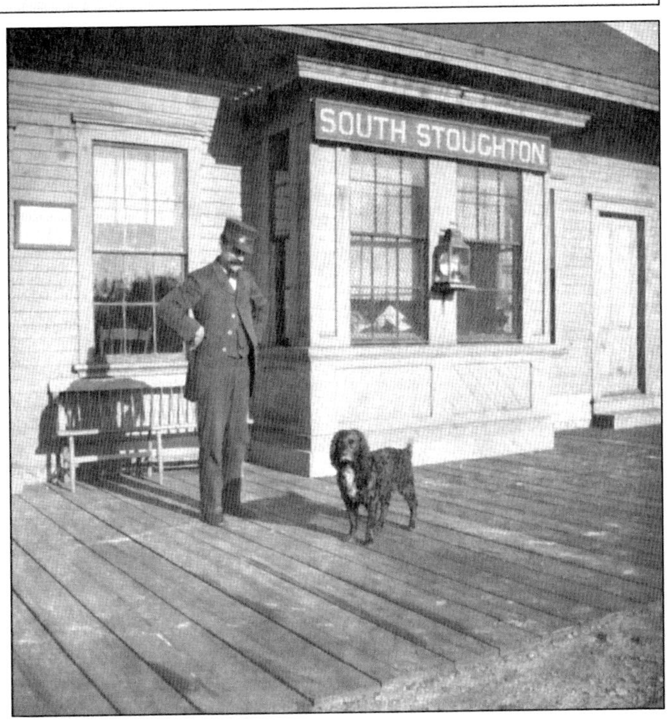

The stationmaster and a small, unidentified friend pose at the old South Stoughton depot off Central Street. This branch opened along the former Old Colony Railroad around 1866 and was closed to passengers in April 1925. The old depot structure was demolished in 1944.

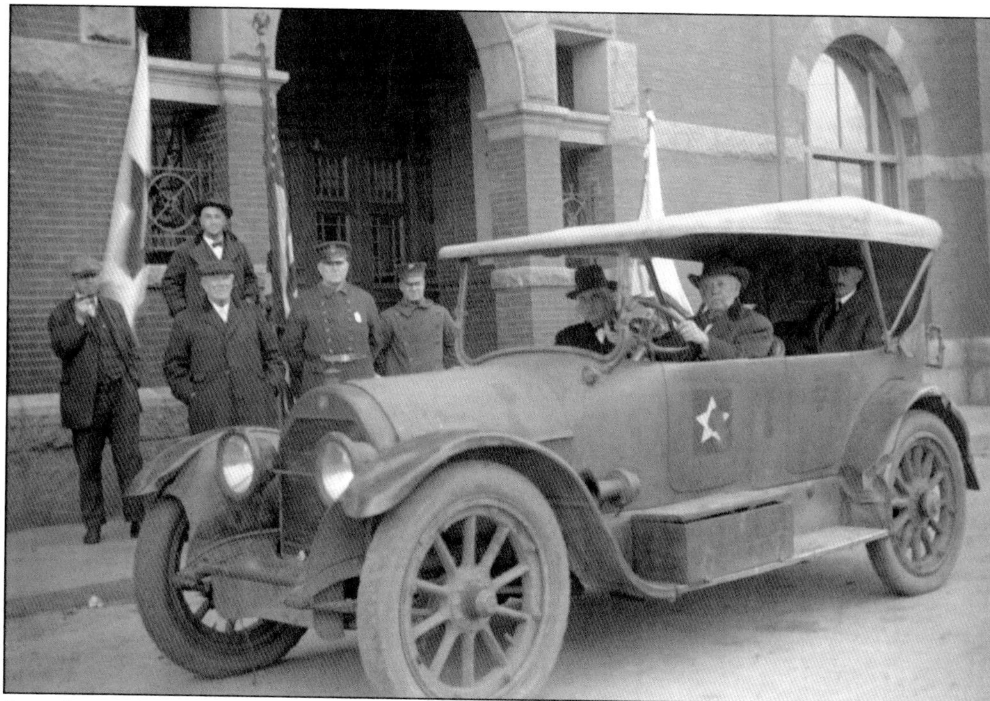

Stoughton selectmen in 1919 pose behind the wheel of a battle-scarred Army vehicle that served 18 months in France during World War I. Behind the wheel is Civil War veteran George William Pratt (1843–1927). In the passenger seat is Cornelius Healy (1868–1928), and in the backseat is George E. Malcolm.

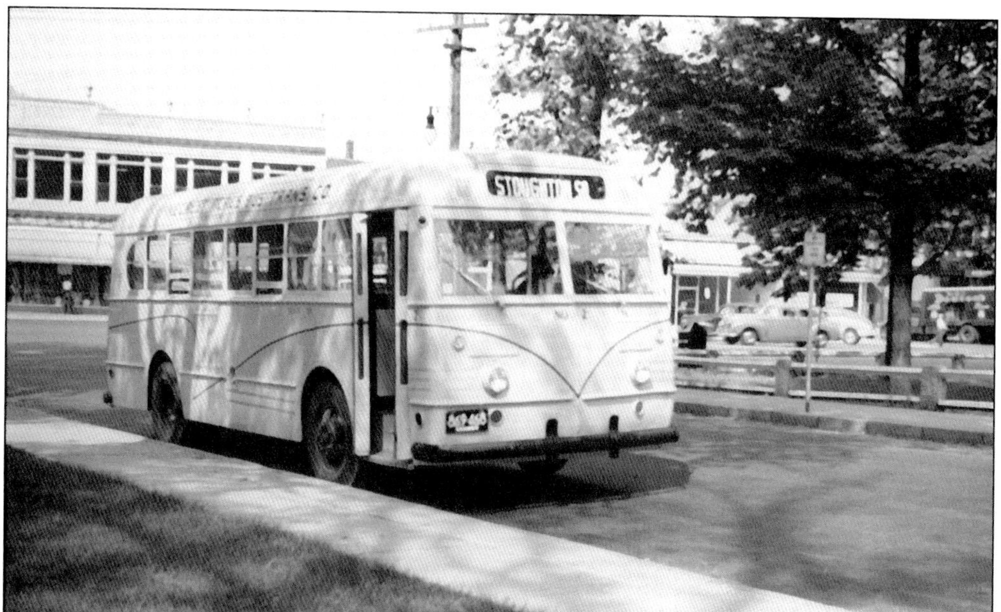

Billy Minuchi operated this bus in the 1950s from the Pinecrest Acres Bus Transportation Co., picking up passengers heading to Pinecrest Acres and to Randolph from Stoughton Square. This same route up Pleasant Street had been handled by trolley cars only a couple of decades before.

Ten

United Community

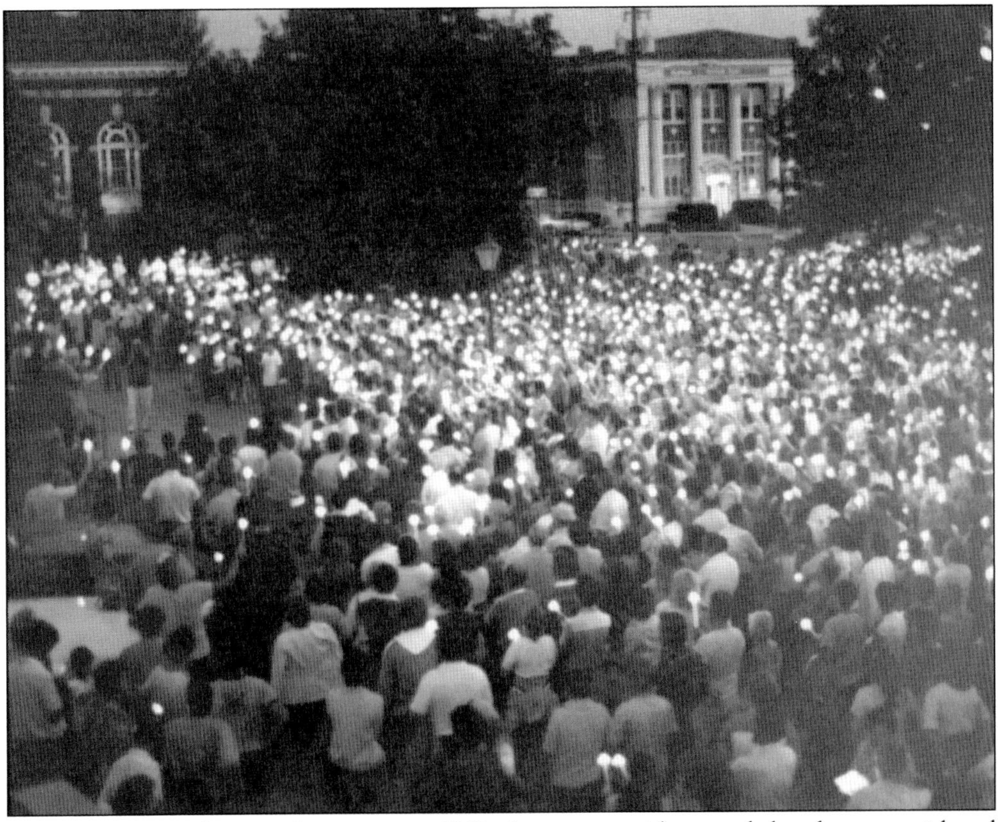

Stoughton received national attention in 1982 when town residents and church groups picketed an adult bookstore at the old Britton Block at Washington and Pearl Streets. Here, hundreds of citizens hold a candlelight vigil on the church green of the Universalist church to voice their opposition to the bookstore.

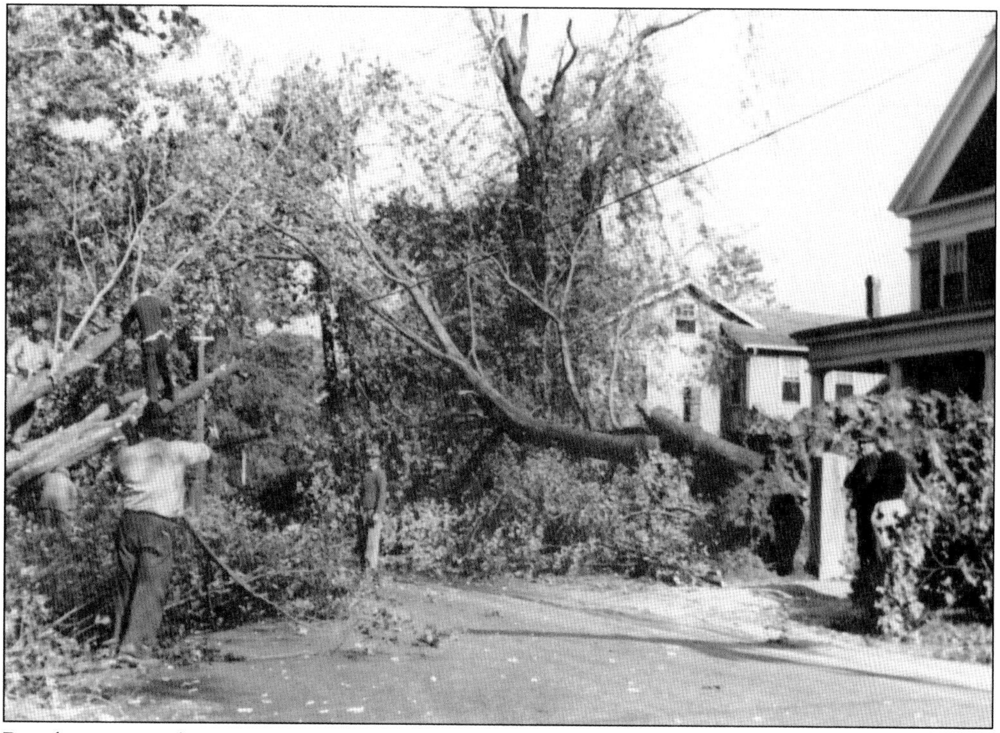

Residents turned out to assist neighbors when the 1938 hurricane struck Stoughton. These uprooted trees were on Pearl Street near Stoughton High School.

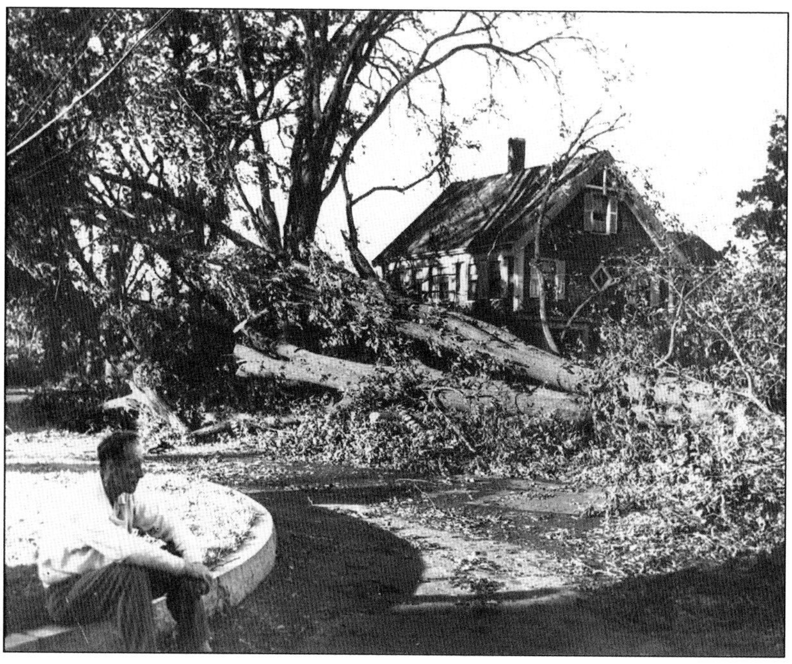

This photograph of the Drugge home in North Stoughton shows the damage from Hurricane Carol on August 31, 1954. This home is now gone. The site is currently home to Target and TGI Friday's in North Stoughton.

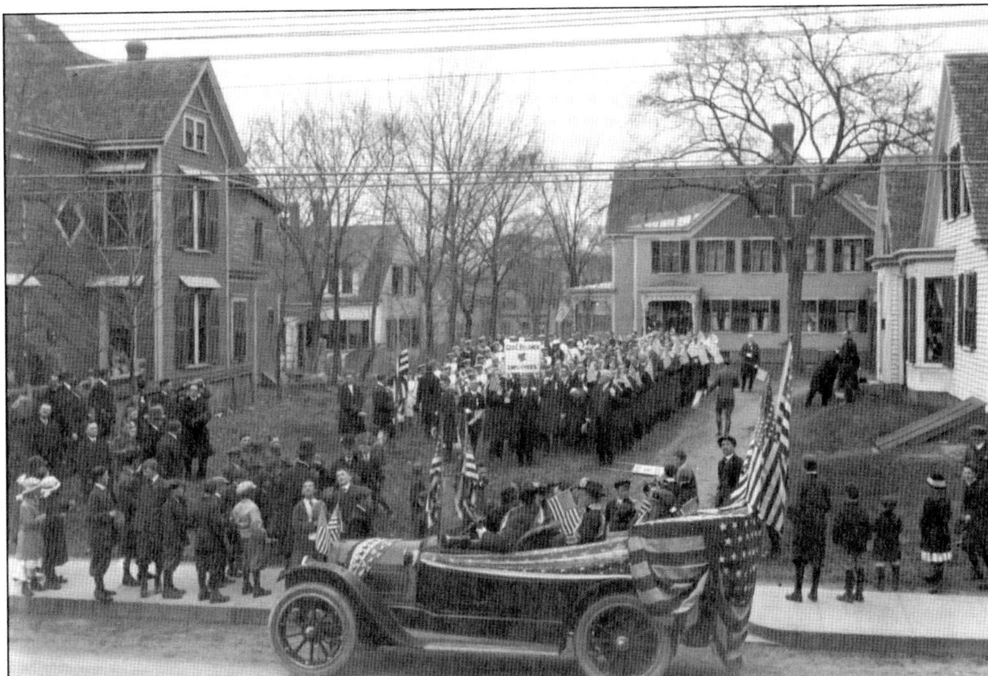

Patriotism in Stoughton has existed since the Revolutionary War. In 1917, employees of the George E. Belcher Last Co. gather for a flag-raising in support of the United States' entrance into World War I.

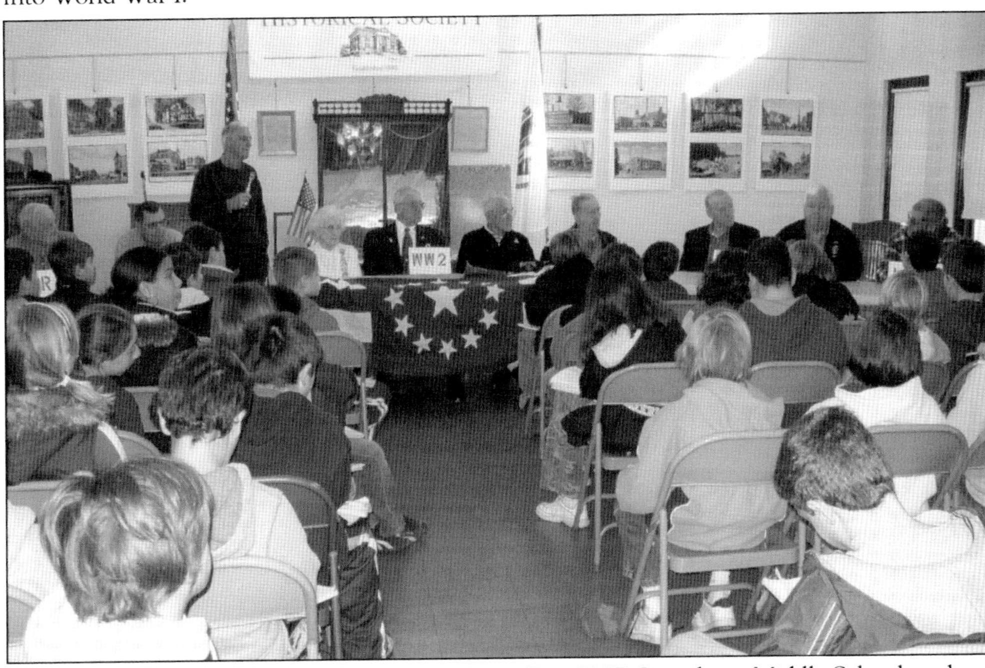

At the Stoughton Historical Society on Veteran's Day 2007, Stoughton Middle School students listened to and interviewed veterans of World War II, Korea, Vietnam, and Desert Storm. Stoughton Historical Society and US Navy World War II veteran Joseph DeVito led the discussion. The future of Stoughton history lies in the youth of the community remembering the worthwhile past.